Darren Allen is from old Whitstable, in the county of Kent. He writes non-fiction, novels, teleplays and graphic novels. His work addresses the nature of reality, the origin of civilisation, the horrors of work, death, gender, mental 'illness', Miss Genius, unconditional love, and life outside the spectacle. He is not qualified to write about any of these things, thank God.

Darren Allen
33 MYTHS
of the SYSTEM

A radical guide to the world

Second Edition

expressive egg books

Published by Expressive Egg Books
www.expressiveegg.org

Text design and layout by Darren Allen.
Front cover illustration by Ai Higaki.

ISBN: 978 1 8384073 8 4 (hardback)
ISBN: 978 1 8384073 4 6 (paperback)
ISBN: 978 1 8384073 5 3 (ePub)
Also available for Kindle.

Disclaimer: the author and publisher accept
no liability for actions inspired by this book.

10 9 8 7 6 5 4 3 2 1

Contents

故至德之世, 其行填填, 其視顛顛.

In a time of perfect virtue, the gait of men is slow
and ambling, their gaze is steady and mild.

當是時也, 山無蹊隧, 澤無舟梁.

In such an age, mountains have no paths or trails,
lakes no boats or bridges.

《莊子》

The Book of Chuang Tzu

Foreword

THE SYSTEM has been at least ten thousand years in the making. During that time it has taken many localised forms—autocratic, democratic, socialist, capitalist—but despite superficial variations in structure and priorities, it has remained the same entity. It is now so sophisticated, so pervasive and so invasive, that it is almost impossible to perceive. We may know that something is very wrong with the world we have made, but it reaches so deep into our experience that when it comes under radical criticism, we defend and excuse it as an extension of our own selves. The myths of the world are our own, and to expose them is to expose ourselves. Even to read of 'the system' can provoke discomfort, the sense of being under attack, or the feeling that the person using the term is an angry misfit.

Chances are though you are somehow aware that something is dreadfully wrong, that the system increasingly resembles hell on earth, that it is cracking up and that we need a radical alternative. This book (now updated somewhat to address a few developments in the world since the lockdown, to add a few extra thoughts here and there, and to more closely integrate the work as a whole with the complementary volume, *Self and Unself*) is an endeavour to strengthen and deepen this insight; to show that the problem is far worse and the solution far more radical than is commonly supposed.

Although brief, I have outlined the entire system, from the left to the right, from scientism to postmodernism, from democracy to fascism. This means that some of what follows may seem obvious and quite right, and some not at all obvious; or dead wrong. Most people have a tendency to complain about the Terrible State of the World, but to keep the part they are most dependent on immune to criticism. This is the part I urge you to look for, look at and look *again* at; and to have patience with those chapters that you are sympathetic to or familiar with.

One final note. I criticise both the left and the right in this book, and in order to do so I occasionally draw on leftist critique of the right, and vice versa. This does not mean that I support any other ideas, much less the entire philosophy, of the authors I quote or reference, with the possible exception of Snufkin.

Preface
The Revolutionary's Paradox

scentate [sɛnteɪt]

vb Not being able to work out whether the problem comes from oneself, or whether it comes from the situation.

- Is your sadness the terrible truth and your happiness a mask, or is your happiness the profound reality of your life and your sadness just a selfish episode? Is your difficult relationship with your lover causing you to be unhappy, or is your unhappiness making the relationship difficult? Is it your train that is leaving the station, or another train you can see moving through the window? *Is it you, or is it the world?*

O N THE ONE HAND it is impossible to change your personal life or consciousness—how you (and others) feel, perceive, think and act—unless the institutions which shape and subordinate consciousness also change.* No matter how spiritually enlightened, cheerful, generous or creative you may be, if you have to go to live in the towns and cities of the world, go to its schools, travel its roads, eat its food, work in its factories and offices, use its hospitals and courts, not only can you do very little with your psychological freedom, but its presence within the system erodes, cheapens and co-opts it. On the other hand, it is useless to change the world while people remain essentially fearful, confused, violent and selfish. Not that people are essentially bad; but anxiety, insensitivity, cruelty and egoism are nearly always successful at resisting or ruining the healthy, the natural, the convivial and the fair. You don't need a historian or an anthropologist to tell you that men and women are exceptionally good at fucking things up.

* Or unless you remove yourself from them.

This is the revolutionary's paradox; a case of SCENTATION. Is the problem out there, or is it in here? Do I change the world, or change myself? People tend to resolve this problem (if they are aware of it at all) by coming down on one side or the other. A prototypical world-changer—a committed socialist perhaps—might say that mysticism, psychotherapy, psychedelic drug use, even art, are kind of frivolous, perhaps self-indulgent; at best of private, personal value or even, in the service of socialism, of collective ('consciousness raising') use; but, in the end, we'll never really be happy until *society* has changed, until it allows us to express ourselves freely, cooperate creatively and reach our full potential. Until then we'll always be frustrated. A prototypical self-changer—a hippy, let's say, in the original sense, a mystic or an artist—might say that faffing about with democracy, riots, unions, activism or revolt changes, essentially, next to nothing. The same groupthink prevails in radical organisations, the same bitchiness, the same dull scripts, the same debilitating compromise and, although material conditions can certainly change for the better, the end results are always, essentially, the same. Changing the world without first changing your *mind* is the quintessence of futility and doomed to failure.

Taken as a whole, the three books in this series make the case that both positions are wrong, and that both are correct. Until the dissident uncovers the radical reality of his personal life, he will never change the world. Until the mystic uncovers the radical reality of social life, she will never change her self. To perceive ego and the world that it built as they are is no easy matter though. They are all-pervasive and all-powerful, and yet the means by which they conceal themselves are extraordinarily subtle. They are so close to us, they pass under our attention, like the smell of our own breath. We are not, after all, talking about aliens living on a distant world, but our own lives, here and now. To understand how humans created, and continue create, the world without first looking at how *you*, the individual man or woman reading this, creates and continues to create *your* world, is like trying to understand a camera by peering at a photograph.

In a book like this, we can, of course, only look at 'photographs'. My intention is to arrange them in such a way that the mechanism which produces them is seen more clearly, and in the seeing, a better camera comes into play.

0

A Brief History *of the* System

'Our society resembles the ultimate machine which I once
saw in a New York toy shop. It was a metal casket which,
when you touched a switch, snapped open to reveal a
mechanical hand. Chromed fingers reached out for the
lid, pulled it down, and locked it from the inside. It was
a box; you expected to be able to take something out of it;
yet all it contained was a mechanism for closing the cover.'

Ivan Illich

FOR HUNDREDS OF THOUSANDS of years, people lived well in peaceful, egalitarian, healthy societies, at the very least in comparison with what followed. We did not work particularly hard and the work itself (if it could be called work; pre-civilised societies don't make distinctions between work and play), was enjoyable, meaningful and non-alienating. Activity is ALIENATING if it makes you feel a stranger, or alien, to your own better nature, if you are forced to do it for someone else's profit, for example, or for no good reason, or if you don't feel 'at home' with its results. For most of human history (actually pre-history—HISTORY begins with civilisation and writing) alienating work and ways of life were unknown; coercion and futility were inconceivable, as were property, religion, law, warfare, much superstition and what we could call 'mental illness'. The fear of *immediacy*, when the senses sharpen to deal with danger in the present, was part of life—because there has always been danger—but the paralysing fear of *tomorrow*, the profound and widespread care, anxiety, and worry that modern men and women are burdened with, was unknown.*

Objectively, it is impossible to know all this directly—but then it is impossible to know anything directly through study. Nevertheless, we can make some reasonably reliable inferences about our pre-historic past, just as we can about the surface of the sun, or the outcome of stripping the earth bare of life. Anthropologists can objectively assess what early people were like from studying soil, bones, tools, cultural artefacts and other archaeological remains, all of which indicate how early people lived, how violent they were, how healthy, how socially stratified and even what kind of universe they conceived themselves to be in. We now know that pre-civilised, pre-historic, pre-conquest

---

* See *Self and Unself*.

folk were happier, healthier and saner than the agricultural and industrial societies that followed.*

Anthropologists can also objectively, albeit approximately, determine the earliest state of mankind by looking at how hunter-gatherers live today. Nobody believes that foragers today are the same as those who lived twenty-thousand years ago; groups which have had no contact with the modern industrial world or with the pre-modern agricultural world no longer exist to observe, but those which, at least until recently, survived relatively independently all shared, more or less, the attributes listed above. Naturally, there is an enormous amount of variation in hunter-gatherer societies—far more than in any other kind of society—but, generally, the further away from civilisation, in time or space, the more egalitarianism, freedom and well-being, both psychological and social.†

There still remains of course a vast, impenetrable void at the heart of our objective knowledge of the distant past. We will never know, objectively, how people lived, felt and perceived for the countless dark millennia before civilisation appeared,

---

* Take warfare. Before around 10,000 BC there is (with a few debatable exceptions) hardly any evidence for warfare, and what there is, clustered around the end of the Palaeolithic era. See Keith Otterbein's review of Lawrence Keeley's *Origins of War*, R. Brian Ferguson, *Ten Points on War* and *War Before History* and Fry, et al. *War, Peace and Human Nature*. The same applies to inequality and ill-health.

† See R. L. Kelly, *The Lifeways of Hunter-Gatherers*, C. Boehme, *Egalitarian Behavior and Reverse Dominance Hierarchy*, A. DeVries, *Primitive Man and His Food*, M. Gurven, H. Kaplan, *Longevity Among Hunter-Gatherers* and D. Lancy, *The Anthropology of Childhood*. See also Daniel Everett, *Don't Sleep There are Snakes*, C. M. Turnball, *The Forest People*, E. Richard Sorenson, *The Edge of the Forest* and many others. Even accounting for the colossal differences between these tribes, the distorting and corrupting effects of living in the twentieth century, the cumulative change to their societies over countless millennia (and repeated, disastrous, contact with more 'advanced' societies), the bias and lies of some authors of who lived with them, the dreadful pains and discomforts of pre-civilised life (e.g. high infant mortality rates), the all-too-human frailties of men and women throughout history and pre-history (nobody imagines that fear and violence have ever been completely absent from the human story) and the tendency many writers have to romanticise hunter-gatherers; the qualities they share—with each other, with what we know of pre-civilised people and with all people at their best—are quite clear.

blindingly over-lit. But if objective knowledge is notoriously limited and unreliable in matters that touch on the essence of human nature, where else are we to gain understanding from? Subjective knowledge is even more unreliable—plain deceptive in fact; it often amounts to little more than wishful thinking and emotional guesswork.

That there might be another, radically different, mode of experience, an awareness of life that is neither objective— based on objects 'out there'—*nor* subjective—based on ideas and emotions 'in here', is ruled out by the science, psychology, history, religion and art of the system and, with a language which inevitably reflects its and our concerns, almost impossible to express in ordinary speech. This PANJECTIVE mode of experience forms the foundation of the companion volume to this book, *Self and Unself*. For now it is enough to note that there is a way we can penetrate human nature without recourse to either rational analysis or guesswork, but this mode of awareness is not available to either wishful thinkers or hyper-rationalists.

The fundamental sanity of early society doesn't mean there weren't problems—pain, frustration, hardship, danger and [increasing] violence—nor does it mean that we should up sticks and return to the trees. It means that what we call 'progress' has been, in terms of quality of life, peace of mind, collective joy and so on, a millennial decline. A few things certainly have improved—technique mostly—but these are almost entirely solutions to problems *caused* by 'progress'.

This 'progress' began around 12,000 years ago, when a catastrophe occurred in human consciousness and, consequently, in human society. Again, the nature and the psychological consequences of this catastrophe, or FALL, is laid out in *Self and Unself*; here we shall confine ourselves to the demonstrable social effects; stratification, violence towards women and children, hostility towards nature, warfare, superstition, shame, sexual suppression and extreme cultural mediocrity, all of which first appeared at the same time and in roughly the same place (the Middle East / West Asia) with the beginning of the process we call HISTORY, CIVILISATION or the SYSTEM.

The civilised system began with intense SUPERSTITION; the belief that ideas—in particular gods and ancestors—were more real than reality. Prior to the superstitious universe, reality was intimately experienced as benevolent, alive and mysterious. This life inhered in certain kinds of things — trees, clouds, rivers, animals and so on — as qualities, or characters, which were then integrated into myths. These stories mirrored the psychological experience of people, or of groups of people, in much the same way as dreams do; indirectly, metaphorically and strangely.

With the coming of the 'proto-civilised' superstitious era these living qualities, and the myths by which they were shared, became objectified; which is to say cut off from fluid, contextual experience and integrated into an abstract mythic system, or [proto] RELIGION. They also became saturated with extremely crude emotions; revolving around sex, violence and, the foundation of superstition, EXISTENTIAL FEAR. Men and women had always been afraid of dangerous things *in* existence, but now they became fearful *of* existence itself, which became separated into two spheres; the reassuring, controllable *known* (the ideas and emotions of the self, 'me and mine') and its opposite, a disturbing-terrifying spectrum which ranged from the *unknown* (foreign people, new situations, etc.) to the *unknowable* (death, consciousness, etc.).

The profound existential anxiety of superstition led, via the coercive absurdities of superstitious shamanism, to the intense abstraction of priests and early [proto] scientists. Prior to 10,000 BC man had thought and reasoned, but now his thoughts began to take on a life of their own, began to seem more real and more important than reality, which now began to be shaped by the structure of thought. It was around this time that a series of interconnected events occurred which were to define the future of the world.

- Cereals were domesticated and incorporated into new agricultural societies (in the Middle East).

- Related to the rise of the cultivation of cereals, which are, uniquely, easy to tax ('visible, divisible, assessable, storable, transportable and rationable'), small, hierarchical and centrally-managed STATES began to grow in the Middle East, which experienced population explosions.*

---

* Large, sedentary, *stateless* societies had flourished before this. There is no reason to suppose that conviviality, equality and liberty are only possible in tiny groups.

- Larger urban areas and more intensive agriculture led to catastrophic deforestation and even more catastrophic soil erosion, which led to the successive failure of the various states of classical civilisation, and to the climate of the Near East becoming drier and more hostile to human society.*

- Writing was invented, in Sumer and Egypt, followed by the Phoenician alphabet, the principle use of which, for thousands of years, was bookkeeping; recording taxation and debt.

- Work became overwhelmingly unpleasant—intensely specialised, monotonous and *managed*. Diseases (such as flu, TB, diphtheria, smallpox, plague and typhus) became, through contact with domesticated animals, common.† Lifespan dramatically declined‡ as did height and general health.

- Finally, and perhaps most significantly, violent male 'sun gods' began to appear in the pantheons of the Middle East (in Egypt and then Judea) which were conceived as being the lords or kings of other gods, which were driven out of heaven, so to speak, until only one, 'true', God remained.

These events took millennia to unfold, spread and integrate with each other, but by the time we reach the third millennium BC the Bronze-age Near East resembled the modern world in every crucial respect. Mesopotamia, for example, was a place of widespread misery, constant warfare, ludicrous superstition, mediocre art, useful science, wasteful over-production, artificial scarcity, massive inequality (the 'original 1%') exploitation of society and nature, over-population, coercive rites, standardisation, division of labour, time-pressure, usury and debt-peonage, taxation, prostitution, ill-health, wretched

---

* E. Hyams, *Soil and Civilisation*, W. H. Kötke, *The Final Empire*, D. Montgomery, *Dirt: The Erosion of Civilisation*, Clive Ponting, *A New Green History Of The World*.

† S. Morand, *Domesticated animals and human infectious diseases of zoonotic origins*, N. D. Wolfe, *Origins of major human infectious diseases*, Burnet & White, *The Natural History of Infectious Diseases*. Diseases of modernity were absent too, such as heart disease and cancer. See A.R David, *Cancer: an old disease, a new disease or something in between?* Immune systems were also far more robust.

‡ Pre-agricultural people were and are as long-lived as modern people. See e.g. M. Gurven, H. Kaplan, *Longevity Among Hunter-Gatherers*.

toil, iniquitous hierarchy, alienation, specialist professionals, slavery, deforestation, soil erosion, repression of minorities, violent subjugation of women, children and outsiders, and rank insanity. This is what we call 'the birth of civilisation', an extraordinarily unpleasant state of affairs which everyone else on earth—the people known as barbarians—was desperate to avoid.

It is possible to chart the spread of this civilisation by following the parallel spread of myths which represent or justify the new state of affairs.* These take the form of a fall from a pre-agricultural garden paradise, or age of gold, into a desacralised, sinful universe of constant toil, presided over by a male sun god (Zeus, Jahweh, Indra, Marduk, etc.) who vanquishes a dark and mysterious female or feminine 'devil', usually symbolised by a snake (Typhon, Satan, Vritra, Tiamet, etc.). This Big Boss in the Sky conquered the mythos of the earth as civilised warriors† and priests conquered and subjugated the freer and far more peaceful populations of Africa, Asia and Europe, who were then forced to accept the new gods with the new rulers.

The next stage in the immiseration of mankind comprised two complementary-yet-antagonistic processes; the rise of Judea—the first society to recognise one 'true' God—and the rise of Greece—the first rational society, and one of the first in which scepticism of divinity appeared. These two events seem to be, at first glance, quite contrary,‡ but the myths and philosophies of the ancient Greek thinkers, and those of the psychopathic old man who ruled over Judea were, in all important points, identical. Jahweh and his Patriarchs, Plato, Aristotle and most of the writers celebrated by classical Greek and Jewish society, hated women, nature, foreigners and ordinary people, and declared that the real world—the earth that is—was devoid of the living mystery which earlier 'backwards' people had worshipped. Greek and Jewish myths are both composed

---

* J. Campbell, *The Masks of God*, M.L.West, *Indo-European Poetry and Myth*.

† Aided by the domestication of the horse—the nuclear bomb of early civilisation.

‡ Like capitalism and communism: see myth 22. Note that a parallel development occurred around this time in China and India also. The entire period, usually called 'the iron age' or the 'axial age', represents a massive intensification of the 'civilised' project across Eurasia; more specialisation, more technology, more rationality and abstraction, more professionalism and more horror.

of psychotic child-men rampaging their way around the world, raping and murdering on the flimsiest of pretexts. We call these stories 'classics'. Greek and Jewish societies also had a veritable obsession with law, which overtook regal—and usually despotic—whim as the means by which society, and by extension, the entire scientific universe, was to be governed. It was through the intensely abstracted reality of the Greeks and the Jews—an abstract rational system, an abstract deity in a distant abstract heaven and an abstract, utterly impersonal, law to which all are equally submitted—that what we understand as 'science', was able to overtake, and then deride, superstition; and what we call 'democracy' supplanted monarchy.* That one nightmare had been supplanted by another, essentially identical, was as difficult to perceive then as it is now.

The baleful universe of the Greeks and Hebrews, conceived in both cases as one of cheerless labour and exclusion from paradise, was founded on the power of severing reality from the *primary technique* of systemic abstraction. This went hand-in-hand with the creation or development of three *secondary techniques* of control, exchange and communication which revolutionised the way people related to each other and to the universe. The first technique was usurious DEBT, first invented by Mesopotamian kings and priests in the third millennium BC to impoverish and enslave their people, but enthusiastically taken up by almost every 'civilisation' which followed. So deeply had debt ingrained itself into the fabric of society that the religions of the Middle East began to reposition reality itself as a debtor-creditor relationship; the debtors, or sinners, being us and the creditor being the Bank of God, managed here on earth by his professional servants; accountants, managers and priests.

The second new technology of control invented by the Greeks, was MONEY—an impersonal, indestructible abstraction which rendered people, objects and, eventually, the entire universe as a collection of homogeneous quantities; *things* which could be bought and sold. It was thanks to the attitude that

---

* After the Graeco-Judaic revolution gods became separate from ordinary life, and the relationship between the two, between *thing* and *god*, became one of command; the beginning of science. 'Abstraction stands in the same relationship to its objects as fate'. M. Horkheimer and T. W. Adorno, *Dialectic of Enlightenment*.

money engendered that Greek philosophers began to view the entire universe as a composite of discrete, rationally-apprehended granules, or particles (a.k.a. 'atoms'), and ideas (or 'platonic forms'), chief among them, *the tragic atom*—cut-off, isolated, alone—we call 'man'.

The third revolutionary technology of civilisation was alphabetic LITERACY, first developed by the Phoenicians but perfected and worshipped by the Greeks and the Hebrews. This technique, for all its potential use and beauty, stimulated a disastrous change in consciousness in those who had access to it, who began to see *inspiration* not as unmitigated experience, but as a function of memory; *meaning* not as inherent quality, but as a series of words; and *society* not as something which man has direct contextual access to, through his senses, but as something which comes to him through the reading mind. Again—as would be the case with every epochal technology which followed—almost nobody saw that the powers being gained were at the expense of faculties withering; in this case, of sensate inspiration, contextual awareness and the ineffable music of speech.

These three techniques had three combined effects. Firstly, they radically enhanced the separation of the individual from his or her context; as money-power requires no relationship to sustain it. Secondly, they intensified the isolated and isolating power of individual possession; as *my* things are no longer tied by tradition, or reciprocity to others. And thirdly, they created or fortified a belief, in all who came under the grip of debt, literacy and money, that reality is, ultimately, a mind-knowable, possessable, *thing*.

And so, by the time Greece ceded civilised power to Rome (which, with the adoption of Christianity, fused Graeco-Judaism into one empire), all the basic components of a brutally subordinating mechanical civilisation were in place; intense social stratification, hostility towards the unknown, an abstract image of the universe which was taken to be real and a sense that money, mind, language and the cosmos are all similarly structured—and equally significant—entities. All the consequences of such foundational attitudes were also in place; namely law and crime, armed forces and war, spectacle and boredom, religion and [proto] scientism, widespread suffering, loneliness, alienation, insanity and ecological ruin. These components, in various forms and combinations, continued to govern the affairs of men and women for the next thousand years in Europe, Asia, large parts of Africa and, eventually, in South America.

Sometimes civilisations fell, such as Rome; an event greeted by relief and an improvement in quality of life for ordinary people.* Sometimes they were kept in check, such as Japan's long history of successful independence, and less uncivilised social systems could then reassert themselves. These FEUDAL systems, although encouraging exploitation—sometimes appalling suffering—represented an overall improvement in the lives of ordinary people. The European medieval peasant, for example, was self-sufficient, had abundant access to common land, did non-alienating labour to an extremely high standard, and very often at an exceedingly leisurely pace, had a colossal number of holidays† and had reasonably healthy social relations with his fellows, even those outside of his class. Subservience to the clock was unknown outside of monasteries, death was viewed as a lifelong companion rather than a time-obsessed 'reaper', madness was rarely a pretext for exclusion and even gender relations, despite many horrendous exceptions, were *reasonably* egalitarian. Medieval men and women were also, particularly in the later Middle Ages, an inspiring, heretical and anarchic pain in the feudal arse.‡ There was sickness, warfare and the psychological miseries of religion, especially towards the end of the period when something like hell descended on the feudal world in Europe, but exploitation such as was practiced before, in Imperial Rome say, or after, in Victorian England,

---

* The so-called 'collapse' of many early states was often experienced as emancipation. Life outside the state could still be violent and precarious, but an end to oppressive taxation, serfdom, warfare, epidemics and all the horrors of civilisation at the very least did not *necessarily* lead to the brutal miseries its defenders are keen to present. See James C. Scott, *Against the Grain* and McAnany & Yoffee, *Questioning Collapse*. Likewise, 'defection' or 'going native'—fleeing the oppressive state and joining 'barbarian' societies that were healthier, fairer and even more ordered—has been a common and persistent 'problem' throughout civilised history.

† Almost one third of the year, and a four-day work week was common.

‡ E.g. the Beguines, the Jacquerie, the Free Spirits, the Lollards, the Taborites and many other mystical radicals of the late Middle Ages.

was relatively low; poverty, the kind that, for example, modern Indians are familiar with, was relatively rare and radical rebellion, the kind that twentieth century Spanish anarchists and European hippies could only dream of, was relatively common.*

All this was to change. In the fifteenth and sixteenth centuries a new form of the system arose; CAPITALISM. In all essential aspects capitalism was a continuation and refinement of the civilised project conceived at the dawn of superstition, first made manifest in Mesopotamia and Egypt—the first societies to operate as if the people who comprise it were components of a mechanism—and then developed by Judea, Greece, Rome, China, the Abbasids, the Mongols, the Ottomans, the Spanish, the Dutch the British and the US. With each successive civilisation the social-machine was refined and improved. The organisation of classical armies, the growth and regimented management of city-states, the repressive institutionalisation and timekeeping of medieval monasteries, the banking systems of the renaissance; each new technique of social control added to the means by which an autonomous, mechanical—and then digital—governing system could be constructed.

From the seventeenth century onwards, every step taken by the elites of Europe (particularly the new class of businessmen and professional technicians) was towards the creation of this self-regulating system. The industrial revolution, the management of a 'free' industrial workforce, the hyper-rationalisation of experience, the conversion of time into money, the proliferation and evolution of schools, workhouses, hospitals, factories, banks, armies and the modern nation state, along with their coercive techniques of surveillance and control (imposing common, standard, uniform names, measurements, currencies, religions, legal systems, urban layouts and so on) were and continue to be to this one end. By the end of the nineteenth century it

---

* The quality of medieval life was erased from the mind of European man by enlightenment thinkers. See, for an antidote, N. Elias, *The Civilising Process*, L. Mumford, *Technics and Civilisation*, J. le Goff, *Medieval Civilisation*, I. Illich, *In the Mirror of the Past*, C. Wickham, *The Inheritance of Rome*, N. Cantor, *The Civilisation of the Middle Ages*, W. Chester Jordan, *Europe in the High Middle Ages*, M. McLuhan, *The Gutenberg Galaxy*, Moore, R. Vaneigem, *The Movement of the Free Spirit* and J. Zerzan, *Revolt and Heresy in the Late Middle Ages*.

had become clear that the creation of a 'perfect' global system was going to lead to the total annihilation of society in short order, and so measures were taken to, firstly, protect the labour force against its onslaught and, secondly, to appease the many revolutionary movements which had sprung up in an attempt to resist their horrific fate. The series of reforms that spanned the century between 1860 and 1960 succeeded in improving life for many, but with the deep foundations of the system ignored, and the common ground beneath those completely unperceived, the juggernaut of civilisation rolled on, untroubled and undiminished—indeed, in many ways, strengthened by reform—until what few brakes men and women had managed to install were, at the end of the twentieth century, 'rolled back', so that the system could finish its business; the amalgamation of the people, ideas, emotions, techniques, tools, objects, behaviours and 'natural resources' (i.e. natural life) which comprise civilisation into a single, monolithic and entirely self-directing mechanism.

Until the end of the capitalist phase of civilised progress, which lasted from approximately 1600 to 1900, the various elements of the system were more or less integrated with nature, human nature and the culture that humans in groups naturally create. The advent of capitalism saw land, labour, energy and time commodified and assimilated with all the other components of civilisation into a multitude of rational-scientific-technological processes, the sole purpose of which was the production of *more output* (profit, production, speed, accuracy, efficiency, etc.). These processes, by externalising or ignoring anything not relevant to the task at hand, inevitably distorted, degraded or destroyed everything they came into contact with. Cotton mills produced more cheap cotton, while devastating local communities, schools produced more compliant workers while terminally corrupting their initiative and sensitivity, farms produced more food while stripping the soil of nutrients and eliminating the wild, factories produced more abstract wealth while chronically impoverishing their workers' actual lives (see myth 11), gadgets produced more 'saved time' while multiplying the work required to build (and pay for) them, and so on. Every technological innovation since has solved one set of isolated problems while producing multiple sets of new problems for which more technical processes have to be developed to solve.

Much fanfare accompanies each new solution—plastic, nuclear fission, high-speed travel, genetic engineering, the internet, bio-fuels, smartphones—or each new prospective solution— smart drugs, virtual reality, cybernetics, nanotechnology, nuclear fusion, vast mirrors in space—while the disastrous pollution, boredom, sickness and madness which they cause are excused, ignored or exploited as new possibilities for technological progress or new markets to expand into.

By the close of the capitalist era, the technical approach to life* had separated itself from human culture and dominated material life on earth. Over the course of the twentieth century this dominance would spread to every aspect of human and natural experience; for the technical approach was not just restricted to the construction of powerful machines, the harnessing of new forms of energy, the refinement of methods of control or the manufacture of merchandise,† but was applied to the full range of natural and human life; indeed it *had* to be applied to everything, because anything which is independent to rational restructuring, impedes or threatens output. Technical development of one aspect of the system, in one place, demands concomitant development in those aspects that supply its inputs and relieve its outputs. A high-tech factory cannot be developed unless there are high-tech supplies, arriving at high-tech speeds and processed by high-tech employees. These employees are no longer allowed to discover their own style of work, train themselves or live the kind of life they want to, but must be entirely integrated into scientific techniques of programming proven to produce the most speed, power, efficiency, accuracy or whatever the desired output happens to be. The same pressures are applied to *literally every human endeavour*. Whether you are a sportsman, a potter, a programmer, a singer, a road sweeper or a police officer, you are not permitted to go at your own pace, to work out for yourself how to work, to create from your own experience or inspiration, to do as you please, when you please or, God help you, to wonder why you are working as you do, in such a bizarrely inhuman manner, or to what end. Independence of thought, action or even feeling is not

---

* a.k.a. 'technique'. See Jacques Ellul, *The Technological Society*.

† The industrial revolution was a *result* of the technological approach, not its cause.

an option, considering the distant or long-term effects of your activity is not an option, any practice or reality which cannot be assimilated to techniques of maximum control, productivity and efficiency* is not an option.

This is one reason why it is useless to reform, refuse or even to attempt to understand independent aspects of the system, in isolation from the whole. Politics, communication, transport, medicine, economics, academia, housing, food, entertainment, management and all work are integrated into a single system of interlocking processes. It is ultimately meaningless to speculate on how the internet has changed human life, or analyse the influence of 'Big Pharma', or attempt to diagnose the problems with 'our education system;' just as it is ultimately futile to reform prisons, or ban plastic bags, or sign petitions; just as it is ultimately useless to oppose the domination of energy companies, medical professionals or state bureaucracy over human life by powering your house with a wood stove, self-medicating or deleting your Facebook account and tearing up your passport. This isn't to say that it is meaningless, useless and futile to investigate, or try to solve or circumvent these problems, *at all*. We are, after all, about to look at thirty-three aspects of the system, each addressed individually. What *is* meaningless, useless and futile is to tackle these aspects without reference to the system as a whole into which each element is inextricably integrated; and those who defend the system understand this. They know, or they unconsciously intuit, that the system is best served by focusing on its isolated elements, which they spend their lives doing. Such people we normally call 'specialists'.

The system more or less forces everyone to become a specialist, to treat separate parts of the universe as objects for technical manipulation. The teacher, for example, must separate the child from his home, his society, his natural milieu and the extraordinary complexity and subtlety of his own life and character, apply fixed inputs to the child's attention (the various books, tests and projects of the syllabus, augmented by whatever games, trips and 'experiences' the school or teacher can add, either officially or *pro bono*) in order to obtain a desired output; namely integration into the system. Doctors work in the

---

* Of which control always comes first.

same way, as do scientists, lawyers, social workers, sportsmen, politicians, managers, designers, plumbers, farmers, kitchen porters... everyone.

A world comprised entirely of such rational specialists inevitably leads to nobody knowing what the effects of their actions are or taking responsibility for them (see myth 16). They aren't trained to do so, and if they do step beyond their allotted roles, they inevitably tread on the toes of someone else, someone whose entire life depends on the power *they* exert over their specialised task. This results in the generation of a near infinite quantity of stupid jobs, created to manage microscopic details or protect specialised power, without the interference of anyone who might know what they are doing.

The system is not, nor can ever be, ruled by men and women who know what they are doing, who perceive the context or who are prepared to put non-systemic ends above the system's proliferation of means. In this sense, the system is entirely autonomous and self-directed; its prime directive being the only one which an autonomous machine can conceive of; grow, expand, reproduce. Never die. Men and women own or manage various parts of the system, but the only actions which the system allows them to take are those which promote its ceaseless growth. Likewise only those who instinctively promote these actions, who have been accustomed to the systemic way of life since childhood, are promoted into positions where they can 'freely' make the right decisions. The system automatically creates filters to remove 'trouble-makers' from the path to positions of influence. If someone who is kindly, well-meaning or intelligent ever gains power, he finds himself completely impotent before the system, which will either do everything it can to expel his useless presence, or just allow him to bash his head against a brick wall until his supporters are disappointed and abandon him.

The pre-modern phase of the system was characterised, then, by the abstracted commodification of space, time and energy. Surveyors divided up the land, clocks divided up the day and the state divided up the people,* and all three were

---

* Or 'labour power', which was no longer independent. The feudal worker could eventually achieve significant independence. Capitalism abolished the mastery

put on the market, where they were integrated into ever more sophisticated technologies of production (or manufacture) and techniques of reproduction (or 'service') which we normally call capitalism. This pre-modern phase then evolved, in the first half of the twentieth century, into the modern or postmodern system we are familiar with, which seeks to commodify *knowledge* (or data), *debt* (via the process called financialisation, whereby the commodified future is manipulated and traded at hyper-speed: see myth 2), *perception* and *emotion* (through the virtualisation of all kinds of social interaction), *matter* (artificial materials, patented molecules, proprietary genes, etc.) and new forms of *hyper-energy* (petrochemical and nuclear power); in short, the removal of every barrier between the system and the last recesses of reality. Ultimately, even our own conscious experience of our own bodies were to be incorporated (or PRIVATISED) into the world-mechanism and forced to conform to its rhythms and laws.

Another notable feature of the post-capitalist world is that it increasingly takes on features of other forms of the system, such as feudalism, socialism and fascism. Financialisation has led to enormous amounts of money sloshing around the higher levels of the system which, in turn, has led to, effectively, a feudal network of favours, kickbacks and sinecures; means to keep friends, family and other allies well remunerated while, effectively, doing nothing.* Large corporations have long depended on government support (via military spending or state-sponsored R&D) and bailouts (during depressions and recessions)—which is, effectively, a form of state-sponsored socialism (for the rich; see myth 6). And the system frequently demands extreme forms of authoritarianism which—particularly under duress—are indistinguishable from fascism and totalitarianism (see myth 22).

The term 'capitalism' might, therefore, be useful shorthand, but it is far from accurate. The 'capitalism' of today is radically different to the one dissected by Marx, which is why some of his key predictions did not come to pass. He had no idea that the entire world, up to and including the psyche of

---

that enabled him to achieve this, forcing labour into a lifetime of service.

* A situation compounded manyfold by technical specialisation. See D. Graeber, *Bullshit Jobs* for further discussion of 'capitalist feudalism'.

everyone in it. would become a 'means of production', nor that, consequently, the working-class would become subdued and domesticated. This is why today's capitalism is now frequently referred to as LATE-STAGE, or sometimes NEO-LIBERAL. But if we accept that these refer to the latest and greatest stage of a project which has been ongoing for at least ten millennia—if we are to understand the entire process, including its decidedly non-capitalistic elements—we need a term which encompasses it. Although, as we shall see, it is also problematic, there is no tool better suited to the task than THE SYSTEM, a term which simultaneously refers to civilisation *in toto*, and the prevailing, encompassing, hyper-sophisticated, post-capitalist world order we find ourselves in today.

Four Kinds of Dystopia

A S THE FINAL manifestation of the system began to take shape, some thinkers began to speculate on what the result would be, of what kind of world was coming into being. Of these nightmarish visions of our present four stand as prototypes, and as models for fundamental aspects of the system. These are the dystopias imagined by George Orwell, Aldous Huxley, Franz Kafka and Philip K. Dick:

ORWELLIAN Rule by autocratic totalitarian people, party or elite group. Limitation of choice, repression of speech and repression of minorities. Belief in order, routine and rational-morality. Erotic physicality and sexual freedom suppressed through violent control of sexual impulse. Constant surveillance and constant censorship. Control of bodies by enclosure, fear, *explicit* violence, repression of dissent and forced obedience to 'the party line' (ORWELLIAN FANATICISM: All must submit). Control of minds by explicitly policing, punishing and suppressing subversive language (ORWELLIAN NEWSPEAK: state-controlled reduction of vocabulary to limit range of thought). Truth cannot be known (a.k.a. HYPER-RELATIVISM or POSTMODERNISM); and therefore we need an *external authority* to decide what the truth is (kings and priests) and to protect society from chaos and madness (the ORWELLIAN THEM: reds, anarchists, extremists, infidels, plebs, freaks, criminals, etc.).

HUXLEYAN Rule by democratic, totalitarian, capitalist, techno-cratic *systems*. Super-excess of choice. Limitation of access to speech platforms. Assimilation of minorities (via TOKENISM: see myth 5), foundational belief in emotional-morality, 'imagination' and 'flexibility'. Control by desire, debt, narcotic, technical necessity and *implicit* threat of violence. No overt control of dissent* (system selects for system-friendly voices and unconscious self-censorship). Erotic physicality and sexual freedom suppressed via promotion of pornographic sensuality, promiscuity and dissolution. Control of bodies through pleasure and addiction to pleasure. Control of minds by proliferating information and enclosing language within professional boundaries (*illichian newspeak*, or UNIQUACK: see myth 28). Truth can be intellectually known (the religion of SCIENTISM: see myth 23) and is obvious when understood (HUXLEYAN FANATICISM: only the wicked can refuse it) and learnt in the process of setting up an *internal* authority (a.k.a. MORALITY or CONSCIENCE) called 'education'.

KAFKAESQUE Rule by *bureaucracy*. Control of world through *putting it in writing*; fixing names, surveying land, standardising measures, tracking movement, quantifying, measuring and recording everything that happens everywhere, thereby abstracting it and making it *manageable*, which, in itself, induces tractable stress and the schizoid, self-regulating self-consciousness (anxiety about low marks, unlikes, official judgements and the like) of the bureaucratically surveilled. In addiction, bureaucratic functions and practices in an expanding abstract system are increasingly designed to manage *their own* abstract output. Having less and less to do with the actual lives of those who engage with paperwork, bureaucratic tasks necessarily become frustrating, interminable, dehumanising and pointless; a state of affairs which is permitted, and even encouraged, as it automatically grinds down that which threatens management; the informal, the illiterate, the spontaneous, the shifting, the weird, the local, the private, the embodied and all those who seek to have a direct

---

* 'A really efficient totalitarian state would be one in which the all-powerful executive of political bosses and their army of managers control a population of slaves who do not have to be coerced, because they love their servitude'. Aldous Huxley.

relationship with their fellows; all of which is intolerable to Kafkaesque systems, which promote into power hyper-normal functionaries who seek an indirect relationship with their fellows and who, through fear of life, seek to control it through the flow of paperwork.

PHILDICKIAN Rule by replacing reality with an abstract, ersatz virtual image of it (a.k.a. the SPECTACLE). This technique of social control began with LITERACY—and the creation of written symbols, which devalued soft conscious sensuous inspiration, fostered a private (reader-text) interaction with society, created the illusion that language is a *thing*, that meaning can be stored, owned and perfectly duplicated, that elite language is standard and so on*—and ended with VIRTUALITY—the conversion of classrooms, offices, prisons, shops and similar social spaces into 'immersive' on-line holodecks which control and reward participants through permanent, perfect surveillance, the stimulation of positive and negative emotion, offers of godlike powers, and threats to nonconformists of either narco-withdrawal or banishment to an off-line reality now so degraded by the demands of manufacturing an entire artificial universe, that only hellish production facilities, shoddy living-units and prisons can materially function there.

These four visions of hell are all founded upon the civilised system. This foundation, or background, serves as the origin and meeting point of Orwellian, Huxleyan, Kafkaesque and Phildickian worlds, which necessarily overlap and interact at key points; namely the fundamental alienation and misery of civilisation, the commodification and rationalisation of capitalism and the hyper-specialised, hyper-technical approach to life of late-capitalism. From this common root grew those branches of modernity and postmodernity which Orwell, Huxley, Kafka

---

* Literacy is not inherently dystopian, but it is the beginning of an existentially degrading process, which starts with societies demanding literacy for participation (devaluing improvised, oral forms of expression) and ends with the eradication of reality. This degradation of existence increases with every step towards virtuality (print, perspective, photography, TV, VR) until there remains no possibility of reverie, transcendence, humanity, meaning or creativity, all of which become suspect.

and Dick explored and described, and which it is helpful to bear in mind as we investigate our world further.

All modern societies, for example, are both Kafkaesque and Phildickian (indeed virtual Phildickia can be seen as a modern refinement of the hyper-literate Kafkastan) with either a Huxleyan or Orwellian overarching framework; modern, Western, 'capitalist' societies have tended to be basically Huxleyan (HKP) and, on the other side of the slit-thin officially acceptable 'political spectrum' (a.k.a. the '*Overton Window*'), pre-modern, Eastern, 'communist' countries have tended to Orwellianism (OKP),* although within these disparities much diversity prevails. We are, while at work for example, largely in an Orwellian mode, where freedom to choose how and when we work is strictly limited (either explicitly or, for modern professionals and precarious freelancer, implicitly), where spontaneity and sexuality are severely punished and where, essentially, we are treated like chattel. When we leave work, however, we enter a Huxleyan world of transcendent freedom, infinite choice, democracy and pleasure; we can comment, vote, consume to satiety, a panoply of sexual and creative opportunity opens out and everyone everywhere treats us (or is at least supposed to treat us) like the capitalist gods we really are (official term; CUSTOMER); at least those of us who can pay are. The dirt poor remain in Airstrip 1.

Ideological managers (academics, film directors, journalists, etc.) prefer to have two (or more) dystopian systems because it makes *us* seem like the goodies and *them* the baddies. Communism is to blame for *their* food banks and breadlines, but capitalism has nothing to do with *ours* (or vice versa). Sure, our masses have the same miserable lives as theirs, reel under the same bureaucratic insanity, stumble around the same shoddy unreal worlds, and witness the same catastrophic destruction of nature and beauty as theirs do, but at least we've got democracy! / at least our families stick together! / at least the trains run on time! / at least GTA 9 is coming out soon / at least the Olympics will cheer us up (delete, or exterminate, as appropriate).

I call this extremely common mental-emotional activity, *biastification*: To excuse one excess of one's self or one's society

---

* The complementary Orwellian-Huxleyan polarity can be traced back at least to the Graeco-Judaic divide. Ancient Greece was roughly Huxleyan and Judea, Orwellian.

by comparing it with its opposame / false antonym. *Our* basically Huxleyan nightmare is excused by pointing the finger at *their* basically Orwellian nightmare. The cult of optimism is excused by comparing it with that of pessimism, cold rationality is excused by comparing it with hot emotion, being 'a responsible adult' is excused by comparing it to being 'an irresponsible child', hedonism is excused by comparing it to boredom, corporatism is excused by comparing it to statism, and the implicit violence of modern uncivilisation is excused by comparing it to the explicit violence of the lawless pre-modern cults which gave rise to and sustain it.

That all these apparent differences are essentially aspects of the same reality or pseudo reality becomes visible during crises. When the Huxleyan world is attacked (or an attack, by terrorists, communists or flu-like viruses,* is simulated) or, at its apogee, begins to break down, it *instantly* turns into an Orwellian nightmare. When the 'law and order' of capitalism disintegrates, those who uphold it are perfectly happy to take their place at the head of feudal gangs and crime syndicates. When the over-excited optimist loses his status he instantly transforms into a suicidal pessimist. When the fun-loving influencer cannot get her fix of excitement she immediately experiences intense, unbearable boredom. When the truth gets close to the rationalist, physicalist, objectivist bone, childish, irrational, solipsistic spleen erupts. When a sophisticated virtual addiction becomes unavailable, the addict switches at once to a cruder antecedent. When a socialist revolution seizes the state, *capitalist professionals hardly skip a step in transferring to one-party rhythms*. When communism falls, commissars switch to raving capitalists in a heartbeat. At no point is a genuine alternative, much less the source of or solution to what ails us, perceived or acknowledged.

Those who build and maintain the system do not have an organ to sense the source, that which is beyond or prior to the biastified opposames of the emotional-rational world. Uncertainty, mystery, femininity, innocence, nature and the context (a.k.a.

---

* Whether the coronavirus 'pandemic' was engineered or not is, as far as the system is concerned, immaterial. The figures were inflated, both factually and emotionally—age-standardised mortality rates were much as they are in any other year—in countries wishing to convert their Huxleyan systems into Orwellian ones.

non-specialist REALITY) are all sources of anxiety to systemoids, who respond to their presence with irritation, hostility and an irresistible urge to either brush them from view or to bring them under comprehensible control. The mysterious and the immediate are met with violence and—the modern companion of violence—rationalisation; the further reduction of experience to quantifiable things, objects, ideas, facts, figures, commodities, prices, wages and so on. Then, as reality is annihilated, and a rational, virtual nightmare spreads over the wasteland where the earth once was, the system proceeds to make a series of extraordinary claims to the effect that because our lives have *quantitatively* improved—because more land or labour has been commodified, because more output has been produced, because the virtual world is faster or more accurately emulates sensory experience, because people are financially richer, or in posses-sion of more amenities, qualifications, knowledge, security or choice—that we are thereby enjoying a superior '*quality*' of life.

Radical critiques of the system necessarily focus on this so-called 'quality', and attempt to show that it is actually just a larger *quantity* of stimulation, movement, security or power (*relative* to boredom, insecurity or poverty). We have more jobs, yes, and more money, and more comfort, and more power; more things—but our lives are not improving. We are becoming lone-lier, sicker, more insane, more bored, and more alienated from a natural world, which is actually dying. A few technological innovations may genuinely serve us, but the system as a whole enslaves and ruins us. The earth is not becoming a better place to live. In fact, everything on it which we deeply value is being destroyed by amenities, choice, prosperity, jobs and progress.

The response of the system to the threat of such a critique is completely predictable. The system and those who serve it inevitably respond to qualitative degradation with quantitative demands and rebuttals: show me your proof, give me your evidence, explain to me the details, my life isn't as bad as all that, look at what the papers say, what does all this even *mean?* Not that there isn't a place for the facts that professional sys-temacrats demand—of course there is—but that the problem with and solution to the unhappy supermind are, *ultimately*, not a matter that can be resolved in this way, technically, ra-tionally, objectively or scientifically. It is to art we must turn to understand our world; which is why those in command of the world spend an enormous amount of energy in debasing art, in stripping it of meaning, or of handing it over exclusively to their quality immune chums.

What follows is a polemic, or as defenders of the system would have it, a 'rant' (a word which, considering its origins, I tend to take as a compliment); a direct attack on the roots of the system. It is not, therefore, as radical or even as truthful as the *indirect* ('non-factual') arts of music, painting or myth can be. But although it is unable to reach the 'existential depth' of those forms of expression, it does appeal, ultimately, to the same experience; a shared sense of quality, or truth, or poetry, or love; words, you will notice, which are meaningless to systemic [capitalist, communist, scientific, religious, institutional, post-modern] thought, not to mention somewhat cheesy, fanciful, perhaps even rather unpleasant feeling.

I mention feeling because it is in *sense*, ultimately, that my case rests. If you do not feel what I have to say as expressing some kind of reality, in your own experience, then, no matter how truthful my account, you'll *already* be starting to feel that it is stupid ('unrealistic', 'amateurish', 'immature') pretentious ('edgy', 'naval-gazing, 'too deep for me!') or, at best, debatable ('who are *you* to say?' or 'that's your opinion, we're all different'); and you'll already be obviating these unpleasant feelings by focusing on the details of what I am saying, removing them from the context of the entire point and objecting to whatever mistakes or inconsistencies you can find. You will, in a word, find it all *non*-sense ('I couldn't get past the first chapter!').

When I say 'feeling', I am not referring to *emotion*, which is also (as explored in *Self and Unself*) a quantitative experience, but to the felt quality of life, which you either experience, or you don't—and which no argument will ever reconcile you to, any more than an essay can persuade you that a song or film you love is shite.

A genuinely different quality of life, to the quantifying self, just *sounds* wrong. It creates an emotion of 'don't like', which the mind then justifies by identifying something else in its memory banks which it also doesn't like. Take for example the proposition *'love is unconditional; it requires no condition to experience it'*. To those who are dependent on conditions for their love—on fun experiences, familiar people, nice possessions and so on—this statement *sounds* abstract, unreal, intellectual, religious, insane, boring, stupid, weird or factually ludicrous ('Oh, so you can feel love if everyone you know dies, can you?'). Or take the proposition *'civilisation is collapsing'*. This *sounds* radical, extreme, exaggerated, angry, edgy, simplistic, dangerous, delusional, hypocritical, socialist or factually dubious ('Look at how powerful the government is! Look at all the experts who disagree!'). Or take isolated claims such as *'murder is worse than rape'*, or *'the Nazis supported Zionism'* or *'Prince Harry helped murder Afghans'* which *sound* prejudiced, offensive, distasteful, insensitive or tactically unsound. Or take someone who utters such propositions. He or she *sounds* like a crank, a weirdo, a fool, a terrorist, a sexist, a racist, a commie, a loser, a nutter, a 'mystic', a schizophrenic (see myth 26), a dilettante (see myth 28), a pessimist, a cult-member, a conspiracy theorist or an out-and-out fiend or fraud.

The reason why all these things *sound* wrong, is because the system-colluding mind cannot bear to be criticised and so it either ignores the criticism entirely or, if that's not possible, focuses on secondary aspects of it; how it feels ('Weird!'), the style in which it is delivered ('Boooring!'), what it resembles ('It's basically a rehash of Buddhism and Marxism isn't it?'), what it means divorced from context ('Racist! Sexist! Madman!'), any isolated errors it might contain ('Ha ha ha! Misattributed quote!'), who is making the criticism (how he sounds, what he wears, who he sleeps with), and so on and so forth.

These reactions are all, effectively, unanswerable—you might as well reason with a child shouting *'no I'm not, you are'* over and over again—but those who own and manage the system are well aware that they are of limited efficacy and, on their own, betray a catastrophic lack of integrity. Hence, the existence of an ideology industry to produce and disseminate myths by which the system can protect itself against radical attack; by which owners and managers can live without conscience and workers and outcasts can die without complaint; by which a counterfeit unworld can justifiably replace the earth we once lived on; myths of the benevolence of the system, of its eternal inevitability, of its unquestionable truth, of its glory, beauty, utility and equity. These are...

1

The Myth *of* Economics

Economics defines the world, the universe,
reality itself, as a rational market system and
human beings as wealth maximising *things*
· · · The purpose of economics is to justify
the activity of the system, and the behaviour
of those who own and manage it · · · This is
essentially a *religious* endeavour.

ECONOMICS EXPLAINS EVERYTHING, for all time. Economists either make this claim openly and directly,* or they just assume that the entire universe and all life within it operates—and will forever operate—according to the core assumption of classical economic theory:

> *Human society is composed of rationally self-interested individuals with unlimited wants competing over scarce resources.*

This foundational premise, upon which a veritable citadel of academic endeavour has been built, is taken to be based on, or extend to, the entire natural world; and once upon a time even to God. All natural forms are self-interested competitors for limited resources, genes are microscopic capitalists, and all evidence to the contrary is instantly rendered invisible or unscientific. Thus, a society which is based on prices and money transactions—a MARKET SYSTEM—is as natural as the human behaviour that economists study within it, a 'propensity to truck and barter',† which has, in effect, been waiting since the dawn of life itself to unburden itself of the obstacles to behaving in the most natural—or most 'developed'—way possible; the perfect system we know as CAPITALISM, which, logically, will endure for all time, or at least as long as human beings behave 'rationally'.

This word, 'rational', is a key component of economic theory, for two reasons. Firstly, because economists, like all capitalists, believe that only the physicalist, scientific method can reveal truth. If something is 'unscientific' it cannot be said to meaningfully exist. Thus, the opposite of rational must be 'irrational'—insane, unreasonable or ridiculous. The existence

---

* Ha-Joon Chang, *Economics: The User's Guide.*

† In Adam Smith's famous words.

or the significance of *non-rational truths* is ruled out *a priori* by economists and the scientific establishment they like to believe they are part of.

Like to believe—but are not. Economics and science do share something in common; they are both founded on a disregard for the context and a focus on what amounts to illusions, but the illusion of science does partly, and demonstrably, mirror an aspect of the physical world* which is how it can be used to make accurate and useful predictions about that world. The *human* world which economics claims to model, is, however, not reducible to ideas in the same way, nor, even if it were, can it be studied using the same experimental method scientists use on physical phenomena. This is why the theories of economists are illogical and superficial, why economists are unable to make reliable predictions, and why the predictions they do make are always wrong. This doesn't stop capitalists following their advice though, because, in the real world, economics is not the study of the economy, nor of human behaviour in it, nor of any of the countless other phenomena that economists presume to explain. Economics, like so much of academia, like law also, and journalism, is ultimately nothing more than a means to justify the acts of the powerful and obscure or confuse any truth which might interrupt their 'freedom'. Contemporary 'neo-classical' economics, for example, examines exclusively abstract models (empirical facts never appear) which assume that all people have the same measurable tastes (which amounts to assuming there is only one person in society) and that these tastes remain the same under radically different conditions (which amounts to assuming there is only one commodity). The resulting 'laws' are perfectly meaningless as far as furthering knowledge is concerned, but such an aim is far from the mind of economists and their sponsors.

When kings wanted to massacre their enemies or impoverish their people, they consulted priests, who were paid to explain to them why God approved of their actions. Now, when

---

* Namely the facts the world can, from the perspective of mind, be said to consist of. These facts clearly and obviously do relate to something in the real world—if they did not, we would be unable to tell it from a dream. The crucial question is what there is in reality which is non-factual and therefore opaque to scientific reasoning.

politicians and CEOs want to do the same thing, they consult economists (or their pseudo-scientific colleagues, psychologists, or doctors willing to sell their integrity in order to keep their jobs*) who explain why it is good for business to enclose the commons, so that self-sufficient peasants are forced to sell their labour; or why it is good for business to introduce starvation to a remote island, so its inhabitants are forced to join the market; or why it is good for business to enslave half of Africa in 'planned villages', or on cotton plantations; or why it is good for business to privatise a country's water supply so that it might be bought up and sold by Nestlé; or why it is good for business to exterminate the bothersome population of a resource-rich country; or why it is good for business to generate unspeakable misery for the population of China, India and Bangladesh, in order to manufacture all the goods sold by Western corporations. Economics magically explains away all this misery and ruin, for such immeasurable qualities as ugliness, suffering, servitude, alienation, exploitation and mounting horror cannot appear in the company accounts or in the minds of economists. They are therefore non-existent.

Take, for example, the 2008 financial crash. All of the attention of the so-called left and right was focused on financialisation, credit and debt, lack of regulation, speculation and banking. Fascinating and significant to be sure (see myth 2); but not a *syllable* mentioned how the colossal economies of the corporate West, and its class of hyper wealthy CEOs, shareholders and managers, actually *gained* their power to gamble humongous sums in the money markets; because this pivotal element of the world economy—the outrageously profitable class-based exploitation of land and labour in 'developing' countries—simply *does not exist* for professional economists and capitalist journalists.[†]

Labour—which is to say, lived activity, which is to say, *life*—is invisible to economists, for whom all happiness, all 'productivity', all 'progress' (see myth 12) is not the result of living

---

* Virologists and epidemiologists are particularly popular these days.

† Economists blame the *effects* of capitalist activity for crashes (reckless risk-taking, lax regulation, etc.) instead of the *cause* (exploitation, inequality, etc.). See John Smith, *Imperialism in the 21ˢᵗ Century*.

creatures doing things, but of prices, commodities and economic relationships such as ownership and investment; in short of CAPITAL. It is, says the economist, capital which produces food and fuel, not nature. It is capital which builds tools and uses them, not people. It is capital which is productive and creative, not life. The economist, both capitalist and Marxist, like the priest and the shaman, thus brings an idea to life, teaches the people to worship his invention and then conceals the outrageous fraudulence of this magical thinking behind complicated language acquired during specialist training. The people then imagine that *their own activity* is really the activity of capital (or 'industry' or 'them'), which leads them to believe that they are only useful to the world while they are producing capital and serving the capitalist system; which is to say, performing activities which they have no interest or control over and paying for goods they themselves have produced with money they received in exchange for this activity, goods which, finally, they admire as alien objects manifested from the heavens above. All of which 'gives new life to capital and annihilates their own lives'.*

For economists such things are as 'noise' is to scientists; background 'externalities', as unremarkable as the air which, nevertheless, must be sucked out of the vacuum of abstract economic thought. The dreamy economic 'reality' which results can then be shown to mirror their inept and corrupt pseudo-science, thereby providing economics with a mask of respectable

---

* Fredy Perlman, *The Reproduction of Daily Life*. 'When an industrial worker runs an electric lathe, he uses products of the labor of generations of physicists, inventors, electrical engineers, lathe makers. He is obviously more productive than a craftsman who carves the same object by hand. But it is in no sense the "Capital" at the disposal of the industrial worker which is more "productive" than the "Capital" of the craftsman. If generations of intellectual and manual activity had not been embodied in the electric lathe, if the industrial worker had to invent the lathe, electricity, and the electric lathe, then it would take him numerous lifetimes to turn a single object on an electric lathe, and no amount of Capital could raise his productivity above that of the craftsman who carves the object by hand. The notion of the "productivity of capital", and particularly the detailed measurement of that "productivity", are inventions of the "science" of Economics, that religion of capitalist daily life which uses up people's energy in the worship, admiration and flattery of the central fetish of capitalist society'.

scholarship. Anyone who attempts to reintroduce oxygen into the void is dismissed, or, if their activities prove to be combustible, locked up or killed.

2. The Myth of Money

scholarship. Anyone who attempts to reintroduce oxygen into the void is dismissed, or, if their activities prove to be remarkable, locked up or killed.

2

The Myth *of* Money

Money converts the *quality* of life, which is ultimately elusive, into *quantity*, which can be grasped, measured, stored and, crucially, stolen · · · Money did not replace barter, but the *gift-economy* · · · The popularity of money was not due to its efficiency, but its capacity to *conceal theft*. The most important of the theft-justifying myths that surround money is that *debt is real*. The dreamworld of *financialisation* is based on this myth.

M ONEY AUTOMATICALLY CONVERTS HETEROGENEOUS *qualities*—the unique and non-duplicable, individuality of people and things, which are embedded in a context—into homogeneous *quantities*—monetary sums, or scores, which are impersonal, abstract and divorced from the context. Money, Shakespeare's 'common whore of mankind', is the opposite of unique; it turns everything it touches into a sum and everyone who touches it into sum-maximisers, with one aim only: to get the best deal. For those with no character—no uniqueness, that is—this is no biggie; money cures all problems that want of character presents,* except lack of love and the inevitability of death; but it provides the stimulating means to push those bad dreams from view also.

There is one other thing in the universe that man can never get enough of, aside from sex of course, and that is *thought*, the bloodless mother of money. Both are abstract, infinite and representative of everything; and so can never satiate the desire they generate. For money, like thought, there is no end, no death, no love, no kin, no character, no quality, no context and so, no rest. There can never be an end to it, because there can never be a beginning. The meaning and origin of money do not exist, or at the very least do not have to. It is inherently, perfectly, clean; it comes pre-laundered, and is, therefore, an essential component of deception, inadequacy, lovelessness, an essentially hollow, meaningless life and theft; theft on a *massive* scale.

---

* '...the more money, the less virtue; for money comes between a man and his objects, and obtains them for him; and it was certainly no great virtue to obtain it. It puts to rest many questions which he would otherwise be taxed to answer; while the only new question which it puts is the hard but superfluous one, how to spend it. Thus his moral ground is taken from under his feet.' H. Thoreau, *On the Duty of Civil Disobedience.*

If money, by hiding and justifying the iniquity of its creation, was vital for early experiments in enslaving barbarians, subjugating domestic populations and tearing up the wilderness, it was positively indispensable for early capitalists who, in order to get the project of a totalising, completely self-regulating market system off the ground, had to commodify labour and land and then to tear them from their contexts so that they might be bought, controlled and sold. That human beings and all of nature were not produced in order to be peddled in the marketplace was as outlandish a notion for early capitalists as it is for their contemporary progeny, who are busily converting water, conversation, childcare, dating, genomes, creativity and consciousness itself into money-measured commodities.

Some troublesome types seriously pursue matters that do not lead to financial-material advantage. These lunatics are best left to their own devices. Worse though, some go so far as to question the need for a money system at all, suggesting that perhaps reality is not best served by reducing everything in it to bookkeeping entries. This has forced economists to generate a secondary myth; *The Myth of Inefficient Barter*. According to Aristotle, Adam Smith, countless textbooks, academic papers and newspaper articles, money, and the market system which uses it, arose because of the inefficiencies of exchanging goods for goods. Apparently, we used to live in a world in which a man with five chickens to sell had no way to get hold of a pair of shoes, because the cobbler had chickens of his own; he had to go around barefoot until money was invented and he could sell to the chickenless blacksmith and buy a pair of shoes with the money. This is a convenient story if, like the inventors of coinage (the 'civilised' ancient Greeks*), you wish to rip up the world in order to sell the shreds—and, crucially, hide (or 'launder') your crimes behind untraceable, contextless cash-symbols—but there is no truth to it.

We use money because it generates and sustains mass-theft, unlimited desire (which leads to unlimited violence) and ego; not because, as the capitalist fairy tale has it, barter was 'inefficient'. Prehistoric society and many pre-modern societies did not use barter to allocate resources, but informal [non-usurious]

---

* Richard Seaford, *Money and the Early Greek Mind*.

credit, centralized redistribution and the so-called GIFT-ECON-OMY—just as friends and families do today. Both money and barter were used only for ritual and for trade with enemies—which is what they are still used for. The difference is that now everyone must be considered an enemy (the official term is COMPETITOR) or as a tool (official term; EMPLOYEE) in the insane activity known as BUSINESS.*

All this has been well known for well over half a century, and is slowly entering common knowledge, but it is, unsurprisingly, never mentioned by capitalist journalists and academics. Economists once made constant reference to the origins of capitalism in primal societies. The moment, however, that it became impossible to sustain this myth was precisely the moment when economists abandoned the study of primitive man as irrelevant to understanding the modern world. No capitalist academic who presumes to make judgements of human nature ever refers to pre-civilised, pre-agricultural or pre-conquest peoples anymore, preferring to base their social theories on the implicit idea that only the last couple of thousands of years of history—minus the unfortunate interregnum of feudalism—*really* represent human nature.

But although the idea that the invention of money removed one of the key obstacles in our attempts to realise our *true nature* as rational, wealth-maximising automatons is never explicitly evoked, it remains one of the foundational money myths (collective term: ECONOMICS) upon which the modern system is based. These myths include; the belief that we need money to organise society, the belief that most money is created by mints or central banks (when, in fact, it is written into existence by private banks—the actual, inflationary, 'magic money tree'), the belief that money exists as a *consequence* of economic activity,† the belief that funds (or resources) are limited (see myth 3), the belief that the post-capitalist economy is based on

---

* Marcel Mauss, *The Gift*, Caroline Humphrey, *Barter and Economic Disintegration*, R.D.Baker, *The Implausibility of the Barter Narrative and Credit Money in Ancient Babylon*, Charles Eistenstein, *Sacred Economics*.

† Ann Pettifor, *The Production of Money*. Pettifor, a socialist, believes that the solution to monolithic corporations creating their own money, is for monolithic states to do it.

anything real (anything other than finance, that is), the belief that money is a commodity or that it represents 'the power of capital', the belief that speculation will somehow, this time, not lead to catastrophic inequality, widespread misery and another horrific crash,* and the belief that, left on its own, the mythic value of money magically grows by itself.

This last hex is one of the founding myths not just of capitalism, but of civilisation itself. We have come to believe that if we store money, not only will it, unlike substances in the real world, not decay, but it will actually *increase in size*. Yes! We have created life! Capitalists call the magical generative powers of stored money INTEREST. Non-capitalists, who understand that this miracle money is coming from someone else, call it USURY, a form of legalised theft (like rent and taxation) which is written into the fabric of Western civilisation.

Usury means lending to make a profit on compound interest. The original debt accrues interest, and then not just the debt, but the debt *plus interest*, accrues interest. The debt doesn't just grow, it grows *exponentially*. Basing, as we have, our society—indeed our entire civilisation—on usurious debt, doesn't just mean that we never have enough to repay, but what we do have to repay multiplies, like the fabled rice grain on the chess board, until it fills up the universe. In order to maintain and justify the abyss of degradation that this inevitably leads to—mass poverty, exploitation, despoliation, anything to scrape together enough to make the next payment to the swelling monstrosity that the lender was fast becoming—a moral duty to repay debts had to be impressed on borrowers; an understanding not just that they owed tribute to this or that lender, but that the universe itself is a debtor-creditor arrangement. Human beings are *born owing* (a.k.a. *sinful*), and can *never* settle their accounts. When they inevitably betray the benevolent gods-by-proxy who pay, feed, house and clothe them, they are then defined as ungrateful, criminal, possessed by the devil or insane. This understanding is also sometimes known as 'religion'.

The powerful lend money to the powerless, who must then pay back more than they borrowed until they are either

---

* Carmen M. Reinhart and Kenneth S Rogoff, *This Time Is Different: Eight Centuries of Financial Folly.*

enslaved, or dead. This self-reinforcing feedback loop of bor-
rowing at interest from the future inflates the power of the
elites, and with it the bubble of the society they control, until it
pops, bringing everyone down with it. The most extensive and
catastrophic version of this process began in the 1970s with the
end of the idea that capital should be controlled, the beginning
of unlimited, unregulated money flow and speculation, and the
creation, manipulation and trading of increasingly sophisticated
forms of debt; a process of, effectively, printing money (instead
of extracting it as tax from the hyper wealthy*) known as FI-
NANCIALISATION, which created unimaginably vast profits for the
financial sector by evaporating the world economy, along with all
the institutions which manage it, and uploading them, and us,
into an inflationary, virtual hyper-economy. This dream-asteroid
we find ourselves clinging to, hurtling towards the waking world,
makes the bubbles before it look like microbial farts, and the
crashes before it look like derailed slot cars.

---

* '...by replacing tax revenue with debt, governments contributed further to inequality, in that they offered secure investment opportunities to those whose money
they would or could no longer confiscate and had to borrow instead. Unlike
taxpayers, buyers of government bonds continue to own what they pay to the
state, and in fact collect interest on it, typically paid out of ever less progressive
taxation; they can also pass it on to their children. Moreover, rising public debt
can be and is being utilized politically to argue for cutbacks in state spending and
for privatization of public services...' Wolfgang Streeck, *How Will Capitalism End?*

3

The Myth *of* Scarcity

The system cannot function unless there
is *never enough.* This we call *scarcity*, which
is the opposite of plenitude, or *abundance*
· · · The system must make the reality of
abundance impossible to depend on and
the idea of it impossible to take seriously
· · · The inevitable end-point of the system
is a reality in which everything is a 'scarce
resource', including jobs, air, water, time,
affection and even conscious awareness of
one's own body.

W E CAN'T AFFORD IT, there is just not enough money. There is also just not enough food, enough energy, enough jobs, enough houses, enough space or enough time. Just as we invent money and then see the world as colourless ideas (sleeping furiously), so we invent capitalism and see the world as a battle for finite resources. The entire universe is reconfigured as a mind-knowable system of facts and all of nature as a war of all against everything for scarce objects. And all this, most extraordinarily, *is how it has to be.* Just as things can only be sold by being rationally ripped from context, so they can only be bought when they are scarce. The market cannot function unless there is *not enough*, and so it must ceaselessly work to make sure that nobody *ever* has enough. If food, water, energy and opportunities for meaningful and enjoyable activity are plentiful there is no need to produce commodities at work or consume them at play. If time is abundant, if space freely available, if necessities are within reach, why bother working for them? Why bother saving them up? Everything crash!

In the real world—a place, alas, so far from most people's experience it appears to them as dreams do—scarcity does not exist. The natural state of man and woman is endless affluence, or *abundance*. This is not, as the systems-man would like to believe, an airy-fairy fantasy, but a demonstrable fact. Scarcity, along with gruelling toil for subsistence, was unknown before civilisation, and was unknown in those societies which, until recently, survived outside of it.* Observers of non-sedentary,

---

* The classic account of 'primitive affluence' is Marshall Sahlins' *The Original Affluent Society*, which demonstrated that modern scarcity and hard work are unknown in pre-civilised societies. Sahlins' work is generally accepted as accurate, if limited, over enthusiastic and a tad sloppy (see for example T. Kaczynski's corrective, *The Truth about Primitive Life*). For a thorough overview of how little

immediate-return foragers are frequently astounded at the profligacy and faith in the future of people who are only ever a few days away from starvation.* Even medieval society did not consider the commons scarce, let alone space or time. It was only when 'civilisation' began generating needs, and when capitalism began multiplying them—only when the monolithic system began curtailing access to necessities and capitalism began annihilating them—that human existence filled up with infinitely increasing desires for ever dwindling RESOURCES; a word which, in modern usage, always implies something there can *never* be enough of.

Thus, what is called 'production' means *withdrawing* capital from circulation in order to ensure a high rate of return on that which is permitted to dribble out through 'investment', thereby guaranteeing inequality. Thus, 'education' means learning under the false assumption that knowledge is a scarce product manufactured in an artificially manufactured 'reality' in which opportunities to use that knowledge, in the activity we call 'work', are also scarce. Thus, 'travel' means locomotion under an imposed need to gain access to scarce road, rail and flight resources and to consume scarce energy resources in order to access scarce production or consumption resources placed artificially far away. Thus, 'aid' means *depriving* foreign people of the means of subsistence.† Thus, 'health' means access to

---

hunter-gatherers work, and what kind of work they do, see e.g. R.L. Kelly, *The Lifeways of Hunter-Gatherers*. Note also this conclusion in the *Cambridge Encyclopedia of Hunters and Gatherers*: 'The most important challenges to economic orthodoxy that come from the descriptions of life in hunter-gatherer societies are that (1) the economic notion of scarcity is a social construct, not an inherent property of human existence, (2) the separation of work from social life is not a necessary characteristic of economic production, (3) the linking of individual well-being to individual production is not a necessary characteristic of economic organization, (4) selfishness and acquisitiveness are aspects of human nature, but not necessarily the dominant ones, and (5) inequality based on class and gender is not a necessary characteristic of human society'.

* Not that this means pre-conquest foragers did not plan; far from it—some of their living strategies required as much forethought and long-term coordination as civilised design—but that these plans were not predicated on a stingy universe.

† Foreign aid means export promotion. Aid money must be spent on goods and

artificially scarce medical resources, 'society' means access to scarce bandwidth, and scarce free time, 'love' means access to scarce mating stock (particularly scarce eggs), 'work' means access to scarce jobs, 'achievement' means access to scarce media attention, 'wealth' means access to scarce money and 'truth' means access to scarce facts, or to scarce 'learning resources'.*

All of which, under a late-stage market system, is inevitable. A usurious, technocratic, debt economy which forces everyone to pay not just more than they have, but more than *exists*, inevitably creates a quenchless thirst to produce and consume our way through a diminishing world of quantifiable resources artificially generated by tearing them from their context and then rendering them as money values. It also creates a huge number of institutions which, in order to survive, must multiply needs and artificially impose deficiencies; which is to say create needy, deficient people, which must then be *cared for* by *caring* people. The disabling system and the crippled men and women it produces, crawling over each other in order to obtain their share of an artificially shrinking pie, is therefore masked by the *service*, *aid* and the *tireless altruism* of professionals employed to *care* for them (see myth 28).

We are told that we cannot take care of our land, or leave nature alone, or build nice houses for everyone, or care for each other, or produce marvellous tools for ordinary people to use... because there is 'not enough money'. 'The state', Margaret Thatcher told us, 'has no source of it; it all comes from what we earn'. And yet, amazingly, these same poor states, affected by the 2008 financial crash, and by the 2020 system-enhancing, poor annihilating lockdown, found *trillions* of dollars to keep the economy afloat. When the poor need to be disciplined, it's time for monkish, belt-tightening 'austerity', but when the system needs money, suddenly there's an infinite, unquenchable, supernatural supply of it.

In actual fact, money is one of the key means by which the power of men and women to live is *made* scarce by the system, which cannot survive unless abundant educational

---

services from the donor nations, which impoverishes local farmers. Essentially a more sophisticated forms of classic, scarcity-creating, colonialism.

* Ivan Illich, *Towards a History of Needs*.

opportunities become scarce resources (provided by 'the best schools'), abundant health becomes a scarce resource (recovered in 'world-class' clinics or maintained at expensive gyms and delis), abundant care for the elderly becomes a scarce resource ('sorry dear, no time to stop and chat, got to clean forty more rooms today'), abundant places for children to play become scarce resources (which must be protected from ever circling paedophiles and the dreaded lurgy), abundant physical affection becomes a scarce resource (Authentic Girlfriend Experience, £240 an hour), abundant water becomes a scarce resource (shipped from the antipodes), abundant nature becomes a scarce, not to mention intensely managed, resource and abundant life is constantly trickling away. Even the opportunity to inhabit *our own bodies*, to rest, to idle, even to sleep, even this, to exist in our very selves, must be a scarce resource under the system in its most highly developed form.

We may never reach the capitalist utopia of pay-per-use bodily organs with operating systems which must be installed every six months, of chairs which decay like mushrooms and have to be reprinted every half-hour, of idea-rental and sunlight-meters and water extracted from the moons of Mars, but there can be only one way forward for the technocratic market system; permanent, omnipresent existential scarcity, a nightmarish, computer game of endlessly proliferating bar-charts which not only never stop diminishing, but are used up at ever faster rates; and any attempt to stop this process, or even slow it down, is, *ipso facto*, criminal or insane.

Ultimately, the process cannot be stopped while its fuel and foundations remain unaddressed. These reach far deeper than the predatory, mechanical and exponentially wasteful system. Scarcity, after all, can only apply to *things*; to isolated objects separated from context and consciousness. Meaning, truth, love and life are *qualities*, and, as such, are inexhaustible. It makes as much sense to talk about 'acquiring' love or 'running out' of truth, as it does to talk about the present moment as a 'resource' which needs to be 'managed'. This is why those who own and manage the system have, from its earliest days, expended immense intellectual efforts in converting qualities *into* objects; to knowledge-objects, truth-objects, quality-objects, and the like, for only this way can life come under control. This is why we are told to view *God* as a person with wishes and desires, *karma* as a cause-and-effect law, *memory* as a text stored in the mind, *happiness* as a chemical produced from amino acids, *ethics* as a collection of things in people's heads which, like 'fibre-optics', must be managed for optimal efficiency, and *meaning* as a pile of ideas which I can empty out of my brain-pocket and into yours (and which 'intelligent' people are sitting on sacks of). This is not a conscious process. The brains in jars that manage the system's intellectual and cultural industries are unable to see reality any other way, nor are the domesticants who live in the thing-world they have helped create.

4

The Myth *of* [Class] Equality

Social class means *power*; how much or how
little of it you have · · · People with power
are terrified that powerless people might
identify with each other, so they promote
the idea that class does not exist · · · In the
most advanced 'late-capitalist' phase of the
system, class distinctions *do* seem to have
been erased, but they have actually been
uploaded and distributed across society,
making them harder to perceive.

SOCIAL CLASS CAN BE UNDERSTOOD in terms of what you own, how much money you have, what kind of job you do, where you live, what kind of language you use, your taste, your education and your attitude to your fellows. But while all of these can be used as social markers—particularly in countries like the UK and India, where class divisions have, historically, been very prominent—they are all secondary effects of what fundamentally divides people in a hierarchical society; power. The 'upper' classes give the orders, the 'middle' classes execute them and the 'lower' classes take them. Ultimately, it's as simple as that; for every country on earth. It is undeniably true that social classes have internal subdivisions,* along with their own complex and shifting 'interests' which intersect with each other, creating a more complex class system than the standard lower-upper-middle model; the working class of the west, for example, took a precarious upward lurch into 'the service economy' when its manufacturing work was shipped wholesale to East Asia a few years back, and the professional class of the West is, as I write, being eroded by artificial intelligence and an extreme polarisation of wealth driving the propertied middle

---

* The upper class is composed of the hyper wealthy ELITES (from multimillionaires, to whom national laws do not apply, up to billionaires who can effectively buy nations) and, below them, the hyper-privileged SALARIAT (extremely well-paid CEOs, civil servants, consultants, etc.). The middle class comprises the PROFICIAN (well educated technocrats and hipsters with the professionally credentialised power to take interesting jobs anywhere, for very good money) and, beneath them, the stressed and threatened DRONE (teachers, junior doctors, social workers, etc.). The lower class is made up of the traditional MANUAL WORKER (also shrinking and threatened), the growing PRECARIAT (zero contract, 'informal' units in the gig economy) and the bog-standard POOR (the underclass, the dregs). See Guy Standing, *Work After Globalisation*.

up into the stratosphere and the merely educated middle down into the gutter. But, despite the many shifting, blurring and in some cases vanishing aspects of class, it is still only possible to understand a hierarchical society, and the formation of men and women's attitudes within it, in terms of power relations; of who, at the top, owns the system, who, in the middle, manages it and who, at the bottom, builds it or is excluded by it.

This is why, when John Major, the right wing leader of the British Conservative party in the 1990s, said he hoped that Britain would soon be a classless society, and when Josef Stalin described the USSR as classless, and when around half of Americans define themselves as 'middle class', and when Adolf Hitler said that the National Socialist State recognises 'no classes', and when upper managers do away with signs of hierarchy in the equalising office, and when the mass media publish article after article, book after book, on class, none of them ever mentions power. They want people who have no power to believe, because they have an exalted job title, a mortgage, a degree, an iphone or shares in Wal-Mart, that 'we are all middle class now', or that class is a quaint out-of-date idea; of interest to Marxists perhaps, or to the English, but inapplicable in the 'real' world.

Elites want the poor, the powerless and the exploited to believe they have more in common with wealthy members of their own group (fellow blacks, whites, women, men, gays, straights, gamers, punks, and so on) than with poor, powerless, alienated and exploited members of other groups. Nothing horrifies power more than the prospect of POWER-BASED CLASS SOLIDARITY*—hence the tolerance, even promotion, of IDENTITY-BASED CLASS SOLIDARITY—the formation and celebration of 'communities', and concerted initiatives to grant them equal status within the system. Not a day goes by without an article being published bemoaning the gender pay gap or a corporate meeting being held on diversifying management to include more women, more ethnic minorities and more disabled people. Only a lunatic Nazi could oppose such initiatives. And yet, there's not *quite* so much fuss about the power pay gap, or about levelling the playing field for the powerless classes, or about

---

* Well, almost nothing. Consciousness-based solidarity is a *far* greater threat, but beyond the scope of the present work.

making serious structural changes so that ordinary working people—whatever their colour, gender or sexual proclivity—are not treated like chattel. *Somehow* the inherent, systemic biases of the power-based market system, and the manner in which the system alienates *everyone* from their own nature, is ignored. But then, how could there be a fuss, when power doesn't really exist?

Elite owners and their managers want classism ('power-ism') to exist on the subtlest level possible, they want lower class students and workers to be unaware of how their relationship to power shapes their experiences and generates their feelings (of self-directed depression at failure or of inadequacy around wealthier types), elites and managers want their hatred of 'chavs', the homeless, the global poor and the *lumpenproletariat* (see myth 31) to be taken as judgements of hygiene (*'ugh! smelly!'*), sexuality (*'ugh! gender stereotype!'*), education (*'ugh! doesn't understand apostrophes!'*) and taste (*'ugh! overdressed!'*)* and they want people with no power to believe that class power is an ideological illusion, or if it does have any reality, that it is nowhere near as important as 'equality issues', professionally-administered justice (squabbling over 'rights', criminalising thought-crimes, etc.) and personal identity† (not to mention the litany of often ludicrous subsidiary problems the media prefers to focus on), or, finally, if ordinary folk don't feel sufficiently middle class, that all they have to do is work hard and, sooner or later, they'll be allowed into the Marvellous Club. The powerful want the powerless to believe these things and they want minority groups,

---

* Empathy, creativity and wisdom do not figure in such judgements, because the lower classes always come out on top in such measures. See, for example, J.P. Brienza, I. Grossmann *Social Class and Wise Reasoning about Interpersonal Conflicts Across Regions, Persons and Situations*.

† This isn't to say that 'gender' or 'race' or other PC concerns are less important than 'class'—in fact in matters of real existential importance to men and women *all* such identity issues are irrelevant next to the alienating influence of the system on consciousness (see myth 32)—rather, that solving manifest problems of sexism and racism *politically* (positive discrimination, teaching black history, outlawing bad words and so on) leaves authoritarian hierarchies, professional dominance of public commons and the misery of the greater mass of humanity *completely* untouched. More homosexual footballers, more black CEOs, more women building laptops... same poverty, same precarity, same powerlessness, same exploitation.

neighbours and even generations* to be continually at war, because *it serves their class interests*. You might not be aware of your class, but you can be quite sure that those who benefit from your lack of awareness are.

And yet. Clearly something *has* fundamentally changed since the days, not so very long ago, when 'working-class solidarity' was a force so powerful that it was able not just to slow the progress of capitalism but, in a few places, for a few brief moments, actually halt it. Class relations do still exist, wealth and power do still alter character and social relations in predictable ways, but exploitation, ownership and production have all been, to an extraordinary extent, internalised.† Who is the capitalist boss oppressing the freelance supply teacher, the Uber or Deliveroo driver, the Airbnb host or the office temp? There *are* owners and managers out there, somewhere, but their immediate physical presence seems somehow to have evaporated, while the exploitative power within their bodies seems also to have magically melted away, leaving Really Awesome People.

What is happening is extremely hard to grasp, yet dominates modern life. Class relations have been obscured in the most subtle and pervasive way imaginable; they have been virtualised in the same way that communication (society and culture), capital and consciousness have; distributed through digital, Phildickian, networks and the hyper-focused minds which create and respond to them, leaving the technical expert very often

---

* Boomers vs millennials is the current generational conflict in the west. 'The tirade against the previous generation presents a false picture; it neglects class. Only a small minority of UK baby boomers went to university, while today half of all school leavers go on to some form of tertiary education. Many in the older generation suffered the ravages of de-industrialisation, as miners, steelworkers, dock workers, printers and so on were shunted into history. And most women had the added burden of economic marginality. The inter-generational interpretation could almost be a diversionary tactic, since it accords with a conservative view that carefully leaves out the role of globalisation (Willetts, 2010). Today's youth is not worse off than earlier generations. The predicament is just different and varies by class.' G. Standing, *The Precariat; the New Dangerous Class*.

† 'The neoliberal system is no longer a class system in the proper sense. It does not consist of classes that display mutual antagonism. This is what accounts for the system's stability'. Byung-Chul Han, *Psychopolitics*. See myth 18.

with more power than the mere owner. Reality exists less and less in tangible form, yet its conceptual projection exerts more and more power over actual, sensate existence.* Class power and capital increasingly exist nowhere, while projecting themselves everywhere, into each atomised, on-line, individual, who has become his own owner, manager, worker, teacher, lawyer, priest, scientist, artist, society and god.† When he sickens or saddens he searches for an external cause, and finds nothing but complaint forms, call centres and discussion threads, all composed of anxious people in the same weird situation. He concludes that *he* must be the problem, and goes out of his mind.

---

* In some crucial respects billionaires and CEOs are, despite their money-power, as powerless as the multitude they crush under their almighty thrones; for it is the system which rules.

† 'Power is no longer in the hands of the owners of capital. I can develop this idea by analyzing the multinational corporations. Here, as we clearly see, capital still exists; but it is now structured in terms of technical demands rather than in terms of the ideas formulated by a capitalist. Today, there is no longer any owner of capital who plays the part that could once be played by a captain of industry'. Jacques Ellul, *Perspectives on Our Age*.

5

The Myth *of* Meritocracy

The system conceals its iniquity with the idea that anyone can rise to a position of power. This is called *meritocracy* · · · The reality is that very few rise from the bottom to the top. Allowing them to rise is actually *tokenism* · · · The masses are not, however, consciously prevented from rising. Instead, the system is structured so that conformity, ambition, highly abstract 'intelligence' and unconsciousness are rewarded *automatically*. Thus *merit*, in practice, means *mediocrity*.

P RIVILEGE BEGETS PRIVILEGE and wealth, fame and elite education produce, in the system, the conditions by which they reproduce themselves. The principle reason why people with posh surnames have been in positions of power for hundreds or even thousands of years, why wealthy accents dominate the media, the arts and elite education, and why top jobs are staffed by elite graduates who grew up in wealthy houses is not merit, and never has been, but family connections, SOCIAL CAPITAL (well-connected friends), CULTURAL CAPITAL (accent, taste, manner, hyper-literacy and elite styles of thinking*), inheritance (and lavish 'inter vivos' gifts of money and property to family members) and the constraints of the market (which force the poor and culturally excluded out of high-cost social networks and unpaid internships), all of which keep power confined to the ambit of the classes which currently wield it.

Elites prefer all of this to be a secret, or, at best, unmentionable. Instead, they like to promote the idea that we live in what they call a 'MERITOCRACY', a fabled land where ability, intelligence, pluck and derring-do determine success. It is not, they want us to believe, through luck, crime, glad-handing, nepotism, and all the massive advantages of family wealth that inept halfmen get their Big Leather Chairs, their exciting jobs as wildlife cameramen, their elite degrees or their *amazing* breaks in the art world, but through talent, attitude, hard work and moral fibre. Certainly we should give a few brainy, tasteful and, crucially, *ambitious* poor people a hand up; get an infusion of

---

* Which require an enormous amount of free time to acquire. Permitting the wealthy to have this time, and denying it to the poor or the excluded, is one of the means by which the system ensures that cultural capital accrues to those who can be trusted with it, although when the domesticated poor do have free time they inevitably spend it tranquillising themselves with 'fun' (see myths 19 and 20).

new blood into the boardroom, deprive the working classes of their leaders and give the impression of equal opportunity to the educational system. The professional left call this INTEGRATION, but the correct name is TOKENISM.* But whatever you call it, there's really only one sort of person who naturally deserves to sit at the banqueting table; the 'best and brightest'. In the past it was the divinely ordained, the twice-born and the genetically superior who deserved to rule. Today it is the cultured, the industrious, the upright and, most especially, the *qualified*.

How the systems-man loves that word, '*qualified*', how very noble it sounds, how dignified, how redolent of rightful, earned authority. That these qualifications are given by the system to those who own it, or have shown themselves gifted at serving it (see myth 17), this does not occur to him. He has *achieved* his success, while the multitude are destined for a life of debt peonage and the misery of actually productive work. All of which is sad, to be sure, but it's also *kind* of fair you see, because it's a meritocracy, and so the excluded, the intractable, the slow and the unlucky *kind* of deserve it.

Those on the bottom floor of the Tower of Earthly Delights are there because they do not have enough *merit*. It's not their lack of security, resources, time or power that has stunted their capacities, it is because they are hedonistic, fatalistic, impulsive, irresponsible, and, the perennial complaint of elites despairing at the weird reluctance of lower sorts to generate wealth for them, lazy.† They should study more, plan ahead, defer gratification, raise their expectations, work harder, learn to spell, have a make-over and cook more risotto. 'Pull themselves up by their boot laces', as the popular idiom has it; which might seem like a paradoxical image, but, on deeper reflection, the image of millions upon millions of cripples rolling around trying to pull themselves onto their own feet by tugging away at their

---

* The same techniques are used to diffuse the threat of revolutionary action from racial minorities. Black people as a whole, for example, will never be permitted to rise from their position at the bottom of the pile, but if the system permits individual black people to go to nice schools and get nice jobs, and gets up in arms about 'racism', perhaps nobody will notice?

† The rich work hard for their success, apparently. Cleaners, builders, factory workers, miners, nurses and waitresses? *They* don't count!

boot laces, for their entire futile lives; well, that turns out to be more or less perfect.

The Myth of Meritocracy is also used to harvest the support of the working class for right wing policies designed to punish the poor and hand more of the wealth they create over to responsible types who [like to think they] run things. It would seem, on the face of it, utterly astonishing that so many people at the bottom of society should vote for representatives of the hyper-wealthy, but, in fact, a large number of the working class believe themselves to be, as John Steinbeck put it, 'temporarily embarrassed millionaires'. They assume the mythic meritocracy will one day soon elevate them onto the Top Floor where the Top People will take care of their glittering assets.* They cannot imagine that there is another kind of wealth, at their very fingertips.

Because all this talk about social mobility, tokenism, 'equality of opportunity', 'equality of outcome' and whatnot masks a far wider and far more disabling restraint on merit, which is never officially mentioned or discussed. When political commentators talk about 'merit' they are referring to the ability to memorise contextless facts, pass intensely abstract 'intelligence tests', innovate in market-constrained directions, work, and hyper-specialise in work, to the point of total physical and psychological breakdown, accept confinement and coercion as

---

* 'I worked on the Conservative advertising for two general elections. This was a subject we gave a lot of thought to, and it's actually simple: a lot of poor people don't think they will always be poor. They have aspirations just like everyone… They think that "OK, I'm not earning a lot now, but one day I'll have a bloody great yacht", so they vote for the party they think will help them most achieve that great leap to riches and the one they identify with in their imaginary alternative life. It's the principle behind shows like "Bake Off", "X-Factor" and "The Voice" and a host of other contests where "ordinary" people suddenly strike it rich. It's deeply rooted in human psyche, and the Tories know it. The Conservatives are quite aware that they are pedlars of what is for most, false hope. They point out the Alan Sugars and Richard Bransons and say that you too can achieve this under their governance.' Nick Schon, Group Creative Director at Saatchi and Saatchi. Note that they are not 'pointing out' the Director Generals of the BBC or the Lord Chief Justices; they know that these 'achievements' are *never* available to the hoi-polloi.

inevitable—or, ideally, as magical and fun—and successfully fuck other people over; in short, succeed at school and at work. *That* is merit, and a system which rewards it is what clever and insensitive mediocrities want; just as white supremacists want a system which rewards whiteness, feminists want a system which rewards women and scientologists want a system which rewards scientology. Genuine creative genius,* true community spirit, radical generosity, sensitivity, unconditional love, honesty, moral courage, craft-skill, self-sufficiency, spontaneity and responsibility do not count as 'merit', and never have, and so the fact that these qualities, and those who possess them, are punished everywhere in the system is neither here nor there. Prejudice towards white people, *that's* a problem (for right wing white people); prejudice towards Jewish people, *that's* a problem (for Jewish folk); prejudice towards women, *that's* a problem (for feminists); prejudice towards working class accents, *that's* a problem (for socialists); but prejudice towards *sensitive* people? Prejudice towards *independent* people? Prejudice towards *honest* people? Prejudice towards *loving* people? Hahahaha! *Those* aren't problems! You can't even *see* those things!

The reader may wonder, as one or two senior editors, CEOs, upper managers and department heads occasionally do, how this punishment can occur; how it can be that principled, capable, sensitive and honest people are prevented from rising through the system while those at the top are given a free pass. 'Nobody tells me what to write!' says the wealthy journalist, 'nobody tells me what to think!' says the elite student, 'nobody tells me what to do!' says the director general; but nobody has to tell them what to write, think or do—which is how they rose in the first place. Those who reject the cruel and pointless restraints of forced schooling—the ludicrous assignments†, the meaningless syllabuses and the mind-numbing tedium of it all—are marked as uncooperative, recalcitrant, undisciplined, strong-willed, unable to function well in a team or, in more serious cases,

---

* As opposed to the technical ability to innovate in a market-friendly manner.

† Stupid ways of working are, of course, endemic to a system run by stupid people for stupid reasons, but it is important to note that making people do stupid things serves as a test for conformity and a means of inculcating obedience. You can't tell who is subservient if you only ask them to do sensible things.

as conspiracy theorists, terrorists or afflicted with a 'mental illness'. Those who defy the manager, who seek to circumvent the paperwork, who question the entire point, such 'difficult' people are passed over for promotion, their contracts are not renewed, their grip on the railings is released and they are 'let go'. In a Huxleyan system there is no need for a shady group of evil capitalists to tell people what to think when the system (and, consequently, the self) is structured so as to *automatically* select for obedience, conformity, mediocrity and, for the top jobs, complete insanity. Because negative personality traits tend to occur together, managers, team leaders and other Heads tend not merely to be cowardly spaniels or cruel monomaniacs, but beset by all manner of weird defects; strangely aggressive, or bizarre, awkward and indirect, or mind-bogglingly boring, or laughably uptight and self-regarding (the David Brent / Alan Partridge type), or skin-crawlingly creepy, or hauntingly absent, not really there. Not that such people don't usually have some kind of human-like core, struggling to get out, or that more recognisably human leaders don't exist; but in both cases the immense pressure that the system puts *on* such humanity tends in one direction only; to breakdown.

6

The Myth *of* Competition

Competition, as far as it refers to productive
activity within the system, is an illusion · · ·
The only people who compete are those who
have no power · · · It is not just the separate
institutions and corporations of the system
who wield a monopoly over mankind; the
system *itself* is radically, or fundamentally,
monopolistic. We are forced to live within,
and thereby conform to it.

C APITALISM, WE ARE TOLD, is a highly competitive system which is antagonistic to monopoly power; and yet here we are in a world in which the ten largest corporations make more money than most of the countries of the world, in which a few tech companies exclusively dominate our ability to communicate with each other and in which seven oil companies wield total control over the world's energy supplies.

In the real world, money makes money, wealth attracts wealth, competition annihilates competitors and ownership of land and private property is inherently monopolistic, as is state power. An aggressively competitive system based on the prerogatives of capital inevitably leads to a few powerful corporations becoming more powerful, owning more and more, and absorbing or merging with their 'competitors', and with the state, until one colossal, state-assisted corporation has a MONOPOLY or, more commonly in late capitalist systems,* a small number of mega-corps working together to 'compete' within mutually beneficial boundaries, form an OLIGOPOLY (or CARTEL). Within this small group of super-wealthy oligarchs there is limited competition and therefore limited pressure to cut costs and multiply surplus (exacerbated by a debt economy which compels everyone to overproduce), but the cartel as a whole (official term; INDUSTRY) works as one to fix prices, lobby for favourable regulation,† dominate resources, curtail self-sufficiency, suppress

---

* Two centuries ago capitalists were powerful individuals in competition with each other. Over the course of the nineteenth and twentieth century the institutions they controlled became larger and larger, effectively taking on a life of their own—in fact large corporations are legally defined as people, with the same rights as people; or, in the case of the corporation, immortal people. See J. Bakan, *The Corporation*.

† Which includes the infrastructure, education and security services it requires to 'safely' operate. All of which the monopolistic state hands over.

labour power, corrupt individual and communal autonomy and, in general, defend the system which they are part of against the threat of independence. Individual companies then disguise their monolithic sameness behind—and generate markets for their overproduced mediocrity with—the varied splendours of advertising (see myths 8 and 9).

The Myth of Competition conveniently side-steps the oligopolistic realities of class power and the total dominance of monopolistic capital, focusing on the occasional fall of a large corporation, the sadistic warfare of smaller businesses fighting their way up and the arena where genuine—indeed pitilessly fierce—competition does exist: at the very bottom.

It is here, at the base of the Golden Pyramid, in a world of artificially scarce resources (see myth 3), that ordinary people have to fight, tooth and nail, against each other in order to gain enough of the Big Pie. Competition, as used by the owners of capital, like the word capitalism itself, actually means competition for *you*, not for *us*. *You* must fight your way to the top of the 'academic league table', in order to get your hands on one of a handful of actually useful degrees. *You* must scrabble over each other to get your foot up onto the next-but-bottom stage of the mountain of filth so that you may, perhaps, one day, earn the right to give more orders than you receive. *You* must fight to win. *You* must have your 'free markets'. *You*, not *us*, because *we* don't want them, *we* don't like them; and anyway *we* were born winners (see myth 5).

Another way to put this, now well recognised by critics of the system, is that capitalism, the lizard-eat-lizard world of constant, pitiless competition, is for the general public. The corporate world is legally, financially and militarily protected by governments, and, in times of duress, generously bailed out by them; the very definition of socialism. Socialism and welfare for *us*, capitalism and warfare for *you*.

The dice are not just loaded for people, but for ideas. Firstly, and most conspicuously, in that ideas are, in the highly developed system we live in, owned by capital. Just as physical property is inherently monopolistic—the prestige land that, say, the Duke of Westminster owns can, while it is his, only be used for his benefit—so intellectual property prevents anybody from 'competing' upon its virtual territory. Ideas, words, theories, characters, songs, patents and the like are locked up, well beyond the reach of ordinary folk, who must compete without access to their own cultural heritage.

There are also monopolistic pressures upon the spread of ideas. There is, we are led to believe, a competitive system of 'natural' selection operating in universities and newspapers, just as there is between businesses, individuals, animals, plants and genes. This is why ideas which support the system rise to the top, because they are *right*, you see, because they have defeated what is wrong, in a fair fight; and not, say, because intellectual competition in a hierarchical institution always leads to ideas which justify the institution, its owners and managers, and the system it is part of. Such ideas include the belief that reality is ultimately mind-knowable; that consciousness is reducible to thought; that psychological problems are physical illnesses (see myth 26); that gender is an illusion (or is real, with one gender superior; see myth 29); or that history represents progress (see myth 12); that climate change is a left-wing conspiracy (see myth 10); that tradition in art is out of date; that quality is subjective; that we are the good guys; that you cannot escape cause and effect; that humans are essentially warlike and selfish; that life was once 'nasty, brutish and short'; that our closest relatives are incorrigibly violent chimpanzees; that the universe and the origins of life were, essentially, accidents (or cosmic rabbits pulled out of God's Big Hat); that anyone who rejects the system is, actually, morally corrupt or laughably naive; that traditional knowledge is rigid and whimsical; that the professional world is benevolent, efficient and fair (see myth 28); that capitalism, or feudalism, or communism, or whatever ideological branch of the system is in control, is normal and natural, indeed is written into the fabric of reality; that sharing is inevitable tragedy; that endless alienated work is a prerequisite for dignity and 'prosperity' (see myth 21); that technological progress is a prerequisite for human health and happiness; that love is a chemical; that genes determine behaviour*; that science (see myth 23) or religion (see myth 25) are the only ways to understand life; that happiness is a product which can be bought; that freedom is synonymous

---

* See R. Bonduriansky and T. Day, *Extended Heredity, A New Understanding of Inheritance and Evolution* and N. Carey, *The Epigenetics Revolution*.

with obedience; that suffering is a primal fact of existence; that disorder and violence are inevitable consequences of the absence of 'law and order', or power and authority, and that poverty is the fault of the poor. In short; all the myths of the system.

Systemoidal ratiocrats working in academia or media spend their lives looking for (or inventing) facts which support their myths, and then beaming them into us 24/7, until they emerge, 'naturally', from the people who surround us—from the conversation of our friends and family and work colleagues—eventually coalescing into what we call 'the normal world', any challenge to which is, *ipso facto*, weird, pretentious, ludicrous, depressing or terrifyingly extreme.

Those who discuss such ideas, the 'unbiased' and 'independent' journalists and academics who 'fairly' rise to public platforms, always *somehow* manage to neglect to mention the monopolistic power of the institution they are part of or, even more taboo, the totalising dominance of the system itself. For monopoly does not just extend to the *individual* institutions of capitalism; these organisations are part of a far more extensive and disabling primary *context*. Individual organisations or cartels may or may not be monopolies, individual billionaires might be able to get this or that law passed to favour his enterprise, and individual drones may or may not be able to choose this or that product or job, but the *entire* system represents a RADICAL MONOPOLY*; an interlinking network of institutions and industries that have become the exclusive means of satisfying human needs—such as locomotion, shelter, knowledge, healing and energy—which once occasioned a social response.

Self is to ego what society, or culture, is to the system. When the former—self and society—pass tipping points of complexity, size and power, they overwhelm the people and groups of people they are supposed to serve and become the latter—system and ego. Me and Us radically monopolise experience at the expense of I and We, replacing individual and collective consciousness with mental-emotional projections. It looks like a person, it looks like a people, but it is not. It is a personality pretending to be a person. It is a social order pretending to be a society. It is an economy pretending to be a culture.

---

* I. Illich, *Tools for Conviviality*.

'Nobody is forcing you!' says the defender of the modern system. 'You can work where you like, read whatever newspaper you like, eat whatever food you like...' He does not understand—or chooses not to understand—that although you may be able to choose between Ford and Kia, or UnitedHealth and Virgin Care, or Oxford and Harvard, or British Gas and E.on, or London and Tokyo—you *have* to use cars to get around, hospitals to get treatment (even in national health services), higher education credentials to get a decent job, the electricity grid to power your house and the supermarket to power your body. You *have* to rely on a totalitarian professionalised system to meet your 'needs' as a client, a patient, a student, a prisoner and a consumer. You *have* to work at some kind of moronic, alienating task. You have no alternative because the omnipresent, ultra-monopolistic, market system demands that humans become entirely dependent on it. This totalising monopoly is invisible—or, at best, not obvious—and so is never addressed anywhere, although, as technology increasingly permits the system to usurp private life, it is exploited, on an unimaginable scale, by oligarchic tech companies which are able to use their monopoly over communication channels to convert personal ownership, personal use and all forms of human creation and activity (media content, houses, cars, friendship, etc.) into corporate control, or POSSESSION BY PROXY. Thus Uber, Alibaba, Airbnb, Facebook, Deliveroo and worldwide systems of contract farming increasingly dominate productive activity without having to own anything* (much as supermarkets dominate food production without owning any farmland), extending the radical power of the system into the final realms of human experience. To say that you have a choice in such a state of affairs is like saying a cyborg is free to plug itself in where it likes, or a Sim is free to build a castle, or you are free, in your dreams, to fall in love.

---

* Except of course the millions of hours of labour 'congealed' in the technology they possess. See myth 1.

7

The Myth *of* Choice

The system is designed to tightly restrict meaningful choice, which is and must be impossible in the system · · · The system only permits meaningless choice. You can do what you want, as long as it doesn't really matter · · · Only those who can be trusted not to make meaningful choices about their lives are free to do as they please.

WHEN OWNERS AND THEIR MANAGERS say that the system promotes choice they mean that it promotes meaningful choice for the ultra wealthy and trivial choice for everyone else.* The market for the masses can only permit choice between products and services which generate profit. Thus, in the Huxleyan wing of the system we are permitted to choose our phone colour, television channel, car badge, pizza topping, and cleaning job; but are prevented from choosing superb drama, truthful news, foot-friendly environments, cheap widespread public transport, carrots that taste of carrots, job-sharing, poaching, foraging, deschooled education and the occupation of unused land.

The fundamental sameness of all products and activities within the market is masked, and *has* to be masked, by the awesome variety and individuality of their packaging and promotional texts. These obscure the fact that the stuff we use is made by miserable people and from tortured animals, and therefore are not stamped with the beauty of free individual attention or of wild nature; the fact that, at least for the masses, our clothes, buildings and furniture are constructed from shoddy materials and built to quickly wear out; the fact that artistic and cultural products are nearly always derivative, imitating successful competitors and precursors and necessarily sucked of intensity, subversion and 'offense'; the fact that craft, and therefore beautifully crafted objects, is a threat to capitalism; the fact that, in short, the universal pressures of cost cutting, corporate concentration, extreme caution and class interest result

---

* Meaningful to *them* that is. In reality, an ugly world of ugly minds only allows the rich to buy ugly things. While the quality of the beautiful things they *can* buy—a nice house next to a deserted beach, a Savile Row suit, a high end meal, a comfortable, silent life away from screens—is all but invisible to them.

in a ghastly conveyor belt of nearly identical goods, services and activities. All this is unmentionable or invisible.

The market cannot function with freedom of choice any more than it can with freedom of speech, thought, movement or feeling. People who are free to choose (psychologically free, as well as physically free) invariably choose things which are good for themselves, their communities and their environments; such as healthy local food, ample free time to take care of each other, active entertainment, sharing of productive surplus, sharing of tools, mastery of tools and spending time with teachers they like. The system, on the other hand, prefers choice to be limited to things which are good for the system; such as food transported from the other side of the world, no free time whatsoever, massively expensive, non-participatory, spectacles, high tech imagination-limiting 'fun', everyone having their own drill, car, lawnmower and printer, imposed motorways, imposed virtual communication, imposed syllabuses, imposed lockdowns and a mechanised world in which contact with human beings is increasingly impossible. These things equal growth, security or stability, therefore you *must* choose them.*

If the people of the system didn't automatically make market-friendly choices; if they didn't automatically elect to talk to their phones before their neighbours, buy bookshelves from IKEA rather than learn joinery, choose work in a ceramics factory over free time at their own potter's wheel, apply moisturiser rather than drink water, drive to the supermarket rather than grow potatoes, consume business-friendly news instead of learning what is actually happening in the world from an independent press or throw themselves upon the latest space-saving or time-saving gadget (as if space and time were really artefacts that can be saved); if they didn't 'choose' such things, the jet plane of the market would instantly run out of fuel and tumble from the sky; and that cannot be allowed to happen.

It is, therefore insane 'choices' which must be promoted within the formative institutions of the system (official terms; SCHOOL and UNIVERSITY), by the propaganda systems of the system (official term; NEWS) and by the restraints imposed by the punitive-legislative wing of the technocratic corporate

---

* Or make choices within the constraints they impose.

world (official term: GOVERNMENT); all other choices must be systematically destroyed, at massive expense, so that new, shoddy, conviviality-corrupting products can be continually generated, continually demanded and continually consumed; while those who generate, demand and consume them are pacified and controlled.

So important is it to promote continual, indiscriminate consumption and production, the manufacture of goods and services must be subordinated to the manufacture of needs, addictions and indoctrinated subservience. Goods must be produced to meet the needs of advertisers (and 'researchers'), news stories—not to mention audiences—must be produced to meet the needs of sponsors, and wars must be produced to meet the needs of weapons' manufacturers. Ultimately, for the market system, what people need, is to *need*, so anything which makes people more needy—and more poorly informed about the nature of their neediness—is good. This is why the history of the system is the history of depriving people of the capacity and the desire to provision themselves. The 'independence' button cannot be found and nobody is looking for it.

Eventually, when the system has dominated human life for long enough, dependence upon it becomes total and with dependence comes shame, denial, hyper-sensitivity to criticism, fear and all the other symptoms of addiction. Meaningful, independent choice then ceases to be visible, let alone practicable, and any suggestion that qualitatively different options might be available are unconsciously registered as an existential threat to be handled in the standard manner; ignore, ridicule, attack and exalt. It is at this point, when inmates of the omni-prison believe their ability to choose is as free as their options are wide, that the system can trust them to 'freely choose'.

8

The Myth *of* Freedom

We are free *within* the psychological, moral,
political and social constraints of the system
· · · Freedom *from* the system is illegal · · ·
The system is so totalising that any attempt
to free oneself partially from it inevitably
ends in failure and pain, thus demonstrating
the necessity of unfreedom.

W E ARE FREE to do exactly what we are told, we are free to buy exactly what we're sold.* We are free to do dull alienating work, or be poor, free to eat expensive, tasteless pap, or starve, free to watch 'mainstream' excrement, or be bored, free to choose any parasitic landlord we like. The limits which compel us into market-consumption, on the one hand, or poverty, starvation, boredom and dependency. on the other, are never mentioned. We are never reminded that we are unable to use our feet to get around, our land to grow food or our mouths to communicate with each other; the fact that land, knowledge and channels of communication—not to mention energy, drugs, diagnostic equipment, motorways and railways—are all owned by, or dependent on, a minuscule group of hyper-wealthy elites, and managed by a slightly larger but immensely powerful and ultimately self-interested professional class, is ignored in capitalist definitions of freedom and in all popular discussions on the nature of liberty.

In fact, the capitalist wing of the system does require free people—in the sense that it needs to *rent* its slaves (HIRE is the official term), rather than own them, so as to be able to call on whatever labour power it requires, and to renounce the responsibility that slave owners and feudal lords had for their chattel. But all system-slaves must be deprived of both the means of production and any meaningful control over the fruits of their labour, forcing them either to sell their bodies to Orwellian slave owners or rent them to Huxleyan hyper-capitalists.

Hyper-capitalists also require what they call 'free markets'; freedom to buy any labour they like, at any price, freedom to buy the laws they need to operate, freedom to trade what they like, freedom to conglomerate into megacorps, freedom to exploit

* From 'Chains', by Matt Elliott, from *Failing Songs*.

any resource they like, freedom to annihilate craft, freedom to tear communities apart, freedom to cover every square inch of our living spaces with exhortations to consume, freedom to upload our social lives onto tightly controlled and permanently surveilled digital platforms and freedom to convert the entire natural world into a poisonous resource. That every other living creature on earth finds that *their* freedoms—to speak, think, move, breathe or simply exist—decrease as those of corporate capital increase, cannot be included in official definitions of 'freedom' which must mean freedom *for* the market, never, ever, *from* it.

Any attempt to curtail the 'freedom' of the technocratic, market system is officially represented as an intolerable attack on 'liberty', anyone who attempts to distribute freedom equitably is instantly recast as an oppressor, or a lunatic, and any suggestion that they might succeed is attended with the spectre of anarchy—a chaotic inferno of shady bomb-throwing punks. For the wealthiest people on earth, and the Uncle Toms, whores and kapos who manage their affairs, 'anarchy', like 'crime' and 'genocide', is what *other people* do—other people who are automatically assumed to be acquisitive, self-interested, cruel and depraved; an assumption shared by a class of people who have been selected, for thousands of years, for their greed, self-interest, cruelty and depravity.

Thus, there is no contradiction in turning the planet into a vast, tawdry prison for ordinary people, as liberty in *their* hands instantly transforms into a lawless free-for-all. This is why the system must force any individual, community, or country which is independent from the market—no matter how peaceful (or aggressive; it doesn't matter)—to 'join the free world'. It's for their own good. Independent states must be wrecked and unable to provide for themselves, independent tribes must be addicted to hooch or to metal buckets, independent communities must be separated from their means of subsistence, independent individuals must be unable to produce anything on their own, independent children must be trained to take their place in an overstuffed labour market made up of meaningless, misery-inducing tasks, every square inch of the globe must be under institutional control and *everyone* must be dependent on the state or in debt. For their own good.

Fortunately, there is no need for capitalist organisations to punish localised moves towards independence. The system is so complete that any attempt to rescue one aspect of life from the totalising whole is, by its inevitably integrated presence in a hostile system, bound to fail—thereby proving its foolish futility. Take your children out of school and, somehow, provide them with a free and meaningful education (one not predicated on scarce opportunities), and they will become unemployable.* Why would anyone hire someone who can actually do something? Prevent fishermen from trawling the seas clean, or loggers from laying the forests to waste, or porcelain factories from sucking the water table dry and entire communities fall apart. Where else can they get money from? Set up a company which slowly and carefully produces beautiful objects for a mass market and you'll be out of business before April 6th, annihilated by the competition (or by your debts). Behave honestly in a job interview, and see how easily you find a job. Tell the truth at work, and see how quickly you rise through the company. Let people do precisely as they please and *initially*† all hell will break loose.

And so, as defenders of the system continually point out, we *need* to live in a prison which covers the entire planet. If we were free, we would all be raping and murdering each other, or at the very least decaying in hopeless, dissolute futility. We just cannot be trusted; just look at how we behave when we're not at work, not at school, outside of the law or working independently. Look at how we suffer, look at how we fail! That we do so because *every* aspect of life must be rescued from the system—such ideas are too horrifying to seriously contemplate.

All this brings us to another aspect of restraints on freedom in the perfected system (of late-stage capitalism, or of the monstrous totalitaria it is automatically morphing into); its intensely invasive nature. Compulsory dependence is not merely a matter of turning up for work bodily, and just doing what needs to be done; your *entire being* must clock in. You are

---

* Or, in a society completely dominated by techno-narcotics, unable to function in their own bodies.

† When unnatural constraints are lifted from an organic system or way of life the initial response is nearly always chaos and pain. See 'Mr. Cerberus' in *The Apocalypedia*.

paid for your 'natural' informality, your 'can-do' attitude, your knowing irony, your 'team spirit', and your 'sense of humour'. If you cannot summon contrived enthusiasms at will, if your love of work doesn't radiate from your pores, if you react honestly to your alienated condition (an event so rare it is always treated with absolute astonishment by all who witness it) then your capacity for conformity and your willingness to give your whole existence up to the market is thrown into terrifying doubt. This guy might not be sufficiently indoctrinated to mob rule (official term: A TEAM-PLAYER). Keep an eye on him.

But it still doesn't end there. Yes, you are forced to rent your entire psychological self to a wealth-maximising Leviathan for one half of your waking life; yes, and to depend entirely on market interventions to remain alive; yes, your every word and act is recorded and scanned for subversive content. But none of this is enough to absorb the over-production of a massively powerfully oligopolistic system. To handle the outrageous surplus of the fully developed debt-enslaved system, you must also be convinced to *continually consume*—to continually want things you don't need and continually buy things you can't use. To this end, the system must continually manufacture low-quality junk that breaks in a few years, or needs to be 'updated' and continually stimulate desire for addictive consumption; sex, luxe, drugs, holidays, films, chat, spectacle, knowledge, success, speed, 'adventure', wheaty-meaty-sweeties, kulcha, power... even transcendence, redemption and revolution. You must want them all, all the time, and you must go through the market system to temporarily satisfy your unquenchable desire for more.

Other methods of reabsorbing surplus include forcibly opening up foreign markets, crippling human beings so that they are in need of market-supplied crutches, investing in the military and financial speculation; all of the most destructive activities of capitalism, which we are free to endure, until we are freed to death.*

And yet. Hold on. All this might be true; I might be compelled by innumerable pressures, inside and out, to conform, submit, obey... but I can still have, or reacquire, *some* liberty, can I not? Can't I, at least to *some* extent, squeeze myself free?

---

* P. Baran and P. Sweezy, *Monopoly Capital.*

Can't I, *somehow*, refuse work (see myth 21) the spectacle (see myth 20), the internet (see myth 12), the vote (see myth 16), the city and the ring road, and the psychological constraints of systemic ideology?

Yes, you can. Anybody can, to some extent; but nobody really wants to. They *say* they want to—one of the consolations of slavery is the freedom to complain—but nobody is willing to act, nor even to hear that they can. They know that actual freedom—the state of not being surrounded by society's signposts, its 'recommended, enforceable and in-drilled modes of conduct'*—entails pain, fear, loss, regret, uncertainty and quite possibly madness; and so they call it slavery. Independent thought, feeling and action, genuine conviviality, self-sufficiency, responsibility and rejection of the system all seem, to the civilised mind, hopeless servitude to cultic ideology or bestial stupidity. As St.Paul, Thomas Hobbes, Georg Hegel, Sigmund Freud, Émile Durkheim, Jordan Peterson and other official ideologues teach us, freedom is really submission to authority and to society, to the system. Freedom is slavery.

---

*   Z. Bauman, *Liquid Modernity*.

9

The Myth *of* Truth

The system manufactures *misery*, which, in turn, generates *revolt*. Misery and revolt must be suppressed. This is done through *distracting* and *confusing* people · · · The manufacture of distraction and confusion is not the conscious work of secret societies or corrupt bosses, but is an output of the system working normally · · · This 'normal working' does not just produce a system-friendly culture, but, through intervening completely between the consciousness of the individual and reality (as the *spectacle*), filters out reality itself.

A PERSISTENT PROBLEM FOR THE SYSTEM is that market-dependence and the demands of infinite consumption spawn immense misery, which, while playing a vital role in generating even more desire for market interventions (narcotics, security, psychiatry, etc.), has a nasty tendency to lead to mass refusal of constraint, violence and, every now and then, revolution. It is essential, therefore, for management to keep the booze, sports, pills and porn flowing, and, crucially, to keep the schools, universities, newspapers, websites, TV channels and publishing companies pumping out pro-market propaganda.*

The ultimate result of such a colossal programme of mis-information, and the *sine qua non* of effective corporate rule, is *confusion*. Nobody must know what is going on, nobody must understand how the world actually operates and nobody must know who or what is responsible for their suffering. The fears and anxieties of the masses must constantly be aroused, their unconscious desire for attention and excitement continually stimulated, their belief that their unhappiness can be alleviated with a sale perpetually fuelled. They must be made to believe that pleasure is the sole aim of life, power equals security and expensive possessions, not to mention expensive qualifications, bring elevated status and self-confidence. They must be constantly reminded, explicitly and implicitly, that nothing is more important than how they are defined, what they know, what they like and what they want. They must be trained to divorce *cause* from *effect*; the demands of the market from war, urban life from misery, consumption of sugar from acne, the torture of animals from chicken nuggets and the horror of factory life from cheap tracksuits. They must be made to feel that humility, mystery, peace of mind, service to others, self-sacrifice, self-mastery,

---

* And, if ever revolutionary pressure does build up, to release it with a few reforms.

health and responsibility are either illusions, unattainable, 'not my thing', available for £5.99 at the chemist, or synonymous with never touching another human being ever again. This way they will be malleable, corruptible, easily dealt with and, crucially, unable to perceive their own confusion; always pointing the finger in the wrong place, at their fellow prisoners, their genes, their gods, their neighbours, their mental illnesses, their parents, their bad luck, their bank balances and their rulers; never at themselves and never at the system.

It is hard enough maintaining such profound, debilitating and widespread confusion, but the work of capitalist 'opinion shapers' is made more challenging by the existence of people who are perversely determined to educate their fellows. Such 'extremists', 'terrorists', 'anarchists', and 'narcissists' can be dealt with in the usual way, but in a Huxleyan system the threat they represent is neutralised before it has a chance to spread; for only those who are heavily credentialised (official term: QUALIFIED), heavily institutionalised (official term: PROFESSION-AL), conspicuously unhappy (official term: FAMOUS) or shielded from reality (official term: RICH) can gain access to the means to speak; everyone else floats through an ocean of useless information in which it is almost impossible to discern quality or truth. Censorship is unnecessary in a system in which everyone can speak, but only those guaranteed not to say anything worth listening to can be heard. This technique, of system-constrained thought-control in a democratic society, is called 'freedom of speech', 'freedom of the press', 'culture' and 'fun' (see myth 20).

It is extraordinarily effective. There is no central control, no proprietor 'spiking copy', there aren't even any, or hardly any, actual lies.* By simply allowing the system to select for system-friendly voices who automatically FRAME the news / PR in system-friendly narratives, a single, unified image of the world is perpetually manufactured by the news media; one in which technological progress, economic growth, compulsory schooling and full employment are unquestionably good; in which our wars of aggression and sale of weapons to client dictatorships are either 'mistakes' or, preferably, invisible; in which insanely destructive weather events, floods, draughts,

---

* 'Everyone must know what the situation is'. Joseph Geobbels.

civil-unrest and distant wars just causelessly happen; in which locking the planet up into Boxes of Merely Existing is, despite no evidence that it works (and scores of studies, not to mention common sense, demonstrating that it does not), the best way of dealing with a virus with a 99.5-99.9% survival rate, and an average age of death of around 80; in which the unmitigated horror of the system is filtered into mere 'tragedy', and, crucially; in which the host organisation, or the role of the media, in supporting the system is never, ever, seriously criticised. A great deal of disagreement on matters of peripheral or trivial interest is tolerated. Journalists and academics can furiously disagree with each other about welfare spending, interest rates, elections, corruption, sex-scandals, the terms of trade agreements, what the royals are wearing and even, at the left-most end of the little window, edgy topics like climate change, economic growth, civil liberties and the deleterious effects of *specific* technologies; but step out of the microscopic range of acceptable thought, write intelligently about how the technocratic market economy exterminates nature and culture, seriously investigate the endemic institutional bias of the entire press, left and right, hold *our* leaders to the same standards of judgement as *theirs*, throw doubt upon middle-class gods (relativism, pacifism, professionalism, monogender and the market), endeavour to explore the entire technocratic system or its origins in the homeless mind, and see what happens to your career.

One of the most popular defences, made by corporate journalists and academics, is that 'The Guardian' (or the BBC, or the Washington Post or whoever), often 'gets it right', that they 'do great stuff on Russia', or their more left-leaning journos write important critiques of corporate corruption and environmental breakdown, and so on. This argument is identical in essence to 'our government is good because it has never bombed Wales' or 'the medical profession is good, because look at all the lives doctors save'. Details, facts and framed generalisations are focused on, in order to avoid addressing the entire structure, filtering system, bias, market-subservience and calamitous harm of the institution in question. The whole, the big picture, the causes and effects, the entire truth... such things are not merely 'taboo', they cannot be perceived by the hyper-focused modern mind which the system represents and normalises.

The purpose of the news is not, and never has been, to tell the truth. It is to sell audiences to advertisers, to support state-corporate power, to normalise professionalism, to provide a voyeuristic window on far away sex and violence in order to distract consumers from their nearby frustration and unhappiness, to excite the restless and needy ego, to smear critics of the system and to bury what they say under an ocean of irrelevance. In fact if it is in the news, it *must* be irrelevant. Truth can no more survive in the media than cats can survive on the moon, or quality can survive in the market. Truth takes too long to generate, too long to express, requires too much attention and sensitivity, has disastrous connections to reality and tends to produces catastrophic effects in those who are exposed to it; such as insouciance, revolutionary inspiration, confidence in the future, love for humanity, weird understanding and spontaneous erotic splendour, none of which does the market any good at all.

The system requires that consumers of news—indeed of any late-capitalist art form—are titillated, entertained, upset, annoyed about the government, nod in sage wonder at the pronouncements of Big Minds, desire the latest tech, are afraid of diabolic foreign powers, or diabolic flu-like illnesses, turn forever away from the implications of mortality, are amazed at magnificent cleavage, in complete ignorance about the true nature of the world, a complete stranger to the mysterious reality of their own conscious experience, regularly swoon over Obama and the Royals (yay!), are up in arms about the communists and fascists (boo!), or about political correctness, or about the damn immigrants... and conditioned to yibber-yabber about Today's Themes with work colleagues during the coffee break. That is what capital requires, and that, you may have noticed, is what capital gets.

And yet. The activity of the news media is trivial in comparison to the entire fabricated reality we experience via the televisions, computers, cinema screens, loud-speakers, adverts, packaging, syllabuses, books, magazines, posters, meetings, laws, ideas, emotions and mediated experiences of the world. We do not experience reality as it is—a mysterious embodied totality—but a comprehensible mind-made topology of isolated individual subjects and objects, continually remoulding, reinforcing and reproducing itself in the service *of* itself. The proper name for this vast, abstract-emotional simulacrum is not 'art',* and certainly not 'truth' or 'reality', although it is taken as such, but the [Phildickian] SPECTACLE, the horrific, hypnotic dreamlife of the world.

The system conceives the entire universe as a constellation of abstractions,† which in the autonomous ego seem as real as reality. In a capitalist system, these abstractions are emotionally-potent (or, in the Marxist tradition, 'FETISHISED') measurements of economic value ('ooh! expensive!'), formal order ('sexy' designs and efficient networks), advertising ('just do it') and the multifarious productions of the public-relations 'industry' (press offices, awarding bodies, rating agencies, think-tanks, etc, etc). These combine with a self-replicating array of system-engendered and system-reinforcing impressions, beliefs, opinions, ideas and vague feelings ('FALSE-CONSCIOUSNESS'‡) to form an ersatz unworld which doesn't just conceal the reality of how people actually live, or how the things they use actually come to be made, but the reality of everything in nature and society; the entire universe, along with the totality of conscious experience. Community comes to be understood abstractly, other countries and cultures are understood mythically, nature is perceived through a sentimental prism, history is reduced to cliché or to quiz-friendly fact-fragments, the objects (and increasingly the ideas, feelings and experiences) which men and women produce appear in their lives as mysterious artefacts dropped from a spaceship ('REIFICATION'), and society rises up before them not as a lived experience formed by their own actions, but as a monolithic *thing* which happens *to* them (this is

---

* Art which serves something other than the spectacular system or the self-informed self, we call GREAT. Not 'high' (although it might be difficult and out of the ordinary) or 'low' (although it might be easy and ordinary), but *true*, expressing ARTISTIC TRUTH, the conscious source of the self and the contextual source of the world.

† Not that there is anything inherently wrong with abstraction, or simulation. The problem, as A.Zijderveld points out in *The Abstract Society*, is when '*there is no homecoming*'.

‡ 'There are no longer human beings, thinkers, lovers etc.; the human race is enveloped by the press in a miasma of thoughts, emotions, moods, even conclusions, intentions which are nobody's, which belong to none and yet to all.' Søren Kierkegaard

the strictly Marxist meaning of ALIENATION). Life entire, which means our own lives, is naught but a schizoid phantasm. When the reality of it is encountered directly, actually, the result is inevitably profound shock and horror.

People who have grown up entirely within the system, within its professional and religious institutions, within its towns and cities, within its managed spaces and its virtual 'spaces' therefore consider *reality itself* to be fake. Not consciously. They are not conscious of believing in something which is not true, nor are they ever consciously imprinted with a fake ideology. Their entire experience is *already* bound by the unreal, the mediated and the represented, leaving them with a sense of permanent, cynical distance from reality, a sense that it's all bullshit and that nothing really matters beyond whatever it is you want to matter. Propaganda can then be applied *to* this sense with ease, even when its untruth is blatantly, crudely, obvious. Human beings raised by the system are quite content to be lied to, because *the truth is really just a useful lie*. If it's not useful, then it's not really the truth.* They cannot be argued out of this stance, because your *argument* isn't useful—so useless, in fact, its laughable. Your attempt to show them reality beyond the coordinates of a self formed by a machine, is like trying to show colour to a man raised in a dark room.

The darkness of the spectacle is not just endless, but continuous, or *seamless*. The witnessing mind passes from rom-com, to sci-fi, to car advert, to browser, to laptop, to the interior of the coffee shop, to the badges and bags of the customers, to their hugs and smiles, to the tones of their voices, to their conversations, to your own conversation with yourself, to ear-worms and sex-anxieties and the shoes you want to buy... and there is no interruption, no disruption, nothing that is actually, existentially, *different*. If anything real does present itself to the system-mind, anything from beyond the knowable, it is either some kind of irritation or pain (a pain which, crucially, cannot be alleviated by following institutional scripts and techniques), or it is registered as such. Because there is no way for the system to perceive the connection between reality and pain it is safer to avoid both. Avoid everything which does not segue seamlessly

---

* The source of such a functional approach to reality is explored in *Self and Unself*.

into the man-made facsimile of nature, culture and consciousness that calls itself nature, culture and consciousness, or that claims to be generated by them, but which is, in fact, produced and managed by the system, which it serves and reflects.

This is why perennial complaints by the left that the 'right-wing' media programme the people into servitude are so completely besides the point. Certainly, the lies and distortions of elite-owned information outlets can disastrously warp public opinion or swing an election for favoured monsters, but it is the entire civilised system that shapes the lives, and therefore the opinions of the masses. Domesticated people have domesticated fears and desires which seek validation in the domesticated news which, ultimately, does not *form* their beliefs but *confirms* them. This is why media reform is useless, and why trying to change people's attitudes through exposing them to different kinds of information is about as useful as trying to make a horse more intelligent by reading Shakespeare to it.

10

The Myth *of* Nature

Civilisation has destroyed the natural world
it depends on · · · The closer we get to the
collapse of the natural world, the less visible
it becomes · · · The system cannot present
the true horror of natural collapse, or its true
cause, because it cannot perceive nature.
What it *can* perceive is an opportunity to
profit from collapse, an opportunity that
goes by the name of 'hope'.

THE MOST LUDICROUS AND DESTRUCTIVE myth of the system is the notion not just that there is a reality in which constant exponential growth can sustain itself indefinitely, but that this is the reality we actually inhabit.

In the reality we do inhabit, the temperature of the Earth is catastrophically rising, Everests of ice are pouring into the oceans, Alaskan and Siberian permafrost, containing billions of tonnes of carbon dioxide, methane and mercury (along with God knows what bacteria and viruses), are rapidly melting, most wildlife has been wiped out, ecosystems everywhere are collapsing and we'll soon be close losing most of our arable land. Data on the effect of the system on the world's oceans and forests, and the consequences of our consumption of energy, fossil fuels, rare earth metals, plastic and water, are all just as horrifying. Meanwhile, a handful of companies are responsible for total annihilation of the natural world and our colossal production of pollutants *continues to rise*.

Some of these facts are, of course, debatable, but, as a whole, the evidence is incontrovertible. Many people now seem to think that because vested interests are using ecological collapse as a cover to develop the system and enslave us all further, that it is *all* therefore an invention. They seem to forget, or not want to seriously consider, that evidence for the catastrophic exploitation of nature has been pouring in for decades, long before it became an excuse to promote green energy; or to consider the enormity of the problem—far, *far* worse than just the hot topic of 'global warming'—or the extent of the system—how little wild is actually left on the earth, or in our selves—and what that must mean for our comfortable world; or to consider the fact that *all* civilisations destroy themselves by, in effect, digging through the bottom of the raft they are floating on; or simply to consider the evidence of their senses.

The next time you hear of ongoing man-made mass extinction, or see piles of animal corpses after a mysterious mass death, or wastelands where there once were rainforests, or seas covered from shore to shore with rubbish, or sea life riddled with plastic, or miles upon miles of bleached coral; the next time you hear that antibiotics are becoming useless, or, that we will soon have no soil left, or that there's just no more wild left, or ask yourself why there are no more insects on your windshield or pretty birds singing in your garden, do remind yourself, because it's sometimes easy to forget; the *earth is actually dying*, and the same system that makes cool cars, smartphones, fibre-optic cables, Oreos, Nintendos, Teflon, Viagra and Jet Skis is killing it; all of which *are* the reason it is easy to forget. The ongoing obliteration of the natural world, like all the other unspeakable horrors of the system, passes the distracted world by, making references to the appalling non-reality of system life seem overblown, exaggerated, hyperbolic, childish. 'What's the beef? It's not *that* bad—I can still buy Jaffa Cakes, the car's running okay and anyway, a new superhero film out soon'. The natural world is dying, human culture is dying, the light of consciousness is dying; everything good is dying. The *real* world, beyond the artificial 'normality' of the wind, security and video screen, is rapidly becoming a wasteland, but nobody *really* notices. Yet.

We are plummeting towards collapse (official term for this process; PROGRESS) and will soon be facing widespread droughts, flooding and famines, along with civil disorder on an unimaginable scale. Not only is it impossible that the system will learn to levitate, but it cannot even slow the speed of its fall (official term; GROWTH or PROSPERITY). Even faced with the prospect of imminent biological annihilation and the collapse of civilisation *in our lifetimes*, the idea that we need massive, immediate, negative growth, or that the system might be to blame, or even exists, or that we should face up to the coming horrors, remain officially unsayable and, in the wealthy West, widely unthinkable. In fact, the closer we get to annihilation, the *less* visible the problem becomes in the news media. Only the *effects* are broadcast; not just silent woodlands and empty seas, but also mass-migration, wars over dwindling resources, rising prices and so on. People are left to invent their own causes for these things, which are very often absurd.

As the evidence for the coming apocalypse piles up—along with the evidence for our responsibility for it—as towns sink into icy mud and once-in-a-million-year hurricanes file up to annihilate the tropics, and crops repeatedly fail, and ships pass unhindered through the Arctic, and countries run out of water, or food, or are submerged under rising rivers, or are scourged by wildfires, and murderous heat-waves become the norm and everyone, everywhere, constantly says to themselves, looking at the freakishly early (or late) blossom, or the silent birds, or the parched fields, 'that's weird', so official mentions of the euphemism 'climate change' diminish to zero, and the privileged classes of those countries most responsible collectively put their fingers in their ears and shout, '*nah, nah, nah, can't hear you.*'*

They'll be listening very soon, although whether they will *hear* is another matter. The entire world is locked up in a planetary panic room comprising, at best, domesticated (and therefore stupid) or symbolic (and therefore unreal) nature. The system—its states, corporations and artificially intelligent machines—is, and has always been, incapable of perceiving nature in anything but the most crudely utilitarian terms. The tree is so many tonnes of timber, or resin, or just *in the way*. The multitude of relations that humans can have with it—much less the infinite subtlety, complexity and beauty of the mysterious thing itself—do not exist, just as they do not for the system-ic-ego, which sees the tree, labels it, says 'ooh nice!' perhaps, and then moves on to something else it wants or doesn't want, or likes or doesn't like.

For the ego and its system, nature does not, actually, exist and so neither does its disappearance; at least the horrific magnitude of it. Isolated cases of pollution are presented and consumed; sad stories of dying polar bears, filthy beaches and whatnot, but the immensity of the situation, of catastrophic climate meltdown, the heartbreaking ruin of all that is materially good and the extermination of life on earth itself—this is ignored or downplayed, offset with 'good news' and David Attenborough

---

* Or at least they do publicly. In fact, the mega-wealthy are prepping for the coming collapse, and researching how to deal with the reality of it; a strong contender for the 'necessity' of lockdown (horde-management), behind the need to cut down on energy consumption and yoke the world into a digital panopticon.

concluding a snapshot of the atrocity with, *'but there is hope...'*
For some reason, newspapers and television channels whose
primary purpose is to get us all to consume are not too interested
in presenting the consequences of consumption, or connecting
the wasteland we have made with the system which made it.
Official pronouncements referring to the terminal state of the
natural world are limited to focusing on scapegoats and secondary matters, such as overpopulation, over-consumption of meat,
volcanoes, cow farts, natural weather cycles; anything but the
system, along with the usual bromides that *we* are destroying
the world and that, therefore, *we* who live in an environment
owned by other people are responsible for saving it. For some
reason, the landowners of the world are not too keen on the
idea that to save the environment what *we* must do is, first of
all, take it out of *their* hands, and so, as they set up a few nice
little recycling earners (such as 'net-zero'), they relentlessly
pump out the counter-notion that we can solve civilisation by
voting, protest our way to paradise and, of course, that 'we are
all in this together'.

Because 'we' are despoiling the earth, 'we' need investment
in green technologies (made from rare-earth metals, plastics and
other petrochemical products) and bio-fuels (made from felled
forests), an unnecessary, low-nutrient, system-friendly vegan diet,
aid sent to ecological disaster areas, green governments, organic
mousemats and state-organised, professionally-run initiatives to
'offset' our planet-cooking gasses. And because 'we' are facing
environmental collapse, 'we' need more green education, more
green professionals, more green security, more green surveillance,
more green technology, more green energy and more green
growth... 'We' might even end up needing ecological martial
law, an ecological world lockdown and a reimagined perfectly
virtual world economy of hideous dystopian ecological control.
But don't worry, because 'we' are all in it together, 'we' will
certainly benefit from what 'we' do.

The system tells us that we are all equally responsible for
'the environment'. In the real world, most people don't *have* an
environment—they can't afford one.* The system tells us that

---

* Not that using a ruinously wasteful IT system to order an amusing t-shirt from
  Amazon that was manufactured in Bangladesh and then carted halfway around

nature is separate from the human world—a kind of painted backdrop in front of which we get on with the 'real' business of living in the world, pursuing, collecting, studying, avoiding and defending *objective things* (The Myth of Scientism). Or the system tells us that 'everything is natural', which is to say, nothing is natural; the word is meaningless, a cultural construct, a subjective no-thing, formed from whatever interpretations you wish to make of it (The Myth of Postmodernism). That objectivity and subjectivity are *effects* of nature is incomprehensible madness to the mind of the world, which will do whatever it can to push the natural *cause* of our ordinary lives from experience. It will continually generate and pursue dreamworlds of future happiness, continually push unmediated contact with nature, or the present moment, from experience and continually obscure, mythologise, ignore or deny the deep reality of nature and the existential sacrifice which reveals it. The mind, in other words, builds the system until the system falls; and then mind goes out of its mind.

---

the world in an oil-guzzling containership; or swanning around the planet on 747s to take selfies on Foxconn phones with the last few dolphin left alive; or munching on burgers raised on cleared Brazilian rainforests while watching a World Cup made possible by exterminating local paupers (etc, etc, etc.) aren't also a significant—foundational—part of the problem, one that the technophilic masses are, curiously, unwilling to address.

11

The Trickle-Down Myth

The advanced system relies on the idea that the more money rich people have, the better off poor people are · · · The fact that a few miserable peasants can now afford Dunkin' Donuts masks the fact that nature is not better off · · · It also masks the fact that by any meaningful, human measure of wealth, *everyone* is dirt poor.

I T IS RICH BUSINESSMEN WHO CREATE WEALTH. Without their ability to spot investment opportunities and invest in the future, everyone else would be sitting around twiddling their thumbs and getting poorer as the economy shrinks.

In order to accept this fantastic picture of the world we have to not only ignore the stupendous growth of the first world during the 1950s, 60s and 70s, when the rich were taxed up to their eyeballs and adequate state welfare handed out to the poor; not only put aside the facts on how fast and how much wealth has increased since the 1970s for the owning 0.01% and for the managing 1% compared to everyone else; not only ignore the fact that money and work do not lift the poor out of misery; not only pass over the fact that, as overall wealth has increased, investment has slowed; and not only pretend that the rich don't do everything in their power to ensure that more and more have less and less; but we also have to assume that a system which gives $500,000,000,000 to five hundred psychopaths, in the hope that a few of their servants might benefit, must be the fairest and most intelligent way of organising society.

The 'trickle-down' theory came to prominence during the 1980s, when Thatcher and Reagan handed the world over to the hyper-wealthy by privatising public services, funding foreign dictators, giving tax breaks to multi-millionaires, dismantling the welfare state and passing a 'financialised' virtual economy over to banks. The idea was that, in order to be persuaded to work, rich people need to be given money, while poor people need to have their money taken away.

Oddly enough, it no work. Funnelling unimaginable sums of money into the ever-swelling pockets of a microscopically tiny group of parasitical rentiers,* via massive tax breaks and

---

* Not just of land and property, but also of intellectual property.

credits, bailouts, enormous subsidies to land-owners, intellectual property rights holders and the like (unproductive rental income, essentially), soft regulation and various other special privileges, doesn't improve the lot of the multitude that the system was built to dominate. Rather, it inflates their living costs, depresses their wages, suffocates their production, sucks the life-blood from their communities, destroys their nature and pushes them into market-slavery, a.k.a. 'debt'.

The Trickle-Down Myth is represented nowadays as the idea that 'a rising tide raises all boats', which is to say 'the principle that the poor, who must subsist on table scraps dropped by the rich, can best be served by giving the rich bigger meals.'[*] Sure, a rentier earning $200,000 a year from a wide portfolio of property and investments now earns 10% more, but so does a Nigerian farmer earning $2 a day. It's fair, you see, because an extra $20,000 earned from doing nothing productive is the same as an extra 20 cents from slogging your guts out all day to grow food. Thus, poor countries are richer and rich countries are richer, and they both got rich through free trade and free markets. The complete ruin of the Third World (forcing poor countries to adopt free-market policies), the annihilation of the natural world—and, incidentally, the 'growth' of states which practice intense state-directed protectionism and discrimination against foreign investors (such as the USA in the 1880s and China today)[†]—are, predictably, swept under the ideological carpet.

'But we're richer now!' cry the Marvellous Ones, living in the Land of Plenty, 'look at my bank balance! look at the price of my house! look at...' actually nobody celebrates their *own* wealth. Focused on the level above, restrained by fear of resentment masquerading as modesty (see myth 15) and hyper-sensitive to microscopic inconveniences, even six-figure technocrats complain they haven't got enough. The [propertied] rich *are* richer though, and the idea persists that their rising wealth is a Good Thing, or that access to middle-class 'financial security' is a Noble Goal. Everyone with eyes in their head knows that wealthy people are overwhelmingly insensitive, that the children and grandchildren of self-made men are notorious morons,

---

[*]   William Blum.

[†]   H. Chang, *23 Things They Don't Tell You About Capitalism*.

that famous people are extraordinarily unhappy, or far less creative than when they made it big, and that the wealthy classes are, as a group, cruel, lonely, miserable, afraid of independent responsibility, terrified of freedom, haunted by their mediocrity, tight-fisted beyond satire and sedated by their affluence; compliant, domesticated and, in the worst sense of the word, ordinary. But none of this will happen to *me!* I can handle money power! Not likely.*

'But *everyone's* earning more!†' cry systemacrats, 'they've got degrees now! and mobile phones! and look at China! and the GDP!' Thereby ignoring the catastrophic madness of measuring quality of life by the transformation of nature and culture into money (an oil spill increases GDP, as does felling a rainforest, as does a new Amazon warehouse‡), along with a billion people who live in slums and do not have clean water or enough to eat§—the money poor—and billions more who are either excluded from the Great Party because they are too old, too young, too female, too sensitive, or too weird; or who are unable to feed, clothe, heal, house, transport or entertain themselves, or live without work, high-tech access to the market (cars, internet, supermarkets, electricity etc.) or the correct paperwork; a world of people who need to get things (and scores) in order to 'enjoy' five seconds of relief from continual, restless, boredom, who have no access to nature or genuine culture (or knowledge that such things actually exist) and who have only crap games to play.

By any meaningful measure of wealth we are *all* dirt poor and getting poorer by the day.

---

* If you've spent your whole life poor, if you are genuinely sensitive and courageous, there is a far-distant chance you can handle money. The litmus test is how quickly, intelligently and splendidly you get rid of it.

† The share of the world living in extreme poverty halved at the beginning of the present century, although it started rising again after the lockdown.

‡ The human misery of such places is soon to be at an end of course, as machines replace warehouse monkeys, who will be deposited into a shoddy welfare system which forces them into criminal activities which lead them to incarceration in GDP-enhancing prisons; run by Amazon.

§ According to *WaterAid* and the *Global Hunger Index, 2010.*

12

The Myth *of* Progress

Progress means a more comfortable decline
· · · Advanced technology may comfort us
for a time, but it always ends up crippling,
exhausting, confusing and enslaving us. We
have now progressed to the point where
human beings are redundant · · · Progress is
entirely rational. Any call to reverse 'growth',
minutely diminish our 'standards of living',
stop working or slow down sounds irrational,
and therefore insane.

WE ARE TOLD THAT THERE IS NO PROGRESS without the system and that the system leads to *innovation, efficiency, convenience* and *rising standards of living*. This is why the poor old feudal peasant runs gratefully into the arms of the modern factory, and why turning away from the advanced technocratic system would necessarily lead to Cholera, TB, the Bubonic Plague, forty-five hellish years behind a plough or brutalist architecture and Ladas.

Turning again to the real world, we have progressed our way into a culture with the durability and beauty of a flatpack, chipboard shed hastily erected on an asteroid that is hurtling into the sun. A shrinking minority, existing in a shrinking pleasure-bubble of artificial calm, intellectual order and spectacular distraction, can convince themselves, and a few of their privileged, salaried, employees, that everything is fiiiiine, while a growing mass rapidly descend into, at best, a state of miserable, numbed fear, at worst, an existential nightmare of schizoid horror.

Capitalism may be able to delay the coming annihilation of our civilised systems for a few moments more by inflating the value of assets held by the hyper-rich (official term: FINANCIAL-ISATION), gambling (official term: SPECULATION), exponentially increasing usurious indebtedness (official term: EXTENDING CREDIT), exploiting global labour to an unheard of extent (official term: OUTSOURCING), stealing from the poor (official term: AUSTERITY) or liquidising their assets, throttling their consumption and making them dependent on state handouts (official term: LOCKDOWN), but more and more people can feel that the shadow of death is descending on us all. With every terrorist strike, every horrendous famine, every punishing blow of nature's fist, every new totalitarian lockdown law, we feel the future-shocks ripple through us, and, as time goes on, more and more of us see these feelings for what they are: WORLD DREAD.

Not that, over the past few thousand years, we haven't discovered how to make a few things that can genuinely serve human beings—ploughs, printing presses, ball bearings, morphine, vulcanised rubber, tinned tomatoes and trumpets; but none of these things were brought to you by the system. It wasn't the system that built your house or produced your food, but *nature* and *labour*, the work of life and of ordinary people, upon which sits the swelling abscess of management, subordinating all activity to its own ceaseless, and, as the economy is now entirely dominated by speculation, financialisation and debt-bubbles, increasingly ephemeral 'GROWTH'.

'Capitalism made your laptop', apparently. The dishonest fiction that a tiny class of exploiting owners is responsible for the work of nature and of labour is not mentioned. The routine conflation of capitalism (or socialism, or whatever) with production, by which the *owners* of land and labour—those people who use others to generate wealth—are always referred to as 'producers', cannot fit onto a car sticker, or in a tweet. And the idea that perhaps we don't need laptops, or the internet, cannot be heard outside of psychiatric hospitals.

Imagine if, using the technologies then available, the same efforts and resources had gone into giving the world what the internet and high powered personal computing now provide us with. Such a world might have a massively well-stocked library in every town connected, via an extremely efficient inter-loan service, to a national or international network. Every town might have an equally well-provisioned concert hall, with thousands of high quality instruments free to borrow, or cheaply buy—and a veritable army of singing coaches, slap-bassists and music theorists hanging around. Each town might have easy access to four cinemas and a well-funded film industry able to take all kinds of risks on new talent. We might have a postal service that collects and delivers five times a day. We might have improvised theatre groups, clay pigeon shoots, playgrounds so fun adults use them, large areas of wilderness, local printing presses, a panoply of art studios, a veritable forest of vinyl and, strangest of all, *actual* social networks.*

---

* The internet brought us two things which we didn't have before, both of which, like so many 'innovations' of the system, were solutions to problems that the system

Although returning to the world we recently left would need an unprecedented slackening of the late-capitalist imperative, and although it might not be capable of undoing the market, much less the system, completely, I put it to you that it would be a better place to live than the 'connected' virtual spaces which we are now *forced* to inhabit. The internet and high powered computing do not give us *anything* qualitatively new and they do not solve the problems of humanity. They solve the problems of the system.

The same can be said of cars, planes, high-speed rail, containerships, electric blankets, air-conditioning units, central heating, antidepressants, power-brooms, string trimmers, smartphones, microwave ovens, professional toothbrushes, and hydro-max 3 elite razors; none of which we need and most of which have been a curse to humankind. When a tool, or a network of tools, passes beyond a finite limit of complexity, power or speed, it ceases serving its users, who must expend more time, energy or attention in maintaining it, than they save through its use. The technology or system becomes autonomous and self-reinforcing, subordinating *all* activity to its growth; including the activities and priorities of its nominal creators, owners and managers. The needs of humans become irrelevant unless they are in service of the mechanism. Thus; high-speed transport slows us down, labour-saving devices make us work harder, smartphones make us more stupid, hospitals make us sicker (see myth 28), centralised agriculture enslaves us,* human

---

itself created. The first was cheap video calls, which helped ameliorate—for the wealthy West—the destruction of local communities, and the second was access to independent, dissident and subversive media, the kind which, as the history of independent newspapers, radio and television demonstrates, the system itself destroyed or restricted.

* Plants and animals were domesticated around 4,000 years *before* we became dependent on agriculture. The theory used to be that we domesticated grains because the environment had become less productive, there were more people to feed and anyway we preferred a sedentary life. Now it is clear that nomadic self-sufficiency had become more difficult and populations had exploded because we had become dependent on domestication, as we had become dependent on the tool of ego before it and as we were to become dependent on every other complex tool or system since. See J. C. Scott, *Against the Grain*.

skill gives way to, at best, operative competence and the closer the virtual world gets to reality, the more the real world becomes unreal. The monolithic technical system that dominates the world subordinates all other values and systems, left or right; another reason why it is misleading to speak of capitalism (or perhaps 'Americanisation') which is actually in service to an all-dominant TECHNICALISM.

The technophile replies that 'standards of living' are rising and poverty is decreasing. Such arguments are too shallow to seriously consider, but even aside from what progress actually means in the world we actually live in—the oceans of misery upon which the fitted kitchens float—it is quite possible for 'standards of living' to rise while exploitation worsens. Standards of living rose during slavery,* Hitler's Germany (which was why he was so popular) and Stalin's Russia. 'Rising standards of living' doesn't justify slavery, fascism and communism, yet is routinely presented as the reason why we must accept hyper-dependence on our disabling, monomaniacal, technocratic system.

The concept of 'rising standards of living' conceals a number of unspoken assumptions which never quite make it to the teevee. Could 'higher standards of living' end up obstructing or harming our physical health, mental well-being, conviviality, access to nature, autonomy or life-purpose? Can we live happily, well, with no rise in 'standards of living'? Did pre-civilised people have a high standard of living? Have the nature of our 'standards' changed over time? Do the benefits of antibiotics, plastics, televisions, smartphones—or even alphabets, ploughs and optical lenses—outweigh the costs they inevitably conceal? Does a rising standard of living in one part of the world entail suffering elsewhere? Have we become 'the tools of our tools'? Are human beings becoming superfluous to requirements? The answer to all of these questions is likely to be yes; but serious investigation of them is well off the agenda. We are progressing, the past was evil† and that's that.

Technicalism prefers to tell us only of the short, brutal lives lived by medieval peasants and pre-civilised tribes, and

---

* See George Fitzhugh for a robust defence of 'rising standards of living' under chattel slavery.

† Except for that of our favourite empires.

of the marvellous benefits of modern technology (particularly of professional medicine, conveniently omitting the fact that changes in public health occur through changes in the environment and that where technology improves general health it is nearly always implemented *despite* the medical profession, not *because* of it) which, it is continually asserted, saved us all from the pox. Somehow we never hear that pre-modern people had enormous amounts of free time, free access to common resources and a healthy attitude towards death, madness, work and nature, and we never hear that pre-civilised people were healthy, happy, long-lived and free, and their societies egalitarian, non-coercive and peaceful, and we never hear of the impoverishment, sickness, stress, violence, inequality and seismic discontent that the agricultural and industrial 'revolutions' brought to men and women—unless the victims are those of official enemies. We hear one crude, brutalising narrative; that history is a ladder, that education is a ladder, that career is a ladder, that technology is a ladder, that knowledge is a ladder... and there is only one sane direction; up and up and up and up and up, infinitely. With every new rung we get a little more power or a little more dopamine, and a lot more dependence on the ladder which provides us with these things, which is why *less* or *lower* are greeted with such horror. Who but a madman would suggest less schooling? less energy? less speed? less education? less medicine? less technology? less growth? less money? less knowledge? A *lower* score!? The sane progress, develop, grow, build, learn, innovate and invest; they are forward-looking, forward-thinking and forever, and ever, in their own words, 'going forward'. The same can be said of cancers, which also put 'progress' above every other concern, but connecting the two is in the diabolic realm of the irrational, the childish and the 'utopian' for defenders of the system. Imagine though how a university educated cancer would justify its priorities to a healthy cell, even as it consumed the body it depends on for its existence.

Just as cancer is bound to the destruction of the body, so the technocratically-fuelled market which runs society is bound to the destruction of that society. First of all by rigidly controlling commodified land and labour, then, in the spirit world of late-capitalist financialisation, transferring every aspect of nature and society into mechanised business concerns. Immense sums of financialised 'easy money' (easy for the rich, that is) incentivise the hyper-wealthy to invest in speculative, or rent earning, rather than productive, creative or convivial activities, to plunder state assets without having to worry about paying any kind of price for destroying the lives of the now helpless unrich and to engage in outrageous, stupendous, levels of fraud and corruption (money laundering, shadow banking, tax evasion, and so on and so forth). In order to deal with the chaos which results, technocrats and economists attempt to eradicate all 'non-rational' elements in society; all mystery, all wilderness, all independence, all truth, all dissent and all freedom.

The system, in other words, is bound to what we would now call 'totalitarianism' and 'fascism'. Technicalism, like the addicts to the narco-porn it manufactures, only understands *more of the same*—*different* and *better* are as unfathomable to a technocratic system as love is to a laptop. When there is more than enough of the same, the system begins, like all drugs, to take more than it gives, until those from whom it takes find themselves completely powerless before *its* needs, forced to continually sacrifice whatever instincts they have for different and better to a now all-powerful totalising dealer. This is why the most rational supporters of the market immediately take up with 'fascists' as soon as they gain enough power, and why rational 'liberals' and 'moderates', after the initial uproar, end up uprooting their principles and, while complaining of being overwhelmed by public stupidity and the poor taste of megalomaniacs, toeing the line, and why everyone in power, despite lip service to whatever green initiatives are flavour of the month, always serves the techno-sphere. If you are part of the system, you have no choice; your only choice is to *not* be part of it.

Likewise, modern fascists and the far-right criticise 'the system', or 'capitalism' while embodying its quintessence, which is why the system always does so marvellously well under dictatorships. Sure, minorities are exterminated, dissidents vanished and the natural world reduced to dust, but these are all small prices to pay for 'stability', 'strength' and 'progress'.

This is why it is so stupendously futile to attempt to reform the system (see myth 31); to change its tech, its laws or its leaders. It may be interesting and of some limited use to identify the influence this or that organisation or individual has over the world, but until the entire system is seen for what it is, and completely rejected, there will be, there can be, no meaningful change, any more than changing a king can make any real difference to monarchism.

13

The Myth *of* Peace

The system depends on mass-murder, mass-slavery and mass-theft · · · These are not very popular, so they must concealed. This is done through ideological management; producing books, movies, academic papers, laws and institutional structures in which the violence that went and continue to go into making the system does not appear · · · There is, however, no need for the system to kill, enslave and steal as it did in the past, as people are trained to *automatically* hand over their labour, their intelligence and their love.

CAPITALISM CAME INTO BEING through something like a gentleman's agreement to put this damn silly feudal business behind us and start bloody well knuckling down. The colonial massacre, enclosure, usury, criminalisation of poverty, curtailment of self-sufficiency, punishing taxation and despoliation that were necessary to impose the market system are illusions. They didn't happen; and even while they were happening, they weren't happening.* There might be the occasional ex-colonel who mysteriously 'makes his fortune' before retiring to one of Jane Austin's vast manor houses; there might be knowing talk of the ungrateful natives in the latest Victorian costume drama (*what beastly racists those old fashioned types were!*') or a socialist in Downton Abbey; there might be the odd glance at our crimes in the paps, or some sad, sad accounts of the bad, bad factories of yesteryear (*factories? we don't still have those, do we?*'); or a suggestion that good old Churchill could be a *bit* of a rotter, or that we shouldn't judge mass murderers of the past by today's standards; or there might be a movie about the 'tragedy' of Vietnam or the 'mistake' of Iraq... but how the upper classes *actually* thought and behaved, what the English *actually* did in India, or the Americans in South East Asia, or why, or Churchill's litany of horrendous crimes, or Kennedy's, or Clinton's, or the structural necessity of a military-based market to invade resource rich countries, or how Israel has come to enclose Palestine in a massive prison camp; none of this makes good teevee. It's too 'simplistic', too 'angry', a naive 'caricature' of a 'complex' past.

The *official* reasons for war are 1) compassion for the weak; to defend them against being bullied by the bad guys 2) to spread *the good*; democracy, civilisation, the Word of God

---

* See Harold Pinter's Nobel prize acceptance speech.

3) justice, law, or fighting *the bad*; terrorism, communism, 'them'
4) self-defence or security, and 5) honour, glory, love and, the
all-time favourite, duty.

The *actual* reasons for war are 1) pouring money into the
military-industrial economy, profitably using up its products and
opening up new markets; which includes destroying everything
so that it all needs to be rebuilt, controlling areas of strategic
importance and stealing resources 2) annihilating the threat and
embarrassment of a square millimetre of the globe being free of
state control or private ownership 3) GROUPTHINK (attachment to
the known) and GROUPFEEL (fear of the unknown) 4) boredom,
sadism and primal, egoic anxiety, and 5) eviscerating dissent at
home by turning the nation into a police state and restructuring
society and nature* so that they mimic an army barracks or a
laboratory. Much the same reasons apply to work (see myth 21).

Because, firstly, the system is unable to operate without
constant warfare and, secondly, because killing lots of people
is not very popular, journalists, academics and other opinion
shapers must continually drum up support for war by ignoring
context, suppressing or denouncing dissent, distorting history,
exaggerating threat, uncritically 'reporting' official pronouncements, eulogising 'our heroic boys', and their marvellous 'team
spirit' and normalising a military society. The horrendous systematic crimes of the system must be downplayed, glossed over
or misrepresented, because to investigate them throws light
on the purpose of warfare, along with the nature and origins
of the capitalist phase of civilisation and the true source of its
wealth and power.

Although upper class wealth is sometimes augmented by
people voluntarily leaving pre-capitalist societies, selling up their
land or heading to the big city to rent themselves to industrial
capital so as to gain money and independence from slave owners
and feudal gangs, the most common tactic by far for gaining

---

* 'The visual sign of the well-managed forest, in Germany... came to be the reg-
ularity and neatness of its appearance. Forests might be inspected in much the
same way as a commanding officer might review his troops on parade, and woe to
the forest guard whose "beat" was not sufficiently trim or "dressed."...The more
uniform the forest, the greater the possibilities for centralized management...'
J.C. Scott, *Seeing like a State*.

control of land, resources and labour power was, and remains, straightforward MASS-THEFT (also known, in Marxist literature, as 'primitive accumulation'), the foundation of capitalism.*

Capitalism originated in massive centralisation of power in England, and the consequent need to commercialise land in order to extract taxable revenue from it, rather than through the previous tactic of plain extortion. Central power began to lease land for profit and appropriate surplus through property tax, rents and accessory tariffs and tolls on commerce, which compelled landowners, and their wealthy tenants, to steal more land from ordinary people ('ENCLOSURE†'), steal people to work it ('EMPLOYMENT'), steal the products they produced ('PROFIT') and develop techniques to augment this production ('INDUS-TRIALISATION'). An entire country—everything living within it—thus compelled to produce for profit and consume from the market—transformed into *things* to be grown, harvest-ed, refined, transported, packaged, sold, consumed and then thrown away—inevitably led to extraordinary suffering, massive over-production, rapid depletion of resources and unheard of financial power for the new wealth-generating class of centralised industrialists, which in turn led to both the power and the urgent necessity to subjugate domestic peoples, expand markets into (i.e. steal resources from) overseas territories, and go to war with competing nations which, in order to keep up with England, all had to do the same.‡

---

* Prior to capitalism the principle means by which states augmented and consol-idated their power was mass-enslavement and domestication.

† 'Stop to consider how the so-called owners of the land got hold of it. They simply seized it by force, afterwards hiring lawyers to provide them with title-deeds. In the case of the enclosure of the common lands, which was going on from about 1600 to 1850, the land-grabbers did not even have the excuse of being foreign conquerors; they were quite frankly taking the heritage of their own countrymen, upon no sort of pretext except that they had the power to do so'. George Orwell; although as James C. Scott explains, 'lawyers', in the form of land-surveyors, often preceded or circumvented the use of force. By codifying land tenure—freezing the shifting, fluid, and infinitely diverse customs which governed land-use in a traditional society into static and 'simplified' laws of ownership—land could, and still can, be effectively—legally—stolen without calling in the heavies (ibid).

‡ E. Wood, *The Origins of Capitalism*.

For the most part, stealing land and labour has been a straightforward case of simply taking it; what we might call DIRECT MASS-THEFT. The earliest ancestors of the noble families of Europe initially gained their power in this way, taking (or 'clearing') the land of their own country's peoples, and then, during 'the great work of subjugation and conquest,*' taking land inhabited or used by other peoples, a practice which has continued for hundreds of years and continues, in various forms, today; in Brazil, Papua New Guinea, China and elsewhere.

Direct mass-theft however is, wherever possible, avoided. It's unpleasant work, exhausting and it's not good for business to have blood dripping from your hands. In earlier days, at the 'rosy dawn' of capitalism, such crude tactics were necessary, as they still are in some parts of the world. Land cannot be compelled or tempted; it must be simply taken; or 'privatised' into ownership by forcibly establishing private-property rights and then buying it all up. Labour, however, is another matter. While pre-capitalist and Orwellian states enslave and press-gang their people, capitalist mass-thieves have always understood that to gain control of people it is vital, not to mention much easier, to use INDIRECT MASS-THEFT; impoverishment (the stick) and addiction (the carrot).

Techniques of pre-modern impoverishment included, and still include, usury, harsh taxation, raising prices on food, capitalising on disasters and enacting laws that curtail self-sufficiency (that make it illegal for people to collect firewood, hunt and poach game) and vagrancy (along with taboos against 'lolling', 'idling' and so on), all of which combine to force people into a state of dependency on the owners of capital and the issuers of money. With no land or access to it, unable to buy the necessities of life, or make them and forced into debt, men and women become poor and hungry, the prerequisites for wage slavery and indentured servitude.

---

* Marx summarises; 'The discovery of gold and silver in America, the extirpation [and] enslavement in mines of the aboriginal population, the beginning of the conquest and looting of the East Indies, the turning of Africa into a warren for the commercial hunting of black-skins, signaled the rosy dawn of the era of capitalist production. These idyllic proceedings are the chief moments of primitive accumulation'.

Early capitalist theorists, such as Adam Smith, were curiously quiet about all of this, although they understood very well the need to remove all barriers to the recruitment of labour. Other influential writers of the time, such as David Hume, Arthur Young and Joseph Townsend, openly extolled the marvellous benefits of deprivation, dependency, poverty, taxation* and the like,† just as their modern counterparts do.

Impoverishment did not end with pre-modern techniques of land-theft and economic deprivation. As capitalism got underway, new methods of crippling people became available. Sophisticated forms of legal, 'non-violent' market transaction (capital flight, financial manipulation, speculation and investment) could reduce entire countries to dependent penury at a stroke. At the same time, the capitalist commodification and control of the *material* world gave way to the late-capitalist appropriation of *immaterial* cultural artefacts (such as ideas and songs), social spaces (via social media), the human genome, the electromagnetic spectrum and all the knowledge locked up in patents. This forced people to become dependent on the technology, energy, transport systems, bureaucratic credentials, high-tech channels of information, 'landlords' of intellectual property and 'consumer goods' of the system, which further hobbled self-sufficiency and broke up traditional networks of mutual aid. While the impoverished pre-modern or Third World worker cannot grow food on his own land, raise his family in his own home or make his own clothes and furniture, the impoverished modern worker cannot use his feet to go where he needs to go—he needs a car—use his mouth to communicate with his fellows—he needs a phone—use his own intelligence and experience to propagate knowledge—he needs the correct qualification or 'a proven track record' in communications—or gain access to the artistic, scientific and cultural achievements of his fellows and forebears—he needs to pay patent and copyright

---

* Taxation, in its purest form means stealing money-power from people. In its modern form it means stealing money-power from people, and then returning a small amount of that into an institutionalised, professionally-dominated system of education, health and transport. In both cases if you refuse the benevolent gift of taxation, your possessions are confiscated and you are put into a little cage.

† M. Perelman, *The Invention of Capitalism*.

owners. Now it is not just land that is owned by the wealthy, but every conceivable form of human capital. Every move we attempt to make outside the market forces us against the point of a spear which forces back into it.

In addition to wholesale appropriation of life, capital also developed powerful and subtle forms of propaganda and indoctrination which, through advertising, film, music, journalism and art, compelled people to put their faith in the modern system, to spurn 'old-fashioned' values, to ignore mass-theft and to embrace the work ethic. These had their roots in the earliest religion of capitalism; protestantism, but they reached new heights of psychological potency with techniques of persuasion developed by the new profession of journalism, designed to manufacture consent, and the new science of psychology, designed to tap into and exploit our desires.

For we are not just compelled into the market by external pressures, but internal addictions. The stick of PLANNED OBSO-LESCENCE (soap that wears out in three days, washing machines that break ten minutes after the warranty runs out, operating systems, and vaccines, that must be updated every year) drives us from behind and the carrot of PERCEIVED OBSOLESCENCE (the 'need' to have the latest version, the newest style*) beckons us forward. From the beads, buckets, calico prints, firearms and hooch sold to pre-conquest people to tempt them into producing for the market, to the smartphones, luxury cars, electric blankets and box sets that compel modern people into a need to earn and consume more; every step the market digs deeper into our addictive fears and desires; every conceivable weakness is exploited by capital, to draw us into the market. Whiskey-addicted speed-freak and closet psychopath? *We've got just the thing, sir!* Loquacious, luxury-addicted bimbo, who needs the constant validation of yearning stares from men? *Step this way, madam!* It matters not *what* you are addicted to, just as long as it is visible, divisible, assessable, storable, transportable and rationable.

---

* A 'need' which fuels a significant part of the entire late-capitalist project, which founders upon the *actual* needs of people, which can be met. This is why so much attention is paid to enhancing the symbolic value of goods; their sexiness, exclusivity and other incitements to *unreasonable* demand, which can never be satisfied.

We are now well out of primitive accumulation and into Adam Smith's creepy 'silent hand' that forces or compels us to consume the products of the market and sell our labour power to it for the credits to do so. Wage labour, as Michael Perelmen points out, appears to be 'a voluntary affair', and capitalists can 'pretend that workers [are] willing partners in a mutually rewarding transaction' because contrived measures to make people work, much less open violence, are now unnecessary. The impersonal market does it all automatically. There are no need for Orwellian techniques of control to keep us in place; the Huxleyan market forces us to keep *ourselves* in place. The explicit orders of the slave owner have been replaced by the implicit compulsions of the contract 'freely made' between the worker and the employer. You are free to start your own company, grow your own food, walk to work, educate yourself, create free communities of mutual aid, work the land, do whatever you please. You're free to do all these things... and yet, so few seem to want to, or be able to. Strange!

And there you have it, here we all are, living on the free, lawful, quiet, level playing field of global capitalist democracy, a state of affairs called PEACE (and all military interventions employed to maintain it called DEFENCE). When capitalist or system-friendly academics (such as Stephen Pinker, Yuval Noah Harari and Rutgar Bregman), and the army of journalists employed to promote and normalise their 'findings', make the claim that we have evolved from a warlike state of misery to a peaceful land of technological milk and honey,* this is what they are referring to; a world of universal boredom, misery and poverty built on an ongoing history of exploitation, mass-theft and mass-murder, where clean, bloodless, pacifistic trade occurs in the highly visible centre fed by warfare, subjugation, private violence, extreme suffering and illegal drugs, arms and prostitution markets on the invisible periphery; and who but a communist, or a terrorist, or an enemy of democracy, could possibly object to this? Who but a madman even?

---

* For demolition of Pinker's fantasies, see R. Brian Ferguson's *Pinker's List*, Edward S. Herman and David Peterson's *Reality Denial*, J. Lewis et.al, *The Myth of Declining Violence*, and Jeremy Lent, *Steven Pinker's Ideas are Fatally Flawed*. See also my review of Bregman's *'Utopia for Realists'*.

14

The Myth *of the* Law

The law prevents individual and collective
intelligence, justifies mass-theft, pacifies
ordinary people and excludes them from
power · · · These are all secondary to the
primary and essential purpose of law, which
is to fix men and women into a written system
of measurement, management and control
· · · The law thereby creates the problems it
is supposed to control.

T HE PRIMARY PURPOSE OF THE LAW is to extinguish or banish intelligence. 'Intelligence' here means awareness of or sensitivity to the context and capacity to respond to it spontaneously or appropriately; which is to say *justly*. Justice is a threat and embarrassment to the law and to those who possess the class power—usually enshrined in property—that the law is designed to protect (see myth 4).

The law works by rigidly defining acts which are undesirable to power; theft, for example, murder, harassment or criticism, and then punishing all those *without* power who are deemed to fit the factual-causal definition of wrongdoer. The outrageous injustice of this behaviour is masked by the fact that, just as a 'stopped clock tells the right time twice a day', so the law occasionally defines and punishes powerful thieves, mass-murderers, professional slanderers and wealthy liars. Should that same definition ever be applied to the *class* of thieves, murderers, monsters and machines who own and manage the world-machine, it is immediately dispensed with or, through a legal system weighted in favour of such power, circumvented. Individual fraudsters and fiends are occasionally targeted and, with much media hoop-la, made an example of, in order to deflect attention away from the monstrous vice and pitiless iniquity of the owner and management class* as a whole which, conveniently enough, can't, like the system they serve, fit into the dock.

---

* Lawyers, like journalists (see myth 9), have no useful skills and produce nothing of value. This forces them to create an integral category of charitable activity, 'pro-bono work', in order to convince themselves and others that they doing good and not merely rescuing a few people from the system for which they work, during their paid hours, to uphold and into which non-professional interference is never tolerated.

Professional law appeared at the same time and the same place as money, democracy and professional science. All four work together to obliterate responsibility by ruling out, from moment one, context and consciousness, neither of which can possibly be admitted into either the bank, the government, the laboratory or the law court. What is happening, and why, are inexplicable noise to the financial, political, scientific and legal mind, which can only see (and record*) descriptions, facts, theories, ideas and objects.

Thus, he who leaks state-corporate data to the public, so it may better grasp what is being done its name; criminal. He who steals private data from the public in order to enrich himself and raise the technologies of state surveillance to unknown heights; businessman of the year! He who works a few hours part-time while claiming benefits; criminal. He who defrauds an entire country, gambles away their assets and buys up their public resources; knighthood! She who wrecks a fighter plane destined for the Saudi Arabian extermination of Yemen; criminal. She who annihilates Libya so that oil companies can move in; feminist heroine! He who kills because he wants someone dead; murderer. He who kills because his government wants them dead; war hero! No need to explain why all this is so; *the facts speak for themselves.*

The second purpose of the law is to permit elite theft through the legalisation of property and the transmission of wealth (a.k.a. INHERITANCE). It's not very complicated, this. The powerful steal land and resources, convert their theft to coin, use their money-power to steal more and to confer their spoils to their children, each step protected by law and, by extension, the professionals that elites employ to justify their interests and remove anyone who threatens them; anyone who acts on the idea, for example, that there is a difference between PROPERTY—an abstract relationship to things, land, resources and people†—and POSSESSION—things that an individual, and by extension her community, actually uses. Owners and managers

---

* *Get it into writing!*

† Which, by virtue of its abstraction must be professionally recorded, managed and enforced. A mind-boggling amount of paperwork, along with an army of pen-pushers to manage it, is created this way.

do everything in their power to discredit such an idea. That absence of property and sanctity of possession has been the basis of human society for *hundreds* of thousands of years* and is never far from the conscience of the great mass of humankind, is irrelevant. All that matters, to property owners and their whores, is that they keep their hands on the loot.

The third purpose of the law, is to put the fear of God into the godless. Law—the harsher the better—takes the place of hell as the source of terror for ordinary people, particularly the lower-classes from whence the only serious threats to the system arise.† The owners and managers of the system couldn't care less about tyrannical legislation, provided it only ever *actually* applies to those without sufficient means to circumvent it. Liberal types might have pangs of conscience from time to time when they see the police and the army go to work, but the security of their gated communities, their bank accounts and their conspicuously privileged children trumps moral qualms about living in a militarised police state.

The fourth purpose of the law is that of every profession; to exclude ordinary people from the meaning of their lives through the imposition of professionally-managed jargon and ritual; in this case the forest of technocratic pseudo-language and the preposterous, quasi-religious legal ceremonies that lawyers spend a large part of their lives learning to decipher and participate in with a straight face. These are unconsciously designed to bewilder, confuse and pacify the uninitiated into submission and, it goes without saying, into dependence on the professional middle-men of the law.

---

* Primal societies go to extraordinary lengths to make sure that property does not build up in the hands of a few people.

† Laws that make no sense must carry absurd penalties. As I write, not wearing a [symbolic] face mask on public transport is punishable in the UK by a fine of £6,400, and coming back from a trip to Portugal without declaring it risks ten years in prison. A complementary tactic, when an unpopular law needs to be passed, is for the government to let it be known that they are considering passing one that is ten times worse. When they 'reconsider' and pass the law they always intended to pass, it is greeted with relief instead of outrage. All of this terrifies and demoralises people, compelling them to take the safe and sure route of meekly obeying, in the hope that, this way, things will, perhaps, one day, improve.

The final and by far the most important purpose of the law, which includes and subordinates the other three, is to keep the wheels of the system running, as a device for administration and organisation. The reason it is illegal to be without the right forms of identification and accreditation, or to act independently of professional authority, or to sell your wares on the high street, or to paint works of art onto bridges, is less because these acts are a threat to established interests, although of course they are, and more because they are independent of or antagonistic to systemic techniques of measurement, management and control. Customs and rights in traditional, pre-civilised societies could be unfair and prejudiced but they were responsive to the incredible complexity of natural and social life, specific to the case, specific to place and people, and alive, adaptable to changing situations; in other words a complete nightmare to the civilising lawmaker for whom all and everything must uniformly conform.

And not merely outwardly. Laws do not just address how individuals act, but how they think and feel, which must also come under unified legal systems of literal measurement and control. Thus gathering mushrooms from the Prince's forest is intolerable to the system; but so is eating them to dissolve time and space. Thus stealing food from the back door of a supermarket must be made illegal; but so must running naked through the front door going 'weeeee, weeeee, weeeeeeeeee!'

But, hold on... what would we do without the law? How would we live? Wouldn't we all be tearing each other apart to get what we want? Don't we need the police and the army to protect us? Aren't justice and security impossible without laws, lawyers, judges and courts? No, no and no. Imagine for a moment we removed all legislation which exists solely to protect class-power, and then we dispensed with all those laws that guidelines, custom and man's innate sense of fairness can far better deal with than the vast, lumbering, context-immune and largely corrupt bureaucratic machine of lawyers, law courts, judges and prisons. Imagine it was impossible to accrue wealth through accumulating property, or power through dominating common resources. Imagine that there were no such thing as money (see myth 2), and that therefore rent, debt, destitution and the wretchedness that goes by the name of 'work', simply could not exist (see myth 21). Would there be crime? The taboo of the law— of 'defenders of the law' and the criminal class of human being we call *the law-abider*—is that the answer to this question could possibly be no. The law, we are told, protects us from injustice, suffering, inequality and ruin. That its purpose is to proliferate iniquity and, via hyper-rational standardisation of human experience, control, is unmentionable; for the obvious reason that dealing with the actual *cause* of crime is not good for business. Money cannot be made by eradicating injustice, redistributing power, land and wealth, fostering self-reliance, allowing ordinary people to take responsibility for their environment or freely shaping it to their needs or those of nature; and so defenders of the law must criminalise such activities and focus exclusively on the deleterious *effects* of living in monstrously unjust, stupefyingly boring and sickening societies. Thus lawyers, thus law courts, thus police, thus prisons, which are to crime as doctors, psychologists and teachers are to pollution, madness and stupidity.

And so it is said 'there are a thousand hacking at the branches of evil to one who is striking at the root'.

15

The Myth *of* Nice

Humans are forced to construct, maintain
and defend an inhuman system. They can
only do this by being inhuman · · · Many
people find this unpleasant, and so they
lie to themselves and others. One of the
most popular lies is *being nice* · · · Modesty,
humility, complaint and charity all perform
the same justifying functions.

'I KNOW SOME NICE / hard-working / humble / frugal / kindly / friendly / generous / creative / smart / sensitive (delete as applicable) aristocrats / bankers / CEOs, / managers / landlords / doctors / rock-stars / lawyers / politicians / consultants / teachers / modern-artists / journalists (delete as applicable)'.

The manager or owner may be any kind of man or woman, he or she might be 'a beautiful person' or a 'great boss' or even 'a bit of a lefty', but only when not called upon to defend his class interests or those of the system that provides him with his position. No matter how much someone who has power in the system protests that he 'hates the word boss', no matter how well a workplace is organised to mask class relations with exalted job titles, open plan offices, roles-off teambuilding, collective piss-ups and dress-down Fridays, the second the owner's profits, or the manager's position, or the needs of the system come under threat, he or she will pull rank; gently, perhaps, with infinite concern, implicit solidarity and many protestations that 'I have no choice' and 'I hate to say it'. This unconscious sliding between the psychological states of human being and employer-employee is a form of 'SCRIPTING*'.

Members of the owning / elite or professional / management classes can—indeed *must*—script between Mr. Jekyll the fellow human and Mr. Hyde the Responsible Lord or Professional, and then deceive themselves about Hyde's part in the system, and justify his shifty cruelty and cowardice as tragically unavoidable, logical, 'realistic' or even, most ridiculously, fair. Occasionally, emperors and technocrats have vestigial consciences informing them that they are actively participating in a profound wrong. This compels them to consciously deceive themselves, which in turn gives rise to great moral stress; but

---

* See The Apocalypedia.

more often than not they have no idea that they have achieved their power by amputating their humanity, and effortlessly script from nice colleagues, to nice tyrants, to nice lunatics.

And so it is everywhere there is a middle or management class there are calls for decent housing, decent education, decent broadband, decent brioche—but never decent class relations*; and everywhere there is class inequality there is aid, protests, petitions, pro-bono representation and advertising campaigns for being lovely, tolerant and peaceful—but never a step taken towards actual equality or genuine independence from the system, unless and only unless mass agitation seriously threatens established systemic power; and everywhere there are slaves there are 'kindly' owners and 'friendly' managers, convinced that they are good or doing good, convinced that the madness and rebellion of those who generate their wealth is due to every other imaginable cause than their slavery or confinement† and, coincidentally, getting a lot more out of the workforce by being nice to them.

In contrast to the manager and professional, the owner or senior manager often knows very well that he or she is extracting profit at the expense of the alienated worker and the terminally exhausted planet and, at least when out of the glare of the public eye, can openly despise the powerless classes. Learning not to let this mask slip is one of the more important tasks of elite education. When the young elite produce outrageous expressions of snobbery, their parents wince and grimace. Don't worry though, she'll soon learn the value of compassion, hard work, charity and modesty.

Modesty (humility, frugality, etc.) is a central technique of expiating self-justification used by the wealthy during times of potential social unrest. When everyone is clamouring for wealth in an expanding economy, the individual capitalist can afford to look and feel rich, but when poverty strikes the masses, and fear and guilt strike those who benefit from the impoverishing

---

* D. Harvey, *Companion to Capital*.

† School shootings? Workplace massacres? Slave rebellions? What *could* be the cause? Why, it *must* be due to mental illness, smartphones, alcohol, moral turpitude, guns, video games and radicalisation. It *can't* have anything to do with the experience of being a student, a worker and a slave. See M. Ames, *Going Postal*.

system, the colours become muted, the gold is locked away, a rosy tinge of socialism is applied to philanthropic acts and there is much complaint of hardship and tightening of belts. The corporations which hold and augment elite wealth continue to build ever vaster monuments to their world-eating power, allowing the wealthy themselves to dress down, save money, cut costs and be just like the rest of us.

Likewise, the exploiting classes love to work hard, to be busy. They moan about it, but the proud subtext is 'I deserve my privilege'. The poor are supposed to be grateful that the rich pay them to produce their comforts and privileges, or that the state pays them to remain in a state of bare existence, not complain about criminally impoverishing class relations. This is why the wealthy are so eager to present to the world the classic excuse; 'I work hard for my money!'

Another increasingly popular tactic used by the wealthy to atone for the intense mediocrity and sickening guilt of their lives, is to develop depression, OCD, clinical anxiety, anorexia or some kind of fashionable sleeping disorder. Naturally, the possibility that such 'illnesses' *are* tactics (albeit unconscious ones), that they are culturally determined* or that the patient is in any way responsible for their onset or outcome is greeted with maximum outrage (see myth 30).

But for the systemoid who is threatened by the stirrings of his conscience or, more often than not, by the outrage of those beneath him, nothing comes close—in importance, prevalence or effectiveness in dealing with the fear and guilt of privilege—to reform (directing one's frustrations at the baddies in power; see myth 31) and to *charity*.

My God they love charity; we all love it. In pre-capitalist days guilty rulers and the anxious masses would wash the blood off their hands by confessing their sins or purchasing indulgences from the church—effectively a soul-cleansing token at God's laundromat. Now they donate to a good cause, or organise a fund-raiser. Who, after all, but a *monster* could object to raising money for the poor children in Africa, or for clinics to cure malaria, or for dentists to treat the homeless, or for teams of crippled children to plant buddleia for the butterflies? It

---

* E. Watters, *Crazy Like Us.*

doesn't occur to those who worship our benevolent overseers that 'charity' might be a vast business concern deeply embedded in the system, and profoundly reactionary to its core, or that the word charity—the love of humankind—should perhaps mean working to *end* a system in which the philanthropy of the rich, or of the swindled poor, is unnecessary.

Yes, a very nice person, the philanthropist. Other examples of nice people include your postman, your toddler's kindergarten teacher, your doctor, the guy who came to clear away the wasteland at the back of your house, the woman next door who works abroad counselling people with PTSD, the men who built the first atom bomb and the people who work for BAE systems.* Lots of Nazis were nice, lots of Romans, no doubt plenty of Mongols too, and I daresay there are some nice lads in the Israeli army. President Obama? very nice. The Queen of England? Prince William? Exceptionally nice![†]

Fuck nice. Nice is death.

Which is not an invitation to act like a prat, or to be cruel and insensitive, or to spit on the generosity and sweet nature of *good* people. Certainly not a recommendation to nurse anger, feed off it, or nurture the dark self-righteous delight of the *goody*. It is to see how nice is *deployed*, how it is used—consciously and unconsciously—to conceal or deflect attention away from *not* so nice. Easy to see in other people, this, particularly when you are on the receiving end of niceness. Not so easy to see in yourself. Not so easy to spot your own scripting, from a conscious individual to a *caring professional*. Not so easy to see how niceness instantly justifies avoiding a difficult confrontation, or standing up for what is right. Not so easy to see how your 'pacifism' is actually a means of concealing your cowardice or implicitly justifying a violent system.[‡] Not so easy to see your own shameful lack of responsibility in handing it over to the system. Not so easy to see how deep the system reaches into

---

* I know a few—lovely people!

† J. Zerzan, *The Nihilist's Dictionary*.

‡ 'When there is only a choice between cowardice and violence, I would advise violence'. 'I would far rather that you died bravely dealing a blow and receiving a blow than died in abject terror'. 'Between violence and cowardly flight, I can only prefer violence'. Gandhi.

your own conscience or consciousness. Partly this is because ego cannot allow itself to be seen for what it is, but also because a hugely important component of the system is the generation of justifications and the continual insistence that there is no place on earth for anything but an upbeat can-do attitude, infinite resilience and a cheerful telephone voice.

16

The Myth *of* Democracy

'Democratic' means 'good for business'.
Democracy does not apply to the market,
and it is the market which runs the world
· · · What nobody can accept, on the left
or the right, is that democracy is inherently
authoritarian and coercive · · · The most
destructive outcome of democracy is that it
eliminates personal responsibility. Nobody
is responsible in a democratic system, which
is why nothing intelligent ever happens in it.

THE SYSTEM RUNS ON THE OUTLANDISH ASSUMPTION that we have something called 'democracy', a system in which people can elect representatives who will ensure that the country will be run by and for the 'will of the people'. That's the idea, and many people seem to think it's a good one.

What we actually have, in our actual lives, is a system in which we are forced to spend most of our waking hours in rigidly hierarchical organisations through which orders flow in one direction only; down. We do not vote for the system, nor for its managers, CEOs, councillors, judges, warders, landlords, teachers, doctors, police commissioners, army generals and owners. We do not vote for the technology imposed upon us, nor for the ridiculous laws and legitimations we must obey, nor for the grossly unfair economic system which screws us into our social station. 'Democracy' doesn't apply to the organisations which actually run the world, in which unelected, unaccountable and usually unseen officials *command*, via their financial or institutional power, the workforce (the prisoners, the patients, the student body, etc.), and shape the environment for their own ends. The correct, if now clichéd, term for this system is TOTALITARIANISM.

The 'democracy' we are permitted is one in which we can vote for a handful of wealthy 'representatives' of business, wealth or professional power every four or five years and then spend the rest of the time watching them on television or reading about their democratic exploits in the news. We cannot vote for a different system, 'the government always gets in'; we cannot vote against its technocratic expansion, against growth, progress or prosperity; and we cannot vote for anyone who can meaningfully change the system we do have. We can usually count ourselves lucky if the vote isn't rigged, although we'll never really know if it is or not.

We *can* be sure that vast efforts go into forming people's minds in a 'democratic system' so that they'll be sufficiently confused to vote in the correct direction (see myth 9) or sufficiently distracted and atomised to not cause a fuss if they do perceive the sham. And we *can* be sure that, should anyone get onto the ballot paper who might resist the demands of the technocratic system, there will be 'a crisis of democracy' which the system will use every power under its command to manage. 'Democracy' is good for business. If business suffers, it magically becomes 'undemocratic'.

Finally, we can be sure that if, by an even more unlikely stroke of chance, a government gets elected which has even minimal interest in actually representing the people, or is a *tad* hostile to technocratic capital, those who hold power in society will instantly drop their support for democracy. They will buy off corruptible leaders, wage economic warfare on the enemy and, using the organs of force and coercion they possess non-democratic control of—police, army, media, law courts and so on—they will smear, undermine, 'destabilise' and, sooner or later, obliterate the 'threat to democracy', which is to say; crush the ridiculous idea that the government is supposed to take care of the interests of the people when, in the 'real world', the purpose of governments, democratic or otherwise, is to extend national boundaries, gain control of resources for business, defend the interests of business, protect property rights for the business class, provide labour for business, manage infrastructure for business, hand massive sums of subsidy money over to business, fix deviants, through imprisonment and diagnosis, back into the system, and take care of the interests of those in power and, above all, serve and always serve, the idolatrous needs* of the egoic system, its foundational approach to reality and the laws, legitimations, scripts and techniques it uses to defend or perpetuate itself. The idea that government should look after the interests of the people or nature is useful for public relations, but has zero influence on policy. Unless said interests are forced upon the ruling classes; then small concessions to what the democratic mass want will, to much fanfare, be made to diffuse the threat.

* See *Self and Unself.*

The most common and effective way of dealing with 'threats to democracy', however, is to simply let participation in the system grind down whoever wishes to make significant changes to it. Democracy doesn't just legitimise authority and provide a little hierarchical mobility within the system (see myth 5), but it usefully deflects revolt into manageable channels.*When decent folk with even moderate aspirations to make changes to the system enter democratic structures, they find they can achieve, effectively, nothing (Podemos, Syriza, Lula, etc, etc.). This was well understood by the industrial architects of the modern system who realised that the terrifying revolutionary power of the new urban working class could be moderated and dissipated by absorbing popular discontent into institutional hierarchies, particularly trade unions, the rise of which castrated early modern attempts to dismantle the system (see myth 31).

We do not, then, live in a democracy; nor can we when the power of money, property, professionalism and technique, not to mention the mass psychosis of easily shaped 'public opinion', completely overwhelms that of the fabled ballot. But this doesn't stop writers, academics, politicians and campaigners on the right and the left, striving to reach the promised land. The idea is that once we have a *true democracy*, of whatever kind—socialist, capitalist, Marxist, anarcho-syndicalist; once 'people power' conquers money-power, property-power, technical-power and so on; once the well known small-minded stupidity of huge numbers of emotional people thinking as one has been overcome by the enlightened ministrations of 'good' professional educators and the absence of 'bad' professional mind-manipulators; *then* our political, social and ecological problems will be, more or less at an end; because *true* democracy,† the modern system tells us, is the

---

* 'A Constituent Assembly is the means used by the privileged classes, when a dictatorship is not possible, either to prevent a revolution, or, when a revolution has already broken out, to stop its progress with the excuse of legalizing it, and to take back as much as possible of the gains that the people had made during the insurrectional period'. Errico Malatesta.

† Political democracy that is. Clearly discussions, federations, assemblies, reaching a decision with people you disagree with, and so on can be called 'democratic'—but this is not the political meaning of 'democracy'—rule by the people via majority vote. See Crimethinc, *From Democracy to Freedom*.

only rational way to fairly and freely organise society. Anything else is fascist madness. That democracy promotes irresponsibility, psychotic groupthink, the destruction of spiritual independence and shallow mediocrity; that it is inherently divisive and cruelly competitive; that it suppresses mutual aid, spontaneity, individuality, independence and intelligence; that there might be a source of truth, intelligence or awareness that we don't need democratic decision-making to discover*; that friendships, sweet love affairs, happy families and well-functioning societies throughout pre-history are neither democratic *nor* authoritarian; that nobody in their right mind accepts democracy in any matters of importance if the vote doesn't go their way; and why should they, if they are right? that democracy inevitably entails *exclusion* (those who cannot be trusted to vote the right way; criminals, children, foreigners, 'madmen', etc.) and *policing* (enforcing the will of those who can); none of this can be considered without sounding like you've drifted in from Neptune's blue moons.

The most inhuman element of democracy however, and the reason that it is revered by both inhuman elites and their dehumanised dependents, is that, like the law it is inseparable from (see myth 14), it eliminates personal responsibility.

Who is responsible for global warming? Who is responsible for 'the sixth mass extinction'? Who is responsible for the horrendous conditions in Chinese and Bangladeshi factories? Who is responsible for rising fascism? Who is responsible for the love going out of the world? Who is responsible for our unhappiness? Who is responsible for the death of culture? Who, God damn it, who is responsible for Justin Bieber and Ed Sheeran? It can't be the politicians; they're 'representatives of the will of the people', not to mention slaves to the market system. It can't be the people themselves; they're not in charge of anything, are they? It can't be managers or CEOs; they have a responsibility to their shareholders, and if they put anything nobler than profits first, their company would go under.† It can't be the shareholders

---

* 'Can there not be a government in which majorities do not virtually decide right and wrong, but conscience?' Thoreau, *On the Duty of Civil Disobedience*.

† In addition, although 'the boss' certainly does exist, many of his disciplinary functions are diffused across the system, further obscuring his responsibility. As Ivor Southwood puts it in *Against Precarity Against Employability*: 'The boss is

either; they don't control anything. It can't be the journalists; they're just reporting the facts. It can *hardly* be the policemen, the teachers, the lawyers or the doctors; they're just doing their noble, noble jobs, under very trying circumstances; nor can it be all the technical specialists who develop and operate the system; anything beyond their particular domain of competence is clearly someone else's affair. It can't be the pimps, pushers, pornographers and movie producers; they're just giving the punters what they want. It can't be the mentally ill, the murderers, the polluters, the paedophiles or the thieves, because their illness *made* them do it. And it *can't* be Ed and Justin; they're just regular kids, having a good time. In fact, it can't be anyone, because, 'look, I didn't choose to be me!'

So nobody is responsible. Phew! No need for any of us to worry about doing anything about our lives or about our world then. We can just consume, exploit and produce to our heart's content and let someone else—someone who, insanely, *is* taking responsibility—do something about it all. If such a loon can be found.

But hold on a moment, that can't be right. The world can't have got so phenomenally out of joint just by accident. There must be *someone* who is to blame here. As it obviously isn't *me*, or any group which I belong to, who can it possibly be? Why, of course! It must be *them!* It's the fascists, the Brexiteers, the remainers, the government, Bilderberg, the Muslims, the Jews, the blacks, the whites, the commies, the capitalists, the anarchists, the West, the East, women, men, sexists, snowflakes, feminists, mum, dad, millennials, boomers, Catholics, the Chinese, immigrants, the establishment, the unwashed masses, the bourgeoisie, lizard people from Alpha Draconis or arseholes. Anyone but me. Anything but the system.

It is the system which has power, power over and within all people. This power, it is true, is for the benefit of those at the top—for elites and their managers, who share and repress the largest share of guilt for the system. But our emperors and

dispersed across a whole network of abstract institutions: not just employer but recruitment agency, welfare advisor, landlord, credit card company... all of which are combined in an internalised virtual authority which oversees and audits one's attempts to act as a responsible, hard-working, "employable" citizen'. See myth 4.

mandarins unconsciously created a democratic machine which would carry their conscious responsibility away, and then decorated it with mighty slogans—justice, equality and progress—so that we wouldn't perceive the inhuman monstrosity of its power and our total, humiliating submission to it.

This personal humiliation guarantees the creation of excuses and scapegoats. Because the system infuses the self so deeply, it is able to support those at the top through the thoughts and desires of those at the bottom—through 'public opinion' and 'common sense'*—and through the imposed needs of the technological-bureaucratic interzone through which all must pass, in the daily grind, to get their bread. By having to worry about what the neighbours think, what the boss thinks, what your friends think, and by having to go to school, drive to work, register your dog, pay your taxes, get your shopping, replace your kettle and upgrade your operating system you are more effectively domesticated and disciplined than you could ever be by an Orwellian state, a secret police or the whims of a mad king. But because all these pressures and indignities arise, at least partly, from your *own* fears and desires, from your *own* self, the system remains obscured, impossible to grasp the root and source of it. Much easier to blame over-population, corrupt politicians, a decline in traditional values, neoliberalism, terrorism or the devil.

The democratic system manufactures responsibility-deflecting excuses and scapegoats at the same almighty rate as it pumps out addictions—all of which work in concert. Feel guilty? There's a charity for that. Feel rebellious? There's a march for that. Feel unhappy? There's a diagnosis for that. Feel purposeless? There's an ideology for that. Feel ordinary? There's a *special identity* for that. Feel lonely? There's a Facebook group for that, or a whore, or a robot. Feel bored? There's an app for that, or a pill, or a purchase. Feel like it might all be your fault? You silly! Have a chat with your mates; they don't bother themselves with such mad ideas. And then, when we poison the world, we can point to our donation, our prescription, our t-shirt, our belief,

---

* 'What is done to all by the few always takes the form of the subduing of individuals by the many: the oppression of society always bears the features of oppression by a collective'. Horkheimer and Adorno, *Dialectic of Enlightenment*.

our club and our phone and say 'look! I'm doing the best I can!' or 'I'm sorry, I *have* to let you go' or 'it's all *their* fault', or 'sorry? what? I wasn't really listening'.

The Myth of Democracy first appeared, surprise-surprise, in ancient Greece. It was those insane inventors of money and law, those frauds and fools who first conflated consciousness with thought, those worshippers of rapists and sadists, those haters of women, those slave owners and pederasts, those thieves and despoilers; it was they who first invented the nightmare illusion that the fools paradise of irresponsibility is based on; the democratic mass. They did it! Blame them!

Today the same illusion, as prevalent as ever, is used to justify every form of violence, addiction, selfishness and repression. All responsibility for 'mental illnesses', all responsibility for genocide, all responsibility for the innumerable indignities and deceits we daily suffer are all passed on to something else. Nobody is really happy, everything is dying; but none of that is *my* fault.* This works for everyone, but particularly for the owners and managers of the system. You may have noticed, for example, in 'late-stage capitalism' that nothing really works. This is deliberately planned — as crippling bureaucracy, widespread ineptness, frustrating interactions and omnipresent shoddiness are good for business — while, at the same time, simply allowed to happen. Some of the most appalling crimes against man and woman today are committed by allowing the system to replicate and organise itself shoddily, and for its operations to unfold haphazardly, in agonising slowness. Those who can do something, simply don't. Thus money and power roll up the Magic Mountain as the people who are deprived of both are ground down, dismantled piece by piece, without anybody ever being responsible, with nobody to blame, nobody even to be found. Under such circumstances, it's not surprising that loopy 'conspiracy theories' arise while the system itself gets off scot-free.

---

* Not that we are *guilty* for our responsibility of course. Guilt is just another self-indulgent trick of the self. Or, as Quentin Crisp put it, *'I think that everything that happens to us is our fault… but that's not our fault!'*

17

The Myth *of* Education

Education in the system means compulsory
schooling in a world of artificial scarcity · · ·
Schooled activity stunts maturity, punishes
experience, corrupts initiative, and cuts
the individual off from the world, making
self-sufficiency and self-confidence all but
impossible · · · The most schooled people on
earth are generally the most stupid; the most
heavily indoctrinated, the most insensitive,
the most conceited and the most helpless.

THE PURPOSE OF EDUCATION is to socialise human beings into an existence of complete institutional dependency. Schooling teaches you that justice must come from someone in institutional authority, that meaningful activity must come from a market-friendly 'career path', that if you want to express yourself you must first gain access to centrally controlled speech platforms,* that if you want to do something, you must first of all gain a licence or a qualification and that, above all, your own desires and instincts are invalid.

General incompetence, self-alienation and permanent childishness is the purpose of education; indeed the *stated* purpose. The designers of the modern school were chillingly explicit about what school is supposed to do.† Self-knowledge, self-confidence, peace of mind, sensitivity, spontaneity and autonomy do not figure; indeed they are existential threats of the highest order which must be repeatedly exterminated.

The purpose of education is to train young people in techniques required by the market system; managing large quantities of useless data, doing the same thing over and over and over and *over* again, doing things you don't actually want to do, under extreme time pressure, for no better reason than because someone in authority tells you to, paying no attention to the world around you and unquestioningly accepting given myths. So called 'objective' exams fulfil this purpose perfectly, weeding out those who insist on doing things their own way, in their own time, without any need of overt coercion; although there are plenty of other ways that systemic threats and defective units can be identified. Inability to sit still, staring out of the

* Or to artificially distributed networks, and the system-friendly popularity, or 'likes', which they are founded upon.

† See John Taylor Gatto, *The Underground History of American Education*.

window, refusal to do ludicrous assignments, hatred of authority, bunking off, asking the wrong kinds of questions, 'inappropriate' behaviour and offensive language are all grounds for suspicion, tranquillisation, ridicule, failure or expulsion.

The purpose of education is to postpone the entry of workers into a crammed labour market—forcing them to accrue debts which can only be alleviated by more work—and to give hundreds of thousands of useless intellectuals something to do; namely, go from twenty years of being subjected to education to forty years of subjecting others to it. Institutional brochures exhorting those who have finally escaped school to do something 'inspiring' with their lives by re-entering it don't tend to focus on teachers who inspire their students to do what the fuck they love (or, even more inspiringly, love who the fuck they fuck).

The purpose of education is to transform human beings into continually assessed, continually observed 'cases'. Naturally, teachers are not expected to rate subservience directly or explicitly; the syllabus, rather, is structured to reward, with good grades and positive references, those who check faculty attitudes and faithfully reproduce them in their work, who do not cause problems and who yield willingly to the HIDDEN CURRICULUM. Such students—usually middle class—are destined for superior professional jobs. They can be trusted to direct their curiosity, creativity and critical minds in profitable directions without seriously questioning the entire exercise.

The hidden curriculum exists in the experience of attending school, rather than what is taught in it; in having to spend most of your life there, in being continually measured and disciplined and in suppressing your finer instincts for years on end. Reformist critics (see myth 31) focus entirely on the subjects that are taught in school, how students' progress is measured, teaching styles, classroom management, financial cost and so on and so forth. These are permitted topics when talking about education. The purpose of being there at all is never considered. Just as you may criticise individual politicians, 'fat cats' and corporations, but must never, ever, critically examine the system itself, so, in school, you are encouraged to question what the teacher says (at least in the 'better' schools you are), but to question the point of being in class (virtual or physical) at all is heresy; and to actually do something about your confinement—leave the class, study what you want, say what you feel—is intolerable; in fact, in many cases, it is a crime.

The purpose of education is to crush initiative, self-sufficiency and self-trust. The superficial means by which this is effected is through punishing any serious attempt to cross disciplines or to reject the syllabus which, by virtue of the fact that all socio-economic activity depends on the values and credentials it produces, makes all learning outside of its confines worse than useless; craft, self-knowledge, social responsibility and general non-credentialised competence, all become non-pedagogic in an intensely schooled system, and the entire world beyond the curriculum becomes non-educational, not to mention unreal (which partly explains the shock that graduates often get on their first encounter with it). Schools and universities must, at all costs, be completely separated from society. The idea that students can meaningfully contribute to society, learn from those who do or rely on their own will to determine their development, is preposterous, utopian; because a total revolution of society would be required to 'teach' students in the manner that they have been 'taught' for millions of years, through their own inclination, and integrated with *an educational society*.*

The purpose of education is to make students less intelligent. Ignoring real life and preventing children from having anything to do with it is enough to stupefy them, but if they still persist in being enthusiastic, sensitive, perceptive, creative and intelligent, the school can, and will, effectively extinguish these dangerous instincts from children by imprisoning them in a room for eight, ten, twelve hours a day, by forcing them to

---

* 'One of the most unequivocal findings re childhood from the ethnographic record is children learning their culture without teaching. 'Navahos abhor the idea or practice of controlling other beings in the course of everyday life'... Inuit 'parents do not presume to teach their children what they can as easily learn on their own'... An egalitarian ethos also contraindicates the inherently hierarchical act of teaching... Deciding what another person should do, no matter what his age, is outside the Yequana vocabulary of behaviors. There is great interest in what everyone does, but no impulse to influence—let alone coerce—anyone. The child's will is his motive force... [a.k.a.] respect for an individual's autonomy is also a core cultural value... one does not impose his/her will, beliefs, or actions on others [including children]...' David F. Lancy, *The Anthropology of Childhood*.

compete with each other, by ignoring their unique characters (or, at best, doing almost nothing to allow them to develop) and, above all, by replacing *doing* with a weird activity which goes by the name of 'learning', the breaking up of activity into a series of stages or 'skills' which are fed from above to the student who then labours eternally up the Sisyphean mountain of competence. Every step up is rewarded, every fall punished, thereby inculcating, deep within the student's psyche, a fear of uncertainty (and therefore of experimenting) and a veritable obsession with 'the right answer'.

The purpose of education is also to prevent ordinary people from being able to communicate with each other. This is achieved by using professional academic discourse to generate a technical jargon, invested with the quasi-religious authority of Scientific Truth, that usurps key terms in ordinary human speech, but has no power to express life as it is actually lived by those who actually live it. Ordinary speech is now peppered with terms, like 'energy', 'justice', 'paradox' and 'conscious', which you have to be a qualified expert, or professionally coded computer, to use 'correctly'. Even words like 'love', 'god', 'beauty' or 'reality' carry with them the subtle unspoken sense that one must be a professional expert (psychologist, priest, artist or philosopher) to really understand or use them. As for expressing yourself in a public forum on topics such as politics, art, history, psychology and so on without having *the proper credentials*, this is a form of presumptive mania which only fraudulent maniacs and laughable naifs engage in.

The purpose of education is to separate children from adults, and thus from their own culture. Technology serves the same purpose. Children are not supposed to take guidance from those with more experience (and likewise, adults are not supposed to learn enthusiasm and play from those with less) they are to huddle in same-age cliques. Children are not supposed to absorb the language, the music, the stories, the values or the knowledge of their elders, but of their peers; of children in exactly the same helpless, cultureless void. Growing up without the unconditional love of their family, or the wisdom of adults (not necessarily their parents, but someone older) or the restraints that living in an ordinary, embodied world puts on them, makes young people confused to the point of stupidity and anxious to the point of insanity, but no matter how shambolic their lives they are unable to turn to adults for help and love. It just doesn't *feel* as good. This insane peer orientation might rapidly disintegrate society and cause untold anguish for parents and children alike, but total isolation from society, total dependency on technology and 'youth culture'* are good for business! When children eventually return to the adult world, after years of isolation, they are quite literally good for nothing.

The purpose of education is to generate scarce opportunities and foster anxiety about securing them, to reinforce class by providing prestigious degrees to those with sufficient financial and cultural capital to acquire them (see myth 5), to manufacture, from the raw material of poverty, a mass of dropouts and to stigmatise them as useless and inferior, to breed snobbishness, cruelty, boredom and widespread FUNCTIONAL ILLITERACY (the inability to do anything useful outside of institutional structures), to level out nuance, to homogenise the world in the name of 'multiculturalism' or 'diversity' (or, in Orwellian structures, the chosen people), to make entry into productive life dependent upon market credentials and to perpetuate this credentialism throughout a life spent in dependence on 'education' and 'training' which, like medicine, law, consumption and the spectacle must cover every aspect of life in the system. Ideally, in the 'perfect' education system, *everything* human will require a series of qualifications and licenses; cooking, child-rearing, speaking, cycling, walking, sex, all that we do will exist on a graded hierarchy of 'competences' each unlocked, as in all centrally or remotely managed virtual experiences, by obtaining enough points from the programme.

The deleterious effects of education are not just found in students, but in teachers, particularly long-term teachers and most especially in the widely-hated exemplars of institutionalisation who absorb and depend on the identity of 'teacher'; who *believe* in the activity called 'teaching', who get frustrated with students who find the whole thing a waste of time, who

---

* 'Youth culture' is about fifty years old. Initially it was, of course, a good thing, as the young could nurture truths inaccessible to adults. Now children have *completely* abandoned adults. The consequences of this are plain to see. See Gabor Maté, *Hold onto Your Kids*.

condescend to children ('you've *really* impressed me'), who like nothing better than laying down a load of laws (for *everyone's* benefit, naturally), and who like to think they are on a noble mission to improve the world by emptying knowledge-pebbles into the mind-sacks of the prisoners they are paid to monitor, sort, categorise, threaten, bully, bribe and endlessly bullshit to. Such teachers can be identified by, when they are young, their upbeat, missionary zeal, when they are older, by the drained, cynical, mechanical shells where their character once was, and, in both cases, by an almost outrageous lack of culture or capacity, barely above those they presume to 'teach'. Of course, a few free human beings find their way into the educational system, just as they do into the medical or legal system, but, although they command actual rather than enforced respect, they are as rare as they are threatened; indeed, as in all democratic institutions, they are threatened *because* they are rare.

Teachers like to believe they are employed to teach. In reality, they are employed to *fit* students into the mechanism of society, to determine which of a handful of system-serving tasks the student is *fit* to do and to reward her for doing them until she *fits* in. If she is un*fit* for any task the student is to be humiliated and rejected. If she is particularly 'gifted' (a mixture of technical expertise, ambition and obedience) she is either to be rewarded with fame, so she can show off her 'talent' or she is shown how to manage the system and the human cogs, belts, diodes and processors which comprise it and given a top job, for which, fingers-crossed, she'll be a *great fit*.

This is all possible because finally, and most importantly, the purpose of education is to programme complete acceptance of the civilised system into young people. This is not done explicitly. Explicitly, the student learns whatever the appropriate ideological doctrine is of the local society; communism, capitalism, Christianity, Islam, whatever. This is a test of conformity. The winners will accept the story, the losers will reject it; but *all* will, after ten to twenty years of being deprived of nature and culture, come to accept institutional experience, and a life *fitted* into it, into domesticated captivity, as normal.

Those who make their way through decades of education—both schooled and 'informal'—are unable to really do much and unable to really understand anything. They don't trust their own instincts, they are afraid of nature and strangers to their own bodies. They are notoriously uncreative, repressed and unhappy, while gripping on to what little they know—an ideology, a few facts—and what little they like—a hobby, a narcotic—like their lives depend on it. They sound the same, they look the same. They are trained for a life of desperation, frustration, loneliness, intense mediocrity, humiliating subservience and complete pointless futility trying to find one of a handful of grotesquely unpleasant jobs in a world that is falling apart in front of our eyes.*

---

* See John Taylor Gatto, Paulo Freire, Ivan Illich and John Holt.

18

The Myth *of* Authority

The system demands complete passivity, acceptance of authority and worship of the pomp and ceremony that it surrounds fame and power with · · · A massive amount of academic effort goes into normalising slave-master relations · · · Today however, in the 'late-capitalist' phase of the system, we are not just commanded by external lords and masters, but also by internalised, self-directed oppression.

HUMANS ARE INCAPABLE of looking after, organising, protecting or ruling themselves. They need someone or something in power to do it for them. This creed emanates from every pore of the owner, the professional, the state, the institution and the egoic, unconscious parent. Often the message is an explicit exhortation, or order, to respect authority, obey the prince or know your place, but usually, in the highly developed system, The Myth of Authority is implicit, an unspoken assumption that a world which has the power to command you and I, is normal, right and natural.

Obedience is fostered and sustained by rewarding those who submit and by punishing those who rebel. Schools are structured to identify and filter out children who 'don't play well with others', who 'voice strong opinions', who are 'disruptive', 'insubordinate' or have 'a relaxed attitude'; admission panels of elite universities and interviewers for top jobs are hyper-sensitive to threats from those who might turn out to be intractable; records, references and even whispered reputations, increasingly systematised, follow trouble-makers to their grave; and if, somehow, someone who is resistant to authority finds their way through this minefield to a position of influence, they will be worn down, undermined and, eventually, ejected.

Most of this happens [semi] automatically. The system is set up to nullify threat and reward compliance with minimal human interference.* Those who tend to its operations do so unconsciously, instinctively or without seriously questioning its values and imperatives. Meanwhile, those at the bottom of the pile look up in wonder at those chosen to lead. It seems that the

---

* 'Power is tolerable only on condition that it mask a substantial part of itself. Its success is proportional to its ability to hide its own mechanisms'. Michel Foucault, *The History of Sexuality, Volume 1*.

typical manager is, at best, an unimpressive human being, and, more usually, skilled in little more than dithering, hiding facts, manipulating information, obfuscating class-relations, rolling over like a puppy when those above him shift their weight and paying lip service to fine qualities and instincts while stamping them out whenever they actually appear.* But these are all precisely the qualities which the system demands. Actual intelligence, competence, originality, human-feeling, generosity and integrity are, if they come into conflict with these *core values*, instantly and automatically rejected.

Underpinning the global filtering mechanism for compliance, an equally vast programme exists to validate it. History, biology, anthropology and psychology are all employed to justify, on the flimsiest evidence, the idea that human beings are *rigidly* hierarchical, selfish, warlike, in need of power to function or simply blank slates that exist to be programmed by whoever has their hands on the control panel. Standard system history teaches us that only power is real or meaningful and the corporate media show us, over and over again, in its fawning reports of royalty (alive and dead), its lavish costume dramas, its celebrity gossip, its fascination with Big People and its uncritical coverage of politics† that power is either normal, necessary and unavoidable, or that it does not really exist.

And in some crucial respects, it no longer does. The final stage of the system has migrated a large part of the exploitative architecture of its earlier forms into the psyche of the individual. The disciplinary machinery of institutions still exists, as do positions of authority within armed forces, prisons, governments and so forth; but the uploading of large portions of the self, the digital exploitation of human communication and emotion, and the development of automated techniques of surveillance and control, have led to an introspection or privatisation of key aspects of systemic subjugation and power. Just as collective urges for sociability and communication have been redirected towards exclusive desires and personal ambitions, so frustration at the boss or the dominant classes is now directed at one's own lack of creativity, health, happiness, productivity, marketability

---

* The correct meaning of 'like a boss'.

† Critical of parties and players. Uncritical of politics, democracy and the Big Play.

or will-power. This is why, as Byung-Chul Han points out, the oppressed are today more inclined towards depression than revolution.* Power appears to have been redistributed, but it is ARTIFICIAL DISTRIBUTION, meaning that inequality persists—worsens—while the emotionally-potent techniques which create and perpetuate it diffuse into the abstract, Phildickian cloud.

The Myth of Authority is one of the foundational myths of the system. If man realised, in his own experience—rather than as a mere theory—that the source of meaning *is* his own experience, his own consciousness, and that he does not need to be told what to think, what to feel, what to want and what to do, the system would vanish like a bad dream on waking. But of course *this* bad dream has a much greater hold on him than any sleeping nightmare, as the source of his conditioning is not merely a mistaken intellectual belief, a system-serving lie that he has picked up on the way, but his *entire self*, shaped from birth to accept the form of the given world as ultimate reality.

This is why systems-man is such a pathetic coward; his self, from the moment it enters of the world, is deformed into a subservient appendage to the Way Things Are. As soon as he can walk his steps are directed towards a life made by others; his games are provided by others, his explorations shaped by others, his learning given from above and his life decided for him. The world he looks upon—overwhelmingly, *massively*, powerful—is *entirely* mediated, *entirely* made by other minds. He doesn't have to *learn* to submit to these others, or ever even think about them, he is completely dependent on the reality they have made for him and so, by the time he is an adult, he is anxious about upsetting authority, apathetic about resisting injustice, unable to think for himself and terrified of sticking his neck out. He doesn't just know, he *feels*, on the deepest level of his being, that to do so is gravely, existentially hazardous. This is why there is hardly any need to control or indoctrinate people, to discipline them, or to instil the Myth of Authority in them. Human beings come pre-subjugated, with each generation more afraid, more dependent and more subservient than the one before. The system manufactures *fear-machines*, and with every year that passes it gets better at doing so.

---

* Byung-Chul Han, *Psychopolitics*.

The advanced system, of course, makes it very easy to be a coward. Why, for example, should I stick my head above the parapet when I am in a trench full of strangers? Who cares if a few Jews or a few foreigners vanish? Who cares if a few radicals or dissidents go missing? Who cares if someone with integrity gets fired or arrested for their integrity? Who cares—I don't. Not really. I don't even know these people. And yes, yes, I know, it *is* sad and terrible that rainforests are being cleared and communities uprooted and all those poor folk in foreign lands have to work in nasty factories to make my trousers, but I've got more important things to worry about. There is just no real, concrete, reason to worry about my neighbours, my colleagues, the hundred species that went extinct today, or the people who make all the objects I use; and so the courage to do so also appears abstract and unreal.

Compounding this unreality is the glacial progress of the system, which makes it even more difficult to revolt. Those who own or manage the system, understanding that humans are more likely to resist sudden changes, work at the same piecemeal pace, enslaving their peoples and annihilating nature by degrees. Everything that happens is worse than the last thing that happened, but only a *bit* worse, so it is bearable, and nobody else is acting, so, again, why risk your own neck? Who knows, the next step downwards might be the one that sparks off a revolution, *then* you'll do the right thing, *then* you'll join in. Who knows? For now it's better to hang on, stay quiet, keep your head down, not make a fuss. I'll be brave a little while later.*

---

* 'You don't want to act, or even talk, alone; you don't want to "go out of your way to make trouble." ...So you wait, and you wait. ...But the one great shocking occasion, when tens or hundreds or thousands will join with you, never comes. That's the difficulty. If the last and worst act of the whole regime had come immediately after the first and smallest, thousands, yes, millions would have been sufficiently shocked—if, let us say, the gassing of the Jews in '43 had come immediately after the 'German Firm' stickers on the windows of non-Jewish shops in '33. But of course this isn't the way it happens. In between come all the hundreds of little steps, some of them imperceptible, each of them preparing you not to be shocked by the next... And one day... you see that everything, everything, has changed and changed completely under your nose. The world you live in... is not the world you were born in at all. The forms are all there, all untouched, all reassuring, the

Because the Myth of Authority, the idea that we need a person, a group, a system or our own alienated consciences to tell us what to do, is an inherent consequence of living within the civilised system, it is common to all civilised ideologies; to communism, capitalism, monarchism, fascism, professionalism and nearly all religious traditions. Each of these constituent ideologies makes a great deal of its differences to the others, of its own unique claims to legitimacy—our leaders were chosen by the working class / meritocratic education / the free market / science / God... but yet, strangely, the result is always the same. One group of people telling another group of people what to do and making a misery of life on earth for everyone and everything they, or the system they manage, control.

Earlier I mentioned 'you and I', because *you* know and *I* know that *we* don't need these people. *We* don't need laws to know what's right and wrong, or states to direct every aspect of our lives, or institutions to tell us how to live, or telephones to direct our desires and evaporate our embodied selves. Although we might need the authority of tradition, or of wisdom, *we* don't need the authority of systemic dominance and control; yes, but, perhaps you're thinking; it's *them*—*they* are the problem! Without princes or parliaments or professionals *they* would be out of control, *they* would be rapin' and pillagin', *they* would be sick and stupid and inefficient and unable to control themselves.

Yes, maybe, but we can deal with *them*, for *they* are our neighbours. *They* are human, and within reach. Shape the world into a monolithic ziggurat with unimaginable power at the top and nothing but automated phone lines between the planet-wide base and the glittering peak, automate exploitation and plug it into our own needs and desires, and we are left devouring ourselves and swiping at ghosts in an electronic vacuum.

---

houses, the shops, the jobs, the mealtimes, the visits, the concerts, the cinema, the holidays. But the spirit, which you never noticed because you made the lifelong mistake of identifying it with the forms, is changed. Now you live in a world of hate and fear, and the people who hate and fear do not even know it themselves; when everyone is transformed, no one is transformed. Now you live in a system which rules without responsibility even to God. The system itself could not have intended this in the beginning, but in order to sustain itself it was compelled to go all the way.' Milton Mayer, *They Thought They Were Free: The Germans, 1933-45.*

19

The Myth *of* Culture

The system's cultural industry suppresses originality; both individual creativity, or *genius*, and collective creativity, or *scenius* · · · It does this because genius and scenius both come from outside of the system, and therefore cannot be controlled, categorised, or packaged by it · · · Suppression of genius and scenius occur through the automatic, unconscious activity of the market, which prevents people from accessing their own society, and the ego, which prevents people from accessing their own consciousness.

'INNOVATIVE' AND 'NEW' are two of the most used words in the capitalist lexicon, but, as with 'growth', 'freedom', 'democratic' and 'newsworthy' innovative only really counts as innovative if it serves business. Capital seeks new answers to one question only; how to accumulate more capital. New ways to extract more work from labour, new technologies to increase production, manage consumption, or suppress dissent, new methods to fix people into the system, new inducements to buy more, new techniques of generating profits, new products, new markets and new marketing campaigns all represent the needs of the system and therefore the acceptable direction of innovation.

The nature of the limits to systemic innovation is exposed in the contradiction that exists between 'innovation' and 'risk'. In the literature of the system the word 'risk' always refers to *minimising* risk to the lowest possible levels, thereby 'maximising return on investment'. Anything which cannot be predicted or controlled—creative inspiration, autonomous choice and all spontaneous natural and social processes—represents an enormous threat to the system and must be, at all costs, restrained or controlled. This is either achieved through *direct compulsion*—which is why capitalists *always* seek to control governments, which can indemnify risk and control those who upset capital by not paying their rents or turning up for work—or through *indirect influence*—by reshaping the environment* to funnel awareness towards its priorities, forcing activity down canalised, controllable, predictable pathways. Genuinely free choice, inspiration, life itself, must be *induced*, only under such conditions are capitalists prepared to 'take risks' in a 'free' market.

---

* Including, via advertising, media ownership and academic sponsorship, the intellectual and emotional environment.

Annihilating the threat of uncertainty results in the endlessly proliferating omni-identical suburban death-zone we term THE TOWN (and, especially, THE SUBURBS), the monocultural agricultural wasteland, devoid of free, natural life, we call THE COUNTRY, and the predictable sameness of all graduates, professionals, jobs, schools, films, books, songs and newspaper columns; in short, *the death of nature* (See myth 10) and *the death of culture*. Only such a MONOWORLD (a.k.a. THE INTERZONE), one in which all components are comprehensible, predictable, controllable and interchangeable, is acceptable to the system. More of such a world counts as 'innovative' or 'new', less—no matter how original, useful, vivid or beautiful—is automatically rejected.

The rejection of originality, truth, creativity and so on is not a personal, explicit, focused activity, but a systemic output. Collective originality (a.k.a. 'SCENIUS') is *automatically* suffocated by time-scarcity, absence of conviviality, digitisation of experience and other consequences of the expansion of the system into the cultural realm, which forces artists to depend upon the machinery of the system to realise their work. The culture industry in turn judges art by how suitable it is for the system, pouring its energy into ensuring that system-friendly titles will be successful. This premium on market success means that art cannot be produced that will antagonise any class, stratum, geographical or religious section of the prospective readership. Murder and mayhem are fine, as is a little bit of controversy, but the serious suggestion, for example, that religion, scientism, feminism, capitalism, communism, nationalism, professionalism, sexism, consumption, mental illness, democracy or communications technology are bobbins will not sell, and so cannot be produced. Genuinely radical social criticism, which concentrates on laying bare the roots of social evils, is taboo among all publishers, producers and critics (*'too incendiary, too controversial, too angry'* or perhaps, *'cliched'*), as is any work which crosses genres (*'falls between two stools'*) as is any song, novel, film or work of art which expresses the nature of human life, as opposed to its systemic appearance and priorities (*'I like it, but I'm afraid I won't be able to sell it'*), as is any work that meaningfully suggests there might be a natural, social or existential reality beyond the self (*'I didn't understand it'* or *'it didn't speak to me'*).

There is nothing like a recognisable social reality in system fiction. When it does appear it has the strangeness of an alien world. In fact alien worlds usually seem *more* familiar to readers and viewers. In the art of the system, man scarcely lives in a social world at all. Or a natural one. Ponderous imitation of nature is permitted, as is the sickening relativist sentiment of green and neo-green doomers, but the essence of natural majesty or harmony in artistic form is as rare in painting and literature as the wild is in society, and greeted with the same incomprehension.

Market priorities, and the intense conservatism of the cultural industry, also demand that preference is automatically given to producers of culture (authors, artists, musicians, etc.) whose fame or whose imitation of other successful cultural products, provides advance assurance of a large market. Over time, Big Names dominate the mass-media in the same way that huge corporations dominate the mass-market, no matter how mediocre or meaningless their output.

Another pressure on cultural scenius is the destruction of the society from which it naturally arises. Massively inflated land prices* drive up the cost of living, which prices out the free time required to make great art. And just as gentrification forces up rents in the physical world, so the 'gentrification of the arts' excludes poorer people and the working classes, who have neither the time nor the connections to enter public broadcasting or gain access to the means of artistic production†; not to mention understand their own cultural tradition or the reality its greatest contributors endeavoured to express.

This is why internet on the beach, pianos at school, William Morris graffiti, Ozu on teevee, Beethoven's seventh on the London to Brighton or any other kind of 'democratisation' of the arts are all next to useless. Consumers of entertainment are supine before neoliberal 'creative industries' which have completely colonised cultural life, replacing meaning with novelty, technological

---

* Due to property speculation taking over from productive investment.

† Which are increasingly dominated not just by wealthy artists but by layer upon layer of artistic bureaucrat—producers, curators, design managers, 'creative consultants' and God knows what else—all of whom stifle actual creative output even further.

'innovation', 'diversity', and other market-friendly ideological
instruments, which are then taken to *be* culture; anything else
feeling 'weird', or 'boring', or 'offensive', or 'hopelessly out of
date'. In addition, such consumers are harried, stressed, lonely,
working all day at meaningless tasks for the enrichment of others,
living in ugly accommodation owned by others or bamboozled
by a lifetime of emotional overstimulation, hyper abstraction,
sensory deprivation, alienation, advertising or grinding poverty.
Under such circumstances the eternal truth and apocalyptic
beauty of great art and wild nature, their revolutionary harmony,
subtlety and power, have either been co-opted, or they cannot
be perceived at all. The organs to do so have withered; and even
when the problem is grasped or the solution glimpsed, the energy
required to do something about them, much less create enduring
works of beauty oneself, is absent. Most people do not know
what to do with free time and when it appears they feel only
an anxious need to consume corporate fun or, at best, cultural
familiarity. This is also why media reform is, ultimately, useless.

Talking of familiarity, it is worth pointing out the cultural
ruin that peer orientation has resulted in. As mentioned in
myth 17, culture is no longer handed down 'vertically' from
adults to children, but is now only passed 'horizontally'. It can
of course be a very good thing for children to reject the values
of their elders, but for the young to break *entirely* with adults,
to reject tradition completely—to dress, think, talk and act like
other children—is a social disaster. The young no longer seek
to express themselves through the long-evolved scenius of their
cultures but through the tastes and preferences generated by
cliques. That these are sterile and degraded is putting it mildly.
Just take a look at the cultural icons of the youth—happily
provided by corporate power—to get an idea of how far we have
fallen in just forty years. And it will get *much* worse.

The final, and one of the most catastrophic means by
which scenius is degraded and banished, is the curtailment
of play. Children have no opportunity to play outside of artificial, mind-made, intensely managed institutional or virtual
environments. And nor do adults. Joyous laughter, 'inappropriate' language, satire and uncensored play are banned in all
workplaces everywhere, supplanted by 'fun days', 'informal
working spaces', 'bonding exercises', 'jolly good fellows' and

other market-friendly morale-boosters. Non-work play usually amounts to intoxication, competition or passive consumption of fun. Free cooperative creation, unmanaged joy and psychologically liberating ritual—the living foundation of collective genius—are now so far from most people's experience that there is no need for centralised authority to bust the party; general awkwardness, apathy, confusion and the uptight distaste of the internal censor are far more effective police. We do not need the authorities to direct our behaviour when we have an inner voice which tells us that spending free time on anything but enhancing employability is frivolous ditz, that playing with other people's children is tantamount to paedophilia, that spending a weekend engaged in improvised theatre in the forest is 'not my thing' or that *being silly will expose you*. Such instructions cut subversion off at the root, and with it subversively original culture.

The result of all these pressures is that almost nothing by way of genuine living culture* is now fed into those most in need of it, the poorer classes, who are overwhelmed by mass produced pap which, in lieu of their own direct experience of reality, they tend to reproduce in their shoddy and superficial artistic output; an omnipresent pornography which deadens the souls of a great many young men who would otherwise have been sanely wanking their guitars.

When ordinary people no longer hang out together, jam and idle, when they no longer have access to creative resources, when they are priced out of their own neighbourhoods, and when they are as far from the wild, and from a dignified, natural life within it, as it is possible to be, a self-reinforcing cycle of cultural degradation takes hold, whereby only the most mediocre (albeit technically competent) painters, producers, directors, musicians and writers can *afford* to produce art and gain an influence over culture; which they inevitably use to expand the reach of second, third and fourth-rate work, which, in turn, conditions artists no longer able to create beauty, into believing that the word 'genius' refers to hairdressing, phone manufacture, burger recipes, graphic design, digital effects saturated fight sequences,

---

* As opposed to that imposed and acquired; such as that of those most cultured of people, ancient Romans and modern Nazis. Cultivation of culture from above is a sure sign that its living roots are dead.

luxury porn, literary characters that sound like middle-class graduates, reboots, hyper-bland aural pap, bleak, titillating or 'ironic' modern art, modern artists that look, sound and behave like upper-managers, hip-hop, superheroes, rich kids with deep voices who can do impressions taking the place of actors and oceans upon oceans of pornoid mediocrity.

We have lived in such a cultural wasteland since the 1990s (although the death-blow was delivered at the beginning of the 80s). Since then, joy has given way to mere excitement, surreality to mere randomness, vividness to mere intensity and the superb insane strangeness of working-class comedy has given way to the witless sniggering of bourgeois 'comedy'.* The difference can no longer be detected because artists no longer have access to a reality which forces them to discern it. Those who would create the art we need are isolated from the harmony of lived nature and genuine culture, and can no longer detect its presence. Cultural ugliness and aesthetic squalor colonise the earth and come to seem normal, until the building of a great work of art comes to be as difficult, and as unlikely, as the building of a cathedral, while those who look back with longing at the cathedrals we once built appear hopelessly out-of-date.

Thus the control of cultural output and the control of the multitude from whence it must arise, go hand-in-glove. The freedom of ordinary people to produce original works of art or culture is intolerable to power, which must convert their lives into commodities and then counter the effects of the resulting misery with a pacifying spectacle of fun and authoritarian normality, bonding the population to the status quo by endlessly promoting or reproducing those ideas and ways of life which serve both it, and the ego which feeds it.†

---

* Check out contemporary comedy on the BBC, or the (bitchy-yet-politically correct) 'jokes' that journalists and wealthy professionals share on social media.

† 'One of the contradictions of the bourgeoisie in its period of decline is that while it respects the abstract principle of intellectual and artistic creation, it resists actual creations when they first appear, then eventually exploits them. This is because it needs to maintain a certain degree of criticality and experimental research among a minority, but must take care to channel this activity into narrowly compartmentalized utilitarian disciplines and avert any holistic critique and experimentation. In the domain of culture the bourgeoisie strives to divert the

This time-bound (or *fashionable*) ego has always been inimical to great art or to any kind of meaningful advancement in human knowledge; the output, that is to say, of GENIUS, the timeless, natural, intelligence of life that great people hollow themselves out to host. Ego, feeding off the intellectual, moral and aesthetic fashions of the group that it huddles to for warmth, is terrified by anything which gestures to a reality beyond what it knows, and what it feels it knows. The unknown—originality, that is—always greets the ego as *an incompatible known*, which is to say, as some kind of violence, threat, offence, or some other kind of *devil* (see myth 25). It is instructive, in this regard, to read of the lives of Jesus of Nazareth, Shakespeare,* Bach, Beethoven, Mozart, Dostoevsky, Van Gogh, William Blake, J.M.W. Turner, D.H. Lawrence and Nietzsche; all of whom were rejected by those around them, passed in and out of fashion, and struggled for money, and all of whose works are now in the hands of critics, curators, auctioneers and other bourgeois guardians of culture; the dust people who haunt classical music recitals and fine art retrospectives.†

---

taste for innovation, which is dangerous for it in our era, toward certain confused, degraded and innocuous forms of novelty.' Guy Debord.

* Was Shakespeare widely praised by his time? Given that you *can't* read of his life—i.e. that we have so little material about his life, not even a reliable portrait—it seems unlikely. We also know that he was soon dumped, lying in obscurity for a century while second-rate dramatists had their strutting hour. See *The Art of Literature* by Arthur Schopenhauer—himself, one of the great ignored voices of history—for a superb, and hilarious, account of how genius is systematically ignored. Presenting artistic truth is, for Schopenhauer, like putting on an astonishing fireworks display to people who are not just blind; but *are also fireworks makers*.

† 'The interior of the temple (of fame) is inhabited by none but the dead who were not there while alive, and a few living most of whom will be thrown out after they die.' Thus, D'Alembert, who could also have added that the Guardians of Culture who manage the temple are as blind as Schopenhauer's fireworks makers. If Johann Sebastian Bach turned up at the Proms he'd feel much as Jesus of Nazareth would listening to an Anglican bishop read the Sermon on the Mount in Winchester Cathedral. It's true that great artists probably felt despair at the larger part of their own audiences, but at least they comprised ordinary living human beings, rather than bloodless stamp-collectors and accountants who *appreciate* great art in their spare time.

Ego will do everything in its power to protect itself against the reality that genius represents; *if* that reality has the chance to get anywhere close to awareness. The unquenchable thirst that ego has for reflections of its own beliefs, desires and fears is enough to drive it away from genius and into the mountains of meaningless drivel (or meaningless doughnuts) that it consumes for reassurance. This reassurance it calls 'pleasure', 'fun' or, if the object is that of a now safely dead, system-subsumed artist, 'appreciation'. Serious engagement with living genius and profound expressions of the inner life of the *individual* (as opposed to the mass or minority *type*) bores, offends, confuses, annoys and horrifies ego, which does whatever it takes to make sure that it does not get in the way of its self.

This is the essence of cultural life in a late-capitalist or Huxleyan system, which doesn't promote ideologies, or force explicit propaganda upon a captive audience, but *automatically* promotes submissive, ego-driven people into positions of cultural power, providing them with a platform to endlessly—'freely'—duplicate stereotypical behaviours, established social roles and reassuring, ego-friendly excrement. The unhappy, stressed, ambitious, insensitive and psychologically imprisoned teacher, shop assistant or factory worker finishes work in order to consume entertainment in which a world of unhappy, stressed, ambitious, insensitive and psychologically imprisoned teachers, shop assistants and factory workers is either normal or given a flavour of paradise. Even cartoons set in the afterlife, fantasy epics set in alternate realities and dystopian sci-fi of the year 3500 must exalt intense specialisation, alienating commerce, infantile technophilia, meaningless or coercive bureaucracy, rigid hierarchies, scientism, relativism, self-obsession, tense emotionality, specious literalism, restless desire, hyper-rationalism, reassuring groupthink and the denial of life. You may, indeed you must, resist enemies within the given world (even, and ideally, 'The Man'*), but there is no space to even conceive

---

* Amazingly, the system actually functions *better* if the mythic bad-guy is the corporation, the bland company man or the monolithic otherness of the modern world. It is superficially accurate, and therefore superficially reassuring, to see one's anxieties projected onto the cinema screen—to see the techno-beast overwhelm us, or the plucky young misfit crushed by work—but it all happens *in the*

of resistance to the world itself, its deep structure. You may even be dimly aware that all this is shit; but, the message is, the ego and its system cannot be changed. It is eternal and omnipresent. It is I and I am it; rebels do not question it and even talking hot-dogs unthinkingly submit to it.

realm of the known. The structure of human society as we find it, modern ways of thinking and feeling and communicating, these are accepted, unchallenged. Except of course in the finest, and rarest, art.

20

The Myth *of* Fun

The system mass-produces, and can only
mass-produce monotony. Life in the system
is, therefore, unbelievably boring · · · The
system permits you to overcome boredom,
but only *through* the system; through the
consumption of *privilege* and *narcotics* · · ·
Privilege and narcotics are sickening, but
they are preferable to overcoming boredom
outside of the system, which can never be
permitted or even considered.

THE SYSTEM IS PLENTYFUN if you have a second home in Padstow, or if the Tate Modern have commissioned a retrospective of your work, or if you exist in an advert for supermarket loyalty cards, or if mum and dad are financing your fascinating internship, or if you haven't logged off since 2010, or if your life-standards are so low that you count being a passive consumer of centrally or artificially organised spectacle as 'enjoyable'. Back on planet Earth, living death prevails; grinding, debilitating boredom at home, at work and, most conspicuously, on the roads (virtual and actual) which connect them. Lack of adventure, soul-crushing futility, deep-grained dissatisfaction with the dreary predictability of living, absence of collective delight and the overwhelming sense that *nothing is happening* are all endemic to the system, which can *only* exist by creating degrading, uncreative and tedious work for the vast invisible majority, by blocking access to individual and collective sources of creativity, by suppressing spontaneous, active, liberating joy (and its concomitants, radical generosity, wild humour and peace of mind), and by replacing it with system-friendly surrogates.

Because work is an activity in which all initiative and energy is extorted from the individual in order to generate profit for someone else, and because it is unbearably unpleasant, futile and barren, 'free' time looms before labour as a garden paradise. Fake sickies are then engineered and labour-saving devices purchased to extend the Pastime Arcadia by a minute or two. But because access to wild nature and genuine culture is curtailed, weekenders are forced to buy their pleasure as they buy everything else, from huge corporations which, to turn a profit, appeal to the lowest common denominator of its demographic, thereby producing, in lieu of satisfying art, addictive titillation and anxiety. In other words, once we have freed ourselves from work, we then have to submit to a world made by work.

Thus life becomes a series of ever more complicated, stressful or boring obstacles to overcome in order to get a few emotionally overactive moments 'free' to browse instagram, watch a superhero film, down half a bottle of wine, have an 'exciting experience' on holiday, pull one off to a webcam or consume any other product you miserably manufactured in your *unfree* time. This addiction to market-produced PORN is what we call fun or, if the activity in question is an attempt to squeeze one's deepest life purpose into a few exhausted moments at the end of the week between the cleaning and the admin, HOBBY. Due to the addictive nature of this process, any attempt to bring it to consciousness is registered as pain and met with instant dismissal, ridicule or antagonism.

The most emblematic entertainment of the highly developed system is probably the video game, in which the system reaches a kind of apotheosis. The typical video game is an unreal, mind-made, soft-porn environment of near constant competition, built on a colossally wasteful technological infrastructure, in which an individual, sitting sense-dimmed and prostrate in a darkened room, staring at a visual display unit, attempts to solve rational problems or exterminate terrifying enemies under extreme time-pressure and resource-scarcity in order to achieve a high score, completely cover the map or achieve total victory over everyone. This is 'great fun'.

The disastrous consequences of fun on one's own body and psyche and on those who must suffer our company, are not so difficult to disguise, but the system provides us with ample opportunities to blame our guilt, loneliness, suicidal anxieties, insomnia, impotence, mediocrity and existential dread on anything and everything but addiction *to* the system (see myth 16), or to annihilate our pain with market-sponsored narcotics, bromides about 'deferment of gratification', hope that we will one day be free of work or courses in so-called 'mindfulness' — which is to say techniques of self-mastery stripped completely of revolutionary action and revolutionary joy so that you might serenely accept corporate sodomy.

A sparkling minority don't need to be pacified. Those who are granted inspiring jobs operating on children's brains, working for the UN or designing actor's hats just don't see what all the fuss is about; yet cling to their wonderful tasks like grim death and turn a blind eye to the compromise and shame of living on the golden peak of Job Mountain. Those who can afford to have meaningful relationships with lions, or are paid to compete in high-tech bicycle races, or swan around award ceremonies, enjoy their fun by suppressing their awareness that the glitzy party is, actually, intensely dull and weirdly repressed; as all spectacles are.

Guy Debord first recognised the pivotal role that passive spectacle plays in the system. The role of the masses in capitalist culture is *and can only be*, that of the fan, the audience or the consumer. This isn't to say that non-participation is inherently sickening, but a society in which ritual, art, adventure, festival and joy can only reach the individual via vast, centrally-directed, technologically augmented *displays* of 'creativity', corrupts the power of ordinary people to create their own culture. You may choose your team, your channel or your journey through Hyrule—you might even actively create the cultural artefacts of the spectacle, which in late capitalism depends more and more upon the work of a 'voluntariat' populating its digital platforms with their work—but you must never be allowed to choose a world of genuine, sensate cultural participation and togetherness.

This is why all fun in the late-capitalist system is, despite much blather to the contrary, intensely *lonely*; because you are prevented from independently, collectively creating your enjoyment, much less your environment. The mad laughter of togetherness cannot be heard in the Twitter feed, the Reddit sub or the massively multiplayer online game, and the notion that we could create *actual* adventures together, IRL, is met with perplexity or anxiety; indeed, very often, with accusations that those who suggest such a possibility are... wait for it... no fun!

The Myth of Fun is usually invoked by highlighting the difference between the multicoloured Huxleyan dystopia of the modern, 'individualist', 'capitalist' or 'democratic' First World and the monotone dystopia of the pre-modern, 'conformist', 'socialist' or 'totalitarian' Orwellian Second or Third World. It is inconceivable that vast, centrally or artificially managed spectacles could be depriving us of actively generating our own rituals. It is inconceivable that access to an endless torrent of stupendous porn could be literally sucking us dry of the energy and presence to love. It is inconceivable that tremendously 'enriching' holidays could be exercises in exotic consumption at the *expense* of faraway lands. It is inconceivable that the fun we are having is pseudo-entertainment unconsciously designed to pacify us. And it is inconceivable that zombie survival games on the x-box could be depriving us of defeating demons or rescuing princesses in the real world. Worse than inconceivable—an active source of unpleasure. This is why such ideas are violently rejected, or superciliously dismissed, before they reach full awareness.

Humans first became aware of the intense boredom of capitalism unlife once it started to overcome the misery of the nineteenth century. For most of the nineteenth and early twentieth century those on the lower stages of the Stairway to Heaven lived lives of horrendous deprivation. When breeze-blocks and tinned corned beef had sufficiently eased the physical pain of the masses, at least in the West, everybody suddenly realised how profoundly bored they were. The response—the sex, revolutionary art, psychedelic drug use, dropping out and interest in Eastern religions which we generally call the 'hippy' movement of the sixties—horrified capitalists, who immediately set about co-opting the movement* (whilst simultaneously ridiculing it), outlawing its practices, expanding work to fill idle spaces and spending more energy coming up with attractive market-friendly alternatives to actual entertainment. These alternatives—blockbuster movies, video games, niche products appealing to consumer identities, a calender of distracting, pacifying spectacles (particularly sport) and, latterly, the internet and social media—effectively neutralised the threat of agonising boredom, at least amongst those sufficiently domesticated to not consciously realise that anything was missing, and replaced it with far more potent forms of social control; anxiety and impotence, the wages of un-experience.

The hypermodernite, existing in virtual or intensely mediated environments, experiences, and therefore expresses, nothing. He is forced to substitute content in his speech† with

---

* By overemphasising its disastrous flaws, most particularly the egoic individualism it inherited from Romanticism.

† Actual or virtual. When the phone is idle, IRL conversation much resembles social

hyperbolic exaggeration of minutia (anecdotes founded on breathless, manic overreaction to microscopic stimulus) or with the reproduction of 'culture' (things that he has read or has seen on the screen, made by the same discarnate minds).* Or he dries up, shuts down, withdraws into a colourless state of neutered anomie, uncanny disinterest and disengagement. Because he identifies with this state—the un-experiencing self— the appearance of experience, or even the suggestion of it, is greeted with more anxiety, sadness, unease, boredom, neediness, hysterically defensive overreaction and craving for un-life. All this is acceptable to the power systems of pre-collapse, which desire anxious, intellectually able, permanently consuming technophiles; cautious, modest, dull, half-dead, socially inept, restless, reactive, semi-schizoid ghosts clinging to an entirely formal, friable, volatile ego. These people are fun.

---

media interaction, just with an added mask of politeness. Much is made of how unpleasant people can be on social media when they don't have to be responsible for their opinions, but they are just as cruel and selfish in real life, behind the fake identities they socialise behind, just less obviously so.

* 'It can be observed that speech becomes gross and hyperbolic, music loud and nervous, ideas giddy and fantastic, emotions limitless and shameless, actions bizarre and foolish, whenever boredom reigns'. A. van Zijderveld, *On Clichés*.

21

The Myth *of* Work

Turning labour into a commodity leads to
exploitation and alienation; from nature,
from society and even from the body · · ·
As the system colonises more and more
experience, more and more of what we
do takes on the alienating and exploitative
character of work · · · This makes people
more unhappy, more stressed and more
stupid; which generates more opportunities
for the market, and therefore more work.

SING HOSANNAHS! WE HAVE JOBS! Joyous proclamations from the capitalist wing of the system are very rare; the coming of the Olympics, the winning of a war and New Year's Eve more or less exhaust the range of official reasons to celebrate, with the crucial exceptions of a 4% growth rate and falling unemployment, which are synonymous with paradise. Nevermind what growth actually means (see myth 12) or what it is like to do these jobs; they 'produce prosperity'. That's all you need to worry about.

What *is* it like to work for forty, fifty, sixty or seventy hours a week turning over five-star hotel beds, turning screws on toasters, trimming cow hides, picking tomatoes, working in an Amazon 'fulfilment centre', making pies for M&S, delivering beer for Drizly, sorting recycling bins in Essex, stitching Gap pants in Islamabad, mining sulphur on Java, teaching children over the internet, tiling luxury flats in Rio or working at any productive (making things) or reproductive (taking care of things and people) task in the system?

Such questions do not trouble those who monopolise the scarcest jobs of joy (i.e. professionals: see myth 28), nor those who express delight at a booming jobs market, nor those poor souls who are so in need of money they confuse five more minutes of survival with gratitude to those who benefit from their slavery; none of whom pause to consider that labour, like land, is not, nor ever can be, a commodity.

Turning labour into a commodity, so that it might form a part—indeed, with commodified land and money, the integral part—of the economic system, destroys it; which is to say, destroys us, humanity. The market system cannot tolerate labour which is in control of its time (able to stop work when it wants), in control of its production (genuinely skilled) or in control of its surplus (what it does with what it produces), and must appropriate this control,* by depriving labour of the capacity to self-sufficiently provision itself, autonomously create or care for itself, without the direction of management or the pressure of market forces, or decide for itself what to do with its surplus, which must always belong to the system.†

Thus labour (or human activity) is transformed into capital (or money and property). The system demands that a proportion of the productive activity of people is stolen by the proprietor in order to enlarge his enterprise and his bank balance with more money and property, particularly land and tools, with which yet more capital can be generated. He who works in the system can therefore *never* be free. He may be able to change jobs, but he must always sell his activity to the system and must always direct his activity within the system to its ultimate needs,‡ which is how he finds himself in the strange position of living in a world in which a billion things clearly need to be done, and yet there are hardly any jobs available to do them. The worker can also *never* be rewarded fairly; he must always hand over a portion of what he produces to the owner, thereby creating the conditions for the further exploitation of life on earth—which must be continually deformed into saleable commodities—and the further purchase of living creatures—which must be made poor, helpless or insane enough to submit to the demands of capital for workers and consumers.§

---

* Labour must be controlled in this way if it is to be commodified; but it must also be stripped of autonomy in order to forestall the capitalist horror of OVER-PRODUC- TION; when not enough people are buying what the system is producing, because they are producing it for themselves. Over-production does not just lead to falling profits; it can wipe out capital completely, which is why forcing people into the role of consumers, or subservient employees, is so important to the system.

† A key component of this control is the eradication of the psychological roots of self-sufficiency; namely, inventiveness and initiative. This is the purpose of schooling.

‡ Professionals are allowed some autonomy. Their work is such that it cannot be mi- nutely directed from above, which is why they are pre-selected by the educational arm of the system for obedience. Professionals also often work for governments which are, ostensibly at least, non-profit organisations; which simply means that the profit accrues less directly to the captains of industry.

§ F. Perlman, *The Reproduction of Everyday Life.*

And so 'drive', 'autonomy', 'skill', 'excellence', 'creativity', 'fairness' and 'commitment', despite forming the larger part of copy for job adverts, are as out of place and threatening in the workplace as generosity, honesty, creativity and justice; but, as ever in a highly-developed system, there is no need to consciously stamp them out. The system does the work of the tyrant automatically, by embedding productive life in the over-arching social mechanism, which cannot operate unless workers are intensely time-disciplined, are terrified of unemployment and unable to handle free time, are unable to provision or care for themselves or their environment, are full of enthusiasm for their given task,* are inured to the hopeless futility of working life, have a trivial relationship with nature (including their own bodies) and are 'trained' (in many cases stupefied and retarded) for a lifetime of HYPER-SPECIALISM.

Division of labour—the natural, pleasant and extremely useful tendency for individuals and groups to do more of what they do best—is mechanically degraded by the system into hyper-specialism, or the fixing of man—*screwing* him—into the mechanism of the system. Hyper-specialism, which begins at school, where humans are sorted according to systemic function, and fully manifests in the working world, comprises two main divisive elements; the *division of activity*; the separation of skilled processes, with all their variety, into a series of minute and gut-numbing sub-tasks which pound to mush the conscious minds of those employed to do them over and over and over and over again, and the *division of purpose*; the separation of physical activity from mental activity and will, and the consequent division of people into two antagonistic groups; on the one hand LABOURERS, focused on a microscopic segment of a productive or reproductive process they once oversaw in its entirety, with

* The classic example of ideological motivation is the 'work ethic'; the idea, which has driven the workers of the West for the past few centuries, that we are morally obliged to work for the system for our entire lives so that, perhaps, one day, we will no longer have to work. A subtler modern example of ideological discipline might be 'team-spirit'—the means by which loss of purpose, dignity, joy and freedom at work is compensated with group-bonding. 'I didn't agree with the purpose of the war; I was just looking out for my buddies'—applies equally to the army platoon, the office department and the school class.

no control over the direction and outcome of their ('blue-collar') work, and, on the other hand, MANAGERS, paid to divide tasks, and thereby people, into the work mechanism, in order to, firstly, make a profit for those who sit at the output end with their big buckets, collecting golden power credits and, secondly, to service the expanding and interlocking sub-routines that the system comprises. The consequence of these two processes—the generation of vast amounts of profit and the generation of tasks designed to measure, monitor, manipulate and manage the ceaseless expansion of the system—leads to the creation of an enormous quantity of BULLSHIT JOBS*; 'white-collar' tasks with no purpose other than to fill a money-making hole, or create and organise pointless information. Examples include teaching English in an Abu Dhabi secondary school, writing user guides for private banking software, writing code for a start-up tech company doomed to failure, managing funds for a custodian bank, and most of the work done by the world's administrators, consultants, clerical and accounting staff, hedge fund managers, political consultants, marketing gurus, lobbyists and corporate lawyers, all of whom could go on permanent strike tomorrow and not be missed. Even the much vaunted 'essential' work of doctors, teachers and scientists is only so by virtue of its exist-ence in a sickening, cretinising and deeply frustrating system.

Divided not just from each other, not just from their land and their communities, but from their own whole selves, the labourer becomes a moron on the (physical or digital) assembly line, a stranger to his class and to his society (both of which become abstract in his experience) and an exile from his own nature, which inevitably sickens, thereby subduing and pacifying him; disciplinary benefits which have been widely appreciated by industrialists for centuries. The manager, for her part, either becomes a tyrant (preferably a chummy one) developing ever more sophisticated techniques to keep the labourer efficiently [re]producing (although, curiously, not quite so interested in developing such methods for 'streamlining' management), or she becomes a zombie, dealing with ever more absurd and pointless administrative tasks demanded by hyper-specialisation,

---

* D. Graeber, *Bullshit Jobs*. Note that Graeber, an elite professional, somehow neglected to include elite professionals in his critique.

hyper-expansion of the power of institutions, hyper-financialisation of the global economy and all the hyper-waste, hyper-misery, hyper-sickness and hyper-boredom which all this produces. All the while she is haunted by the sense that her life is devoid of meaning or purpose. No problem though! The system provides an education system to produce pre-alienated work enthusiasm, a medical system to patch up or dispose of broken units, a legal system to quarantine defective units, an entertainment system to distract exhausted units from the cause of their misery with amazing experiences, and an academic-media system to justify the indignity, futility, fraudulence or outright evil of their working lives; all of which at great profit to the market and the professionals employed to maintain it.

A key component in the management of labour is the welfare system. In advanced capitalist states this is used for two purposes. Firstly, to keep the so-called 'reserve army of labour' in a state of disciplined readiness to work (i.e. in near starvation). These prime movers in the job-seeking industry are (along with shipped-in immigrants*) used to discipline those *in* work with the knowledge that twenty thousand others, just like them, are desperate to take their place. They must, however, be closely monitored and tightly controlled, because they are never far from comprehending the meaning of the word 'fair'.

As the system piles on the pressure, it generates revolutionary heat in the mass of miserable, exploited labourers which it depends on, and is then forced to throw a few more bones to the dogs. These scraps from the elite table—a minimum wage here, an NHS there, an income support payment perhaps or a bit of housing benefit†—are accepted as fair by the subservient classes, who have forgotten all about the *community* welfare we had before states dismantled it. This is the second reason why the system tolerates the *state* welfare system; it can be used to diffuse revolutionary pressure.‡

---

* Who serve other purposes as well of course; principally boosting diversity for leftists, mowing the lovely lawns of the right and sewing tractable discontent amongst the native working class.

† Which goes straight into the hands of landowners.

‡ Particularly important during times of economic contraction. If the drip-dripping of food-tokens, furlough money or welfare cash dry up, so does obedience,

Can, but certainly doesn't have to be. Simply allowing people starve to death, or locking them up, or even exterminating them, are also disciplinary options. The important thing is to shaft workers from every conceivable angle; to force them to work more hours, for more years, for smaller wages, shrinking pensions and non existent benefits; to reduce their power in the workplace, rarely imposing, to non-existence; to enable management to put intense pressure on workers, to make it easy to shift them into precarious roles and 'release' them if they prove recalcitrant or if a machine can replace them; to make sure that everyone, everywhere, works harder (the so called shadow work at automated tills and so on) and pays more (for everything we do, everything we eat, everywhere we live and everything else we need—with a few notable and much vaunted ecologically and socially ruinous exceptions, such as clothes and electronics); and, all the while, pump them full of fear of destitution, guilt for not working hard enough, desire for consumer delights and, crucially, the absurd but entirely necessary illusion that because they have 'worker participation', 'profit-share', access to suggestion boxes, a union card and a friendly t-shirt, that they are somehow in charge of their working lives.

Labour then—like the unemployed, like nature, like consciousness itself—is *automatically* disciplined by being integrated into the system, which compels workers to expend every last calorie of energy in service to it and to mutilate themselves in order to fit into whatever role the system has determined they are best able to fit. As the world-mechanism entered its terminal, late-capitalist, phase and migrated into instantaneously transmitted virtual channels, the nature of this compulsion, along with the modes of engagement it demanded from workers, changed from relatively obvious institutional constraints to extraordinarily subtle forms of Phildickian coercion. Old-school tyrants still exist of course—for it is still the case that only the subservient and insensitive are promoted to, or can endure to be in, positions of management—but as the system perfects itself, so it distributes its command across the Magical Cloud. Just as there is no-one in the call-centre that can be held to account for

---

leaving a flammable mass of desperate subjects. See F. Fox Piven and R. Cloward, *Regulating the poor; the functions of public welfare.*

the various administrative nightmares of free time, so there is no-one at work in charge of work time. Those who endure the horror of working poverty find themselves constrained more by schedules, spreadsheets and smartphones than by kapos and commandants.

As more and more tasks are automated and outsourced, the postmodern company owns less and less land, or material resources, and hires fewer and fewer people. Labour, cut 'free', transforms into the PRECARIAT—a condition of chronic rootlessness, crippling working poverty and tractable anxiety whereby the individual is transformed into a corporation of one, working 'in partnership' with 'fellow' transnational organisations—and the VOLUNTARIAT—in which the component parts of the condition we ordinarily refer to as 'living' (talking to each other, helping each other, making things, playing and so on) are 'harvested' by postmodern institutions, which either own the networks by which such activities occur or, more simply, which can simply take what is freely created.

A precariat workforce finds that it must sell not just its activity during working hours, but its entire being at all times, forever. 'Labour is done everywhere, and discipline or control over labour is exercised everywhere'.* Success in the final phases of the system increasingly becomes a measure of how well one sells oneself, or *performs* (in both senses of the word); meaning how well one can meet the targets of the system (SELF-MANAGEMENT) while projecting informality, friendliness, creativity, engagement, enthusiasm and whatnot (EMOTIONAL MANAGEMENT). The stress that this induces—exacerbated by invasive surveillance and exposure to 'peer review' in the virtual panopitcon of the internet—is prodigious, but because it is one's own self that is compelling the worker to *act* (in both senses of the word), it is impossible for the self to perceive the cause and nature of its estrangement from reality, or recognise the solution. It's not unlike a real-life version of *Invasion of the Body Snatchers*. You smile, you nod, you meet your targets and answer your phone. It's not you doing it, but there's no you to notice that anything is missing; just a vague sense of emptiness which can never be filled.

---

* Guy Standing, *The Precariat; the New Dangerous Class.*

Work then, in the system, is inherently alienating. Alienated from his society, or context, and from his own conscious self, the worker looks down on what he produces, and on the manufactured objects around him, as if they were alien artefacts beamed down from Betelgeuse, which, in effect, they are.* The job of the highly developed system is not to do away with this [highly profitable] alienation, which is impossible, but to stimulate and coddle the subjectivity of the worker so that he embraces it. Work, ideally, is comfortable, purposeful, sociable, *fun*; comprising 'uniquely valued individuals' with complete 'autonomy over their work', 'sharing in company profits', spending six hours a day in an eco-friendly Scandinavian tech company, before hovering home on a solar-powered tram to spend the evening baking artisan bread and planning a rousing hike. Ideally, the worker's body will be curled up at home on an artificial cumfi-tummy, suckling warm lightly drugged milk from a big synthetic tit while his uploaded mind hovers in a miraculous cloud, alternating between fact-manipulating 'work' and

---

* This is, at least partly, why nothing beautiful is made. Listen to William Morris talking about 'that side of art which is, or ought to be, done by the ordinary workman while he is about his ordinary work, and which has got to be called, very properly, Popular Art. This art, I repeat, no longer exists now, having been killed by commercialism. But from the beginning of man's contest with Nature till the rise of the present capitalistic system, it was alive, and generally flourished. While it lasted, everything that was made by man was adorned by man, just as everything made by Nature is adorned by her. The craftsman, as he fashioned the thing he had under his hand, ornamented it so naturally and so entirely without conscious effort, that it is often difficult to distinguish where the mere utilitarian part of his work ended and the ornamental began. Now the origin of this art was the necessity that the workman felt for variety in his work, and though the beauty produced by this desire was a great gift to the world, yet the obtaining variety and pleasure in the work by the workman was a matter of more importance still, for it stamped all labour with the impress of pleasure. All this has now quite disappeared from the work of civilization. If you wish to have ornament, you must pay specially for it, and the workman is compelled to produce ornament, as he is to produce other wares. He is compelled to pretend happiness in his work, so that the beauty produced by man's hand, which was once a solace to his labour, has now become an extra burden to him, and ornament is now but one of the follies of useless toil, and perhaps not the least irksome of its fetters.'

superheroic fucking; still a machine, but now no longer a rusty analogue contraption; now a sexy cyborg! If that's not possible, if the worker is on the lowest rung of the productive ladder, where things are actually done, and it is too costly to eliminate his anxieties, then the worker himself must be eliminated; either attached to a shock-collar and connected to an AI manager, or replaced with a literal robot, ejected entirely from the machine and left to suffocate in its prodigious waste.

Pseudo-you accepts all this as not merely normal but as actually desirable. Work, like slavery, debt, democracy and war, gives man a reason not to be free; a reason to avoid having to face himself (or his wife), a reason to complain about his sad, sad story, and a reason to do nothing about it. Everyone says they want to be free of the nightmare of work, yet fall apart when they are granted such freedom, and immediately start scrabbling around for more work; or for more fun, which amounts to the same thing.

22

The Myth *of* Uniqueness

The system must promote the idea that its internal factions and ideologies are all radically different to each other. This is an illusion · · · The late-capitalist system must also promote the idea that all its people are radically different to each other. This is also an illusion · · · These illusions are called diversity. *Actual* diversity is a threat of the first order to the system and must be stamped out wherever it occurs.

'DEMOCRATIC' CAPITALISM IS RADICALLY DIFFERENT to totalitarian communism. That's what we're told; and yet all these systems had and have the same attitudes to nature and society; domination, exploitation and annihilation. The alienating principles of 'SCIENTIFIC MANAGEMENT',* along with the hyper-rationalist ambitions of modernists to completely subordinate nature and culture to centralised, specialist, scientific control, were eagerly taken up by American capitalists, German fascists and Soviet communists, none of whom regarded either land or labour as anything more than resources; which is why they all end up with the same misery, poverty and ecological ruin.

For capitalists it is generally private power that decides how productive life is to be managed and where surplus is to be allocated (with a cursory nod towards 'democracy', see myth 16). For so-called fascists and communists it is generally the state that makes these crucial decisions. Nowhere is the worker meaningfully consulted,† nowhere are ordinary people free to direct their own fate and nowhere is land excluded from the market. The centrally directed market of communism gives nominal ownership of the means of production to the worker while functionally denying him any power over what he produces; which is to say communism, like fascism, is, as Lenin conceded—indeed *as Engels himself recommended*—a form of bourgeois STATE CAPITALISM.‡ Genuine libertarian socialism, or

---

* a.k.a. FORDISM and TAYLORISM. These have, in ever subtler forms, governed industrial output for over a century; although elements of time-obsessed scientific management can be found throughout history, as far back as the inventors of modern time measurement, the proto-capitalist ancient Mesopotamians.

† Only in the most 'progressive' companies does the worker have any input, and then only over matters which pertain to productivity, never to the allocation of surplus.

‡ 'Communism' and 'capitalism' both share common base assumptions. The

anarchism—the practice of dismantling the market, the state and the system—such as was practiced, to some extent, by the Soviet councils of the Russian revolution, was crushed just as violently by Lenin's 'socialist' Bolsheviks as it was by Mao's 'red' army and Hitler's national 'socialists'.

Huxleyan capitalism is at pains to position itself as the opposite of Orwellian communism, fascism and totalitarianism, and to efface all commonalities* in order to project an ideological antagonist, a bad guy to justify military intervention abroad and suppression of criticism at home. We do not invade countries to gain control of resources but to defend against communism. *We* do not silence critics because they threaten power, but because to criticise capitalism *must* equal support for the bad guys.† *We* do not build walls to keep poor Mexicans out of jobs, *we* let one or two climb the Diamond Ladder (see myth 5) and structurally exclude the rest.

Another component of The Myth of Uniqueness is the useful idea that capitalism exists in splendid isolation to the bad old autocratic systems of yore. Overt violence, constant warfare, bizarre rituals and superstition, these are all things of the past.

---

communist state owning the means of production entails a slightly different system to private ownership, but in both cases ordinary people are powerless. A system based on different *power* arrangements in society was never even attempted in the USSR, and Lenin said as much.

* 'It is futile to be 'anti-Fascist' while attempting to preserve capitalism. Fascism after all is only a development of capitalism, and the mildest democracy, so-called, is liable to turn into Fascism when the pinch comes. We like to think of England as a democratic country, but our rule in India, for instance, is just as bad as German Fascism, though outwardly it may be less irritating. I do not see how one can oppose Fascism except by working for the overthrow of capitalism, starting, of course, in one's one country'. Thus, Orwell; although it is important to note that Orwell is talking about the modern definition of fascism (authoritarian and right wing; see myth 31); socialism tends in exactly the same direction.

† Likewise, criticism of model capitalists such as Clinton, Blair, Obama and so on *must* equal support for Trump, modern fascism and the far-right. The idea that they are *all* rabid capitalist warmongers cannot be countenanced, ever, by the capitalist 'left' (the managers of people) and the capitalist 'right' (the producers of things) noisily battling out with each other, in the capitalist press, their procedural disputes about how the system should be managed.

We would never behave in such an uncivilised manner. *Our* wars don't count as violence, *our* military-sporting spectacles, professional rituals and 'common-sense' beliefs don't count as superstition, *our* poverty isn't *really* poverty.* Likewise, so-called 'neoliberals' criticise stuffy old 'neoclassical' folk while relying on precisely the same state interventions (and extremely strong ones), the same money and property system, the same professional dominance of the commons and, at base, the same egoic experience of the universe.†

But by far the most pervasive and paralysing element to the system-serving idea that 'we' are different to 'them', is the idea that a difference exists between the [Huxleyan] 'left' and the [Orwellian] 'right'. The range of thought that lies between, say, Tony Blair, The Guardian, Adam Curtis, Laurie Penny, Alain de Botton and Hollywood on the 'left', and David Cameron, George Bush, The Mail, Sky, William Buckley, Katie Hopkins, Henry Kissinger, Roger Scruton and the BBC on the 'right' is roughly the thickness of a blade of grass. Despite an enormous amount of highly visible disagreement ('lively debate' it's called) between them, they all accept the underlying assumptions of the market system, they all, ultimately, serve the business class (despite profitable left-wing claims to the contrary: see myth 31), they all have the same foundational attitude to reality, love, truth and other so-called 'subjective' illusions and they all turn, as one, to repel the threat of those who seek to strike at the root of the system; unless of course it temporarily serves their professional interests.‡

---

* 'We cry shame on the feudal baron who forbade the peasant to turn a clod of earth unless he surrendered to his lord a fourth of his crop. We called those the barbarous times. But if the forms have changed, the relations have remained the same, and the worker is forced, under the name of free contract, to accept feudal obligations. For, turn where he will, he can find no better conditions. Everything has become private property, and he must accept, or die of hunger'. Peter Kropotkin, *The Conquest of Bread*.

† Not that neoliberalism didn't represent a new form of hyper (or late-stage) capitalism; it did. See Philip Mirowski, *Neoliberalism; The Movement That Dare Not Speak It's Name*.

‡ 'Future students will be as much confused by the supposed differences between capitalist and socialist professional institutions as today's students are by

In the real world, the entire media spectrum—along with all governments, businesses and professional institutions (which also like to pretend they are unique, autonomous units and not integral parts of the one system)—runs from the FAR RIGHT (which the media calls 'left'), to the EXTREME RIGHT (which it calls 'right'). To the right of this microscopic *official* OVERTON WINDOW, lies a small pocket of pure modern FASCISM and to the left lie the CENTRE (the political position of most of the world) and the *unofficial* LEFT (inhabited by socialist reformists).

Much is made of the difference between these groups, but they are all, functionally, identical. Take the difference between official leftists—so-called 'socialist' politicians and writers—and the unofficial left, comprising Marxists, socialist liberals, socialist anarchists (i.e. anarcho-syndicalists) and similar 'dissidents' and 'radicals'. This latter group has precisely the same *fundamental* attitude towards civilisation, technology, democracy, the state, work and even reality itself as those they criticise, which is why they think and behave in much the same was as their mainstream nemeses, reacting to genuine criticism in the same way and, upon gaining any kind of power within the system, effortlessly blending into it. Their reaction to the so-called coronavirus 'pandemic' was a perfect illustration of this. 'Radicals' and 'leftists', even those well outside of the mainstream, did not merely refuse to question what was happening, they pushed for *stricter* measures; all to the benefit of the technocratic system and to the ruin of the world's poor.

Alongside the fiction that 'our' system is unique, or that 'our' political position is unique—*The Myth of Systemic Uniqueness*—runs the idea that you and you and you, who form the atomic components of this special we, are also special. You matter, apparently. You are different, so they say. This is *The Myth of Personal Uniqueness*.

Your freedom to 'be who you are' exists within predetermined limits. You can be anything which corresponds to your role in the market, as consumer or producer. You can have any *identity* (definable personality) you like if it helps you get a job or respond to an advert. Nerd? Trans? Buddhist? Carer? Fan?

---

the claimed differences between late Reformation Christian sects'. Ivan Illich, *Disabling Professions*.

Atheist? Black? Foodie? Fussy eater? OCD? Retro-porn enthusiast? Welcome. If we have a job or product for you, step right in; and if you're not sure who you are, then we'll diagnose, test and measure you, and tailor your experience to what we know you like. And if you *still* don't fit in, we'll arrest you—which is to say, we'll give you the identity of 'prisoner'.

What cannot be tolerated by the capitalist economy is a refusal to *ultimately* identify with skin colour, body shape, gender, diagnosis, race, religion, sexual preference, ideology (left, right, green, red, black...) or market-directed interests and talents. The inability of the system to acknowledge the indefinable is enthusiastically—if implicitly—welcomed by the individual ego, which is trained, from birth, to cling to its fears and addictions and to defend itself with its constructed identity and its definable world. Ego is as terrified of genuine self-knowledge—which comes from *de*constructing identity definition—as the market is; both the systemic ego and the capitalist market will greet genuine independence, uniqueness, originality and psychological freedom from addiction with incomprehension, ridicule and contempt.

In short, you can be a black, half-Nepalese, transsexual, communist midget with high-functioning Asperger's, a talent for graphic design and a breakfast bar in Dalston, or you can be a tall, ripped, straight-A, white supremacist all-American marine with a cruel mother, a farm-equipment fetish and a python. Fine—as long as you are both dissatisfied in your love lives, unable to be on your own, addicted to consumption (porn, video games, food, fitness, heroin, whatever), forced to work for fifty hours a week or dependent on the state, have no idea who your neighbours are, cannot fix or make anything you actually use, become anxious whenever a moment's silence falls and spend most of your idle time wanting or worrying; which is to say, *as long as, underneath your 'identity', you are just like everyone else*.

And so we come to the marvellous *Myth of Diversity*, the idea that the institutions of the system value or produce vast collections of thoroughly unique and independent individuals, while, in the real world, what they actually need, demand and manufacture are schools, offices, cities, farms, factories and forests comprised entirely of obedient, isolated replicants.*

---

* 'In clear cutting, you clear away the natural forest, or what the industrial forester

These can be measured and managed. Nature—countless unique people, living amongst countless unique species—cannot.

And, lo, it comes to pass that ever newer and more fantastic kinds of food are produced, ever stranger and more novel ways of clothing, heating or housing ourselves appear and an ever wider variety of personality profile fills the feeds; ever narrower and finer forms of sexuality or gender, ever more refined and hyperspecific interests, ever new disorders and syndromes, ever more specific personal identities assiduously constructed to achieve the holy grail of psychological capitalism: *specialness*... while, at the same time, local languages, regional accents and the musicality of speech are everywhere levelled out, eccentricity is banished, all forms of dress begin to resemble each other, all houses are constructed from IKEA, all music begins to sound the same, movies become entirely predictable rehashes, schools, hospitals and airports the world over become indistinguishable, as do factories, farms and forests; of nature we see little more than pigeons, cats, rats, foxes, dogs and flies, of the world we see little more than food, sex, sport and war, of ourselves we feel little more than what we want and what we don't want; and that's it. Everyone talks about the same things, has the same narrow range of opinion and reacts in predictable ways to the same kind of life lived everywhere in the same kind of way. Officially this is 'diversity'. Actually—to those sensitive and aware enough to perceive actuality that is—it is excruciating MONOTONY, the inevitable consequence of which is *sickness*.

Genuine diversity—natural systems, that is, which integrate innumerable unique but mutually cooperative (or even uncooperative) and contextually beneficial elements—is extremely

---

calls "weed trees", and plant all one species of tree in neat straight functional rows...Then you dump on chemical fertilizers to replace the washed away humus, inject the seedlings with growth forcing hormones, surround your plot with deer repellents and raise a uniform crop of trees all identical. When the trees reach a certain prespecified height [not maturity; that would take too long] you send in a fleet of tree harvesting machines and cut the fuckers down. All of them. Then burn the slash, and harrow, seed, fertilize all over again, round and round and round again, faster and faster and tighter and tighter until, like the fabled Malaysian Concentric Bird which flies in ever-smaller circles, you disappear up your own asshole'. Edward Abbey, *The Monkey Wrench Gang*.

robust. Factory chickens, factory timber, factory corn, factory houses, factory children and factory workers on the other hand are vulnerable to infection, disruption and pain, and so must be continually pumped full of artificial supports, nutrients, fertilisers and antibiotics. They must be continually and aggressively defended against the slightest incursion and they must be continually justified or normalised by a professional class paid and privileged to keep the rickety monocultural huts of civilisation from toppling in a fart.

23

The Myth *of* Science

What we call 'science' is really the technical operation of the system and the opinion of its favoured technicians · · · Actual science is useful and interesting, but impotent to explain anything of importance to men and women; including its own origins and limits · · · Basing society entirely on the literal illusions of science leads to mass ignorance and existential insecurity.

THE PRACTICAL-MECHANICAL component of the modern system—its machinery—was largely founded on the activities of working mechanics, the technical and ideological basis of which was but one element in a much wider philosophy of rational systematisation which had been progressing since the dawn of history, but which, with the advent of the modern era, began to supplant human activity completely, replacing it with a series of output-maximising technical practices. We ordinarily call this approach to life—the abstraction or isolation of a few elements of experience, the complete disregard for everything else (technical term; 'noise') and the manipulation of these elements in order to produce a definite result—SCIENCE.

Towards the end of the nineteenth century the elites of giant corporations realised the extraordinary potential of this 'science' as a means of furthering the accumulation of capital, at which point it instantly overcame the classics as the principle purpose of 'higher education'. Powered by the energy sources and potent organisational procedures discovered by a new class of professional 'scientists' and their reduction of the immeasurable complexity of life to manageable 'simplicity' (i.e. monotony), capitalist organisations were able to massively expand their generative powers and their geographical reach, and the system, which had hitherto concentrated on managing a few aspects of production and output, could now, with new techniques of analysis and new mechanisms of observation and manipulation, concern itself with converting every minute aspect of life into a process, a resource or a product. Nothing, but nothing, systems-man began to understand, could evade the technical-scientific process of abstraction, measurement and, crucially, total control. To be sure, servile human beings were still necessary for wealth-creation, and a great deal remained to be incorporated into the market; sunlight, air, the use of bodily organs, fertilization and face-to-face conversations, for example, continued to be, to the frustration of scientific management, beyond the reach of the market, and there were still a few organisational and disciplinary functions which were yet to be fully automated, but the end finally drew into view; the bright utopian moment when human beings could, once and for all, be made completely redundant; a prospect, incidentally, celebrated by a rising movement of left-wing thinkers who look forward to a day when all work (yes, *all* of it) will be done by machines, leaving us 'free' to prance around on silver spaceships, gravity all nonsense now. No problem building, fuelling and maintaining this champagne world, apparently, and no chance that omnipresent technology will alienate us even further from our own nature. These child minds, choosing to ignore the fact that the over-production of technology accompanies and hastens the decline of all terminal civilisations, call themselves 'fully automated luxury communists', in order to disguise the fact that they are actually 'fully addicted and domesticated state-capitalists'.

Returning to modern *institutional* science; its primary purpose is not to explain certain objective aspects of the world or to improve our lives, but to justify the system, to further its techniques (software) and technologies (hardware) and to adjust nature to fit its requirements (the proper term for this process is DOMESTICATION). Each advance always begins with optional, innocuous, helpful improvements and inventions and always ends by further enslaving people and deforming human nature. We begin with cars that help us get around, or phones that help us communicate, or antibiotics that help us overcome infection, or washing machines that help us 'save time', and we end by becoming completely dependent on motorways, computers, drugs and home appliances, unable to use our legs to get to where we need to go, our mouths to speak, our bodies or our environment to heal ourselves, or our time to get things done. Meanwhile, nature dies, communities decay, 'traditional values' break down,* bodies sicken, minds crack up and we become

---

* 'The conservatives are fools: They whine about the decay of traditional values, yet they enthusiastically support technological progress and economic growth.

estranged from our own nature, but none of this is enough for any but a few scattered cranks to suggest that many of our gravest problems might be a consequence of living in servitude to industrial technology and the hyper-rationality it is built upon.

The modern system may have seized on the technical power of science only recently, but the common root of system and science reaches as far down as the foundations of civilisation. All three—science, system and civilisation—were built on the mind's ability to isolate subjects and objects from consciousness and context, represent those subjects and objects as abstractions and—in the tertiary process we normally call science—systematise those abstractions into testable narrative theories. The abstract world created by this 'isolating-representing-systematising' activity slowly became, as civilisation progressed, more and more useful, 'accurate' and, crucially, *neat* (internally coherent*) which served to conceal the fact that science has almost no bearing on ordinary existence (life, death, love, creativity, beauty, self-knowledge and so on) which is far better served by myth, folk-knowledge and art, and that, ultimately, the entire project of mind was founded on an illusion. The utility and factual accuracy of science conceals this truth; that the world *as mind understands it* was brought into existence *by the activity of the mind.*†

Civilisation, in other words—the man-made 'world' as we ordinarily experience it—is ultimately built on abstract sand. *All* of its dominating ideologies—superstitious, religious, philosophical and scientific—are founded on a world made by the mind and on the foundational belief that what the mind creates is real or that it is capable of apprehending reality. Thus shamans, priests, philosophers and scientists may believe

---

Apparently it never occurs to them that you can't make rapid, drastic changes in the technology and the economy of a society without causing rapid changes in all other aspects of the society as well, and that such rapid changes inevitably break down traditional values'. T. Kaczynski, *Industrial Society and Its Future.*

* See *Against Method*, by Feyerabend for the classic critique on the spurious neatness of science, and how it is better served by anarchic systems and practices.

† See Zerzan, Numb and Number, in *Why Hope?* for a good overview of how early scientific developments, specifically number, were used primarily as techniques of control. See also *Self and Unself* for a more thorough critique of physicalism.

different things, and violently disagree about their beliefs, but they all *behave* in exactly the same way; treating reality as a mind-knowable mechanism (operated by laws or by gods), conflating consciousness and thought,* subordinating experience (what is actually happening) to knowledge (what I know about what is happening) and widening the gulf between them, restricting access to knowledge or technique to the uninitiated, dressing up Big Men in gowns, dressing up language in jargon, taking metaphor (the scientific metaphor of measurement or the religious metaphor of myth) as factually true, completely dismissing the testimony of the individual, being reflexively outraged by attacks on orthodoxy, and either sucking up to power or monopolising it.

Because the 'civilised' hyper-literal mind has, on its own, no standard by which to judge that which precedes or transcends itself, any foundational experience of reality which is paradoxical, non-dualistic, qualitative or impossible to grasp with abstraction is *automatically* rejected as false, heretical or insane. God, says mind, is a *literal thing*, consciousness is a *literal thing*, matter is a *literal thing*, society is a collection of *literal things*, reality, or the context, is a collection of *literal things*, labour, land and life itself are *literal things*, and all these literal things relate to each other literally, in ways which mind can also reveal. Thus, to fit in with God's plan, or to harmonise with the 'natural' order revealed by science, or to take your place in capitalist society, or to accede to professionally determined reality you—*who are also a literal thing*—must relate to them in the correct way. Any other approach is heresy, madness or pure fantasy to literal systemoids; to laws and lawyers, to cults and religious fundamentalists, to third-wave feminists ('no means no'), to anti-racism extremists and modern leftists, to technophiles (and the social media they create or use), to standard psychology, to journalism (left and right), to management, to scientism, to postmodernism, to the ancient Greeks and their heirs, to batty conspiracy theorists

---

* All Western philosophers before the nineteenth century believed that consciousness was synonymous with thought. After the nineteenth century they began to believe a different, but equally false idea; that consciousness was synonymous with emotion. Finally, postmodern thought introduced the idea that consciousness (along with quality, truth, love, meaning and so on) doesn't really exist.

(the moon was invented by the Bilderberg group to turn frogs gay) and to all chronically boring people everywhere. To all these people *truth is literal** (either exclusively or ultimately) and paradox, implication, metaphor, mystery and quality are sources of existential discomfort which must be obliterated.

And yet, strange to say, the ideologues of uncivilisation never tell us what the literal things they worship or depend on *actually are*. Neither religion nor science *ever* explain or express what anything actually is, only how they can be described and how they behave. What things are (the thing-in-itself) is utterly and inherently opaque to the scientific mind, which can only perceive *representation* (via measurement). This is why science concerns itself entirely with cause-and-effect, and why it is unable to explain *anything* of any importance (the creation of the universe, the origins of life, the nature of consciousness, the reality of death, how to write a timeless love song or what to do about a moody). Everything that happens is said to happen as the result of a prior, mind-isolable, event. Consciousness, the ineffable quality of existence 'behind' its sensible spatial forms, its freedom from all cause and its consequent responsibility (see myth 16) is completely intolerable to the mind-made world, and must be ignored or annihilated. This is the project of systemic science, and its partner in crime, law (see myth 14) which seek to define everything out of existence; because only the defined can be controlled.

It is the chronically and perpetually insecure ego which seeks to control reality. It seeks to transform the universe into a network of rigid, literal definitions, just as it seeks to transform sensual reality into a controllable simulacrum (see myth 9). This habit-comfortable *pseudo-self* is in charge of the world's scientific institutions, just as it is in charge of every other institution, which is why the abstract scientific world-view is presented as uncritical orthodoxy, why 'the scientific establishment' is uniformly insensitive, selfish and stupid, and why it sees, wherever it looks, a reality which is insensitive, selfish and stupid. The universe, according to the 'consensus', is a *literal mechanism*, nature is *constant warfare* and man is *inherently egotistical*; because those who form the consensus—predictable, belligerent,

---

* See *Self and Unself* for an enquiry into the bedrock of the system; literalism.

selfish mediocrities*—can do nothing but go looking for literal mechanisms, conflict and reflections of the 'reality' they know.

It was convenient for the system that after a religious ideology which defined life as inherently sinful lost its power over society, a scientific ideology arose which defined the universe as essentially meaningless and life as inherently selfish. It was also convenient that, as the focus of attention shifted from the organism to the gene—lo! we find that the gene is meaningless and self-interested too! What extraordinary good luck! Granted, there were a few heretical movements which challenged the doctrine of original sin (medieval Christian mysticism) as they did Darwinism (Lamarckism and Kropotkinian theories of mutual aid), as they do neo-Darwinism (Epigeneticists and Neo-Lamarckists), but somehow these ideas don't *quite* make it onto the box. Somehow they always manage to get *proved* wrong.

Proof is vital because it absolves individuals of responsibility for their philosophies and theories. 'It is not *me* who believes humans are sinful and in need of salvation or selfish and in need of control; it has been *proved*. Look, it is in The Bible / On the Origin of the Species / The DSM / the Wealth of Nations / the Tragedy of the Commons... It is written, it is rationally self-evident, it is indisputable. Much as *I* would like to believe we're all good, or that we are responsible, or that the universe is a conscious organism, I have to remain faithful to the *facts*, you see'.

Honest scientists, those outside the established worldview, understand that everything based on scientific fact—all theories and scientific beliefs—are, *ultimately*, based on faith. They know that science is founded on metaphor, that it is inherently superficial, that it has inherent limits which can never be superseded, that it can never penetrate the thing-in-itself, that it can never grasp the context—only extrapolate from it, that nothing can ever be proved,† that technophilia is an infantile disorder, that all scientific theories are subject to revision, that the reflexive appeal to rationalism is a *political manoeuvre* (the deep

---

* Science *requires* mediocrity. A few conspicuous 'creatives' might further the project, but, as the father of science, Francis Bacon, stressed, the scientific project cannot function without the combined work of innumerable dull, characterless, drones.

† 'I doubt that there is any experiment that could... prove my claim'. R. Dawkins

politics of the system; worship of the legible, the graspable, the literal and the thinkable), and that science has *nothing* meaningful to say about the creation of the universe, the creation of life, the nature (i.e. the quality) of consciousness and, therefore, about love, death, beauty and truth; words which scientists very rarely utter. Intelligent scientists are aware of the primary role that vague—sometimes thoughtless—counter-inductive, counter-intuitive and even *counter-rational* passions and hunches play, not just in life generally, but *in scientific discovery*. They are aware of the limits of scientific hyper-specialisation; the woeful consequences of obsessive focus on tinier and tinier granules of knowledge, and the consequent fear that hyper-specialists, like all deeply institutionalised people, have when faced with qualities and totalities, with consciousness and context, or with any kind of experience outside their narrow domain of expertise; the importance of which they tend to inflate to comic proportions. None of this means that reductionist science, abstract thought or intellectual specialisation are useless—they are, as defenders of science continually remind us, the very essence of use, and only a fool discounts the technical knowledge, or the logical reasoning, that science and the specialised mind provide us with—nor does 'based on faith' mean entirely arbitrary and illusory; if reality were not *somehow* relative, mind-knowable and 'factual', nothing that the mind understands would have any meaning. Clearly facts *do* exist and clearly the scientific mind *can* determine what they are; something which fools and liars (religionists, postmodernists, monogendroids, climate-change deniers, flat-earthers, mystic fluff-minds, revisionists, corporate PR men, economists, politicians, and other believers in conspiracy theories) are keen to deny or ignore. But facts, *ultimately*, have nothing to do with quality, with truth and with consciousness; and truthful scientists know this, which is why they turn to art, and to experience, and to guts, and to mum, for instruction on matters which cannot be dealt with by the mind alone.

Institutional scientists on the other hand, which form the majority, are paid to prostitute their intelligence to the technical needs of the system, to ignore the rightful subservience of science to the experience of consciousness, and to adhere to the insane belief that reality is a mind knowable thing; in short, to uphold that most dismal of religions, SCIENTISM.

24

The Myth *of* Relativism

The system is threatened by meaning; by such things as quality, goodness, morality, truth and beauty, which are meaningless in the system · · · Meaning is intellectually extinguished by the ideology of *relativism*, the assumption that meaning does not exist · · · Relativism is used every day by liars, thieves, murderers and madmen to pretend their lies, theft, murder and madness do not really exist. It is also used by talentless and ambitious artists, academics, journalists and philosophers to pretend their mediocre output is really genius.

SCIENTISM IS THE APPLICATION of the scientific method to all of life, to questions which scientific objectification, conceptualisation and systematisation can never illuminate. There is, for the hyper-rational scientist, no experience which cannot be objectified, conceptualised and systematised. If mind cannot know it, it does not and cannot exist. It is *all* relative. Truth and falsehood, good and evil, beauty and ugliness, art and porn, right and wrong, meaning and meaninglessness, love and hate, sanity and insanity… all such matters, to rational scientism, are either *objective*—inhering in conceptualised neurones, or genes, or atoms 'out there'—or *subjective*—created by the [largely deluded] individual. That they are real—and therefore not subjective illusions—but, at the same time, cannot be objectified by priests or scientists—is the quintessential taboo of both theistic religion and atheistic scientism.*

Although traditional religion is not incompatible with capitalism, it has, for the most part, been ditched, or rather neutered; removed from meaningful ideological influence. Too many educated technicians control the organs of academic power for the transparent absurdities of donkey-age dogma to gain any traction, and science is just too useful to capital to be ignored. But this use doesn't just extend to its role in technique, it also has a dual purpose in the formation of men and women's attitudes. An ideology which positions truth, beauty, justice, goodness, consciousness and so on either as objective matters which can be centrally measured and managed, or as subjective fantasies which can be ignored, is ideal for justifying the dominating role of technocratic management in people's lives, while,

---

* I call this reality PANJECTIVE. Panjectivism, unlike superstition, religion and 'enlightened' scientific abstraction, presupposes no ultimate distance between subject and object, and therefore no dominance of one by the other. See *Self and Unself*.

at the same time, completely dismissing their 'assertions' that, for example, drilling into shale is wrong, that paying bankers inflated bonuses is unfair, that office work is meaningless, that an unmade bed is not art, that love is going out of the world, that the body is conscious or that the universe is an organism; none of which can be verified in the lab.

This isn't to say that the ideologues of the system don't speak of love, death, justice, beauty, quality, the sacred and the profane—they do, constantly—but scratch below the surface of the liberal newspaper column, the sacred thought for the day, the modern art catalogue, the alternative manifesto, the pop-science tract (which regularly hijack words that science cannot understand, like 'beauty', 'god' and 'reality'), the detox yoga-retreat brochure or the middle-class green philosophy of mystic doom and you'll discover that, although there are manifold verbal references to absolutes, or to 'non-materialism', they are all, ultimately, understood relatively—intellectually or emotionally—an approach which, conveniently, just happens to also be the approach of their employers. If the essence of the opinion piece were not essentially relativist, if it took responsibility for love and truth, it would never be published. It would be too weird, too extreme, too political or just not what the punter wants. If the author were conscious, if she directly addressed the reality of love, she would never be allowed to speak.*

So what is the truth? What is beauty? What is love? What is justice? What is consciousness? What kind of experience is neither objective nor subject? How the relativist loves to ask such questions! How he rubs his hands, and clenches his mind, waiting for an *idea* to be produced, something he can *think* about, something he can *grasp*. To actually *face* the truth, to actually endeavour to *create* beauty, to actually *be* conscious, to actually *love*... Nope. Don't get it.

---

* Capitalist artists, writers, priests, teachers and scientists, of the 'left' and the 'right' (see myth 22) never criticise the means by which they gain prominence. For modern artists, newspaper columnists, celebrated academics and prominent bishops it goes without saying that their platform is down to their talent, originality and honesty, and has nothing to do with the fact that the newspaper, gallery, university, church or radio station that employs them knows that they won't rock the boat by taking responsibility for the truth by saying anything meaningful about it.

The relativistic philosophy of the non-existence of truth, love, quality, meaning, justice, responsibility and reality has its roots in classical Hebrew and Greek thought and in the modern scientific movement laughably known as 'the enlightenment*'. The most extreme ideological form that relativism takes, however, is POSTMODERNISM.† While scientism—the objective wing of enlightened capitalism—busies itself with converting reality and quality into concepts, theories, brain scans, genes, particles, structures and the like, postmodernism simply asserts that they do not exist; only 'de-structured' or 'de-constructed' 'representation' does. Thus, the inane, the pointless and the ugly have just as much *right* to be included in the art gallery, the weekend supplement or the discussion show as the finely crafted, the socially useful, the transcendently beautiful and the actually true. *Actual* truth, for the postmodern thinker, is conflated with *abstract* truth and shown to be either nonsense or inherently authoritarian (the authority of the Huxleyan system). In attacking such concealed systems of coercion, the control of knowledge, the lies of the enlightenment and so on, one or two pomo thinkers (notably Foucault, Deleuze, Fisher and occasionally Lyotard) made some important contributions to radical scepticism, but they had nothing to replace them with; just capricious, egoic emotion and a kaleidoscope's nightmare of abstract 'viewpoints' unconnected to each other, or to any kind of social, natural or conscious whole.

This is, at least partly, how intellectual frauds such as Lacan, Derrida and Žižek, can present their ideas with a straight face and be received as if they have uttered profound truths; ultimately there is no such thing *as* a profound truth, so wordy bullshit can effortlessly flow into the void. It is also how purveyors of artistic snake-oil, such as Hockney, Anselmo, Richter, Warhol, Ryman and all the other charlatans of the corrupt, hyper-capitalist 'Modern Art' market, can present a canvas sprayed with child vomit or a bra stuffed with spinach to the Serious Minds

---

* Which, like modern neuroscience, conflated mental representation with conscious experience and then concluded that the latter did not really exist.

† By 'postmodernism' I am not just referring to the output of a few French philosophers, but to the overall outlook of the late-capitalist system, particularly on the so-called 'left'.

of the high-brow media world, and nobody falls about laughing. Just as there is, actually, no such thing as moral truth—and so whatever moral depravity I engage in requires no intelligible justification—so there is no such thing as aesthetic truth, so a banana gaffer-taped to a wall is art.

Actually though, there are one or two qualities which the professional artist and critic must learn to create and detect—irony, formality, irrelevance, titillation and bleakness—but ultimately all a cultural creation needs to gain access to the Tate Modern or the MOMA is for its creator to be well-connected. Politics, media and business work in the same way, which is why they all endlessly replicate a cultural reality which is prefaced on the complete destruction of nature and the natural self,* leaving nothing but an illusory or 'hyper' reality—in truth a schizoid intellectual horror show—in which we are impotent to act, to think, to speak or to judge.†

This 'reality' is the unspoken 'truth' of the truthless world. Postmodernism and scientism both make much of the absence of gods and supernatural 'meta-narratives' (which is to say, any kind of meaning in human affairs) while serving the most powerful myth the world has ever known; the advanced system, to which everyone on earth must submit. The stories and rituals presented by the servants of the system—the origin myths, the tales of heroes, the spectacles, the 'groundbreaking' documentary series, the scholastic debates, the beatific visions of success and the tractates on the secret order of things‡—coalesce into the creed and ethic of the one world religion, preached everywhere at all times by those who maintain that no such thing exists.

---

* 'Postmodernism is what you get when the modernization process is complete and nature is gone for good'. F. Jameson.

† 'Not only does [postmodernism] echo Beckett's comment in Endgame, "there's no more nature", but it also denies that there ever was any recognizable space outside of language and culture. "Nature", declared Derrida... "has never existed". J. Zerzan. See also L.A. Sass, *Madness and Modernism* for more on the relationship between [post] modernism and schizophrenia.

‡ 'The Market suffuses the cosmos; money is the benchmark of rectitude; financial, technological, or professional prowess is the empirical proxy for blessedness; and the aggressive, unapologetic entrepreneur is the eidolon of existential superlativity.' E. McCarraher, *The World is a Business*.

The contradictions inherent in relativism do not trouble hyper-relativists, any more than those in rationalism trouble hyper-rationalists. Value-free modern minds are comfortable claiming that all ideologies are lies—except their own—that language cannot convey meaning—unless it is the claim that language cannot convey meaning—or that there is no such thing as right and wrong—except in the claim that there is no such thing as right and wrong. They are comfortable with these self-refuting claims because they do not justify any truth that can be found in the world; they justify the felt-desire for there to *be* no world.

Essentially, post-modernism, or extreme relativism, is a form of high-functioning schizophrenia, or everyday solipsism, a condition which has afflicted the institutionalised (largely priestly or professional) mind since institutions began, back in the Bronze Age.* Its symptoms include a basic humourlessness, constant watchful anxiety and an aversion to value-laden terms which have the power to expose a foundational lack of qualitative experience. Hyper-relativists don't ever really, or meaningfully, use the words 'good' and 'bad', 'right' and 'wrong', 'ugly' and 'beautiful', or 'sane' and 'insane', because they don't know what they mean. They *think* they mean something like 'I like' and 'I don't like'. They can't refer to anything which exists in the real world, because there *is* no real world, just a collection of value-less objects out there and layer upon layer of interpretations, ideas, angles, 'takes', viewpoints, belief, attitudes and perspective in here, behind which, or under which, there is nothing, the nothing which lies under their personalities, which rises in nightmares and speaks back at them in the truth, love and beauty they fear.

---

* Note that subjectivist solipsism, like objectivist rationalism is rarely—perhaps never—seen in a pure form, any more than masculinity is, or leftism, or any other generalised state or quality. Most people (actually most egos) swing between subjectivist and objectivist stances in order to explain or justify their momentary fears and desires, or to meet the needs of the moment. This is another reason why they are so resistant to seriously explore their beliefs; because they crumble to dust the moment they are poked. See *Self and Unself* for further discussion.

25

The Myth *of* Religion

Religion is the belief that ideas and words
are physically real · · · To the extent they
take ideas and words to be physically real,
and respond to critical ideas as if from a
physical attack, professionalism, capitalism,
feminism, atheism, scientism, relativism,
socialism, theism and sexism are all religions
· · · Religions violently police the borders of
belief (*orthodoxy*), violently persecute non-
belief (*heterodoxy*), and all religionists aspire
to power, usually to state power.

T HE BELIEF THAT IDEAS AND WORDS are real we call SUPER-
STITION. A group of people sharing superstitious beliefs
we call a CULT or, if the group is very large, a RELIGION.
Religions are composed of people whose personality is built on
the assumption that ideas and words are literally real and that
criticism of these ideas and words is capable of causing real
harm. Such criticism may come from non-believers, who reject
the ideas and words completely ('INFIDELS'), or it may come from
believers, who interpret the ideas and words, or some of them,
non-literally ('HERETICS'); in both cases the threat is existential;
the existence of the egoic personality—via the cultic-religious
GROUPTHINK it depends on—is under threat.

The paradigmatic examples of religion are the 'Abrahamic
big three', Judaism, Pauline Christianity and Islam, members
of which tend to venerate the written word and take criticism
or satire as literal attacks. They're not alone though; fanatical
Buddhists, Hindus, atheists, modern leftists, nationalists, socialists, fascists, doctors, journalists and other cult members react
in the same way, for the same reasons. Point out, in a fanatical
communist forum, how petty, spiteful and authoritarian Karl
Marx was (or communism is); point out to a group of fanatical
feminists that (in feminist author, Fay Weldon's, words) rape is
not the worst thing that can happen to a woman (thermonu-
clear war is, for example, a bit worse) or that some of the most
underprivileged people in Western society are poor, white men;
point out to a group of fanatical black activists that, say, more
white people are killed by US police than black people; point
out the farcical all-too-human concerns of the author of the
Quran to a group of fanatical Muslims;* point out the crimes
of Israel (or the disproportionate power of Jews), or the crimes

---

* Or ask extremist feminists 'what would you rather have—feminism or Islam?'

of America (or its clients), or the crimes of Britain to a fanatical nationalist or market-worshipping Anglo-Saxon audience; point out inconvenient facts to a Trump or Blair or Marx supporter; point out that the coronavirus was harmless to all but the old and infirm and that deaths declined at the same rate everywhere, regardless of what local measures were taken,* to a system-intensifying lockdown enthusiast; point these things out, or make fun of a TOTEM (a religiously worshipped idea) or use a TABOO word or expression, and then take cover as a physical response detonates; the sweating, the anguish, the eyes turned to heaven, the hysteria, the quaking rage...

Religious adherents, the fanatical kind,† have extremely fragile selves, composed of nothing more than thoughts and emotions, which is why they tend to see people not as individuals, but *as* thoughts, or categories, backed by extreme emotionality. The fanatical world is a rigid taxonomy, comprised entirely of goodies and baddies. Goodies—Muslims, or women, or black people, or Americans or whoever is on 'our side'—are right simply by virtue of their emotional category. Baddies wrong, simply by virtue of theirs. If baddies silence, exclude‡ or criticise, it *must* be heretical (racist / sexist / ableist / fascist / communist / atheist / superstitious / intolerant / immature / a tin-foil hat conspiracy theory / an over-generalisation or, the classic, *cult behaviour*), while if goodies do, the judgement *cannot* be wrong.

It is not just other people who are perceived as emotional categories. The religious attitude denies the embodied reality of all life on earth in favour of an ersatz projection and belief

---

* Such as social-distancing and imposing the use of face masks.

† Many *non*-fanatical people belong to religions for reasons other than bolstering a shaky sense of self. They may benefit from the psychological insights of its founder or its tradition, they may value the social elements of membership, they may be committed to the general, and non-literal (perhaps even miraculous) 'way of life' that the religion represents, they may gain psychological solace from religious ritual, they might enjoy the practical benefits that their religious tradition confers, they may love the master or they might have had self-rupturing experiences of mysterious otherness which they [wrongly] attribute to the specific divinities and realities of their mythos. I believe that while these instincts can be called 'religious' they are not well served by that term, which I therefore prefer to use negatively.

‡ Religious adherents have a positive mania for ostracism.

system. Initially, mythic idealisation and systematisation blended with and served natural life, but, around 10,000 years ago, it took on a superstitious life of its own, first overcoming reality and then, with the advent of monotheism, subjugating the world-mythos entire, until reality was seen as a poor reflection of an abstract spectacle (platonic ideas, Hebrew heaven, etc.). Although the monotheistic religion began to decline around three or four hundred years ago, the growth of this spectacle did not merely remain unchanged; it accelerated into every area of life.

The religionist today usually does not believe in a monotheistic god or a polytheistic mythos (although such beliefs are not incompatible with the religion of [post]modernity), indeed he can hardly be said to 'believe' at all now that his entire existence is immersed in an artificial pseudo-reality which has completely colonised art, culture, all knowledge, language, thought and even perception. There is nothing to believe in, for there is no position *from* which to believe; nothing left by which to grasp any kind of experience or expression that comes from without. Thus every passing phantasm, provided that the self can benefit from believing in it, becomes hyper-real, while reality, nature, direct experience and any genuine criticism based thereon appear dreamlike, unreal, laughable or, if they get too close to the pseudo-self, horrifying.

This sense of horror lies under the ordinary—ponderously literal, joyless and repressed—awareness of the religionist. It manifests as constant low-lying addiction, anxiety and restlessness, which surface as irritation in moments of boredom (no access to the narco-spectacle), impatient anger at the slightest frustration and a queasy sense of discontent. If the boredom or frustration continues, the horror rises as fury, depression, wild flights of emotional over-excitement, sadism, masochism, terror and finally, outright madness. All of this the cult member defends, tooth-and-nail, for the simple reason that he feels it. Any attempt to question *his* feelings (actually *emotions*), or the boundaries of his carefully organised and vigilantly policed categories, or the existential status of his god or his spectacle, is intolerable and met with instant rejection, insanely rationalised justification or immediate, fantastic, infantile and violent overreaction. Throw into doubt the existential status of modern gods (*rights* or *capital* or *mental illness* or *democracy* or *civilisation* or *progress*, or just *us*); point out the role that sport plays in pacifying the restless mass or the chilling dystopia of the sporting spectacle; question the need for schools, hospitals and prisons; tell people you don't work, don't drink, don't have a smartphone; talk seriously and simply of love or death; take responsibility for your unhappiness; treat words as words rather than as incantations with the power to rend and flay; criticise technology; refuse to engage in everyday feasts of emotional cannibalism; turn off the wi-fi or the background muzak or the news; live differently and happily... and see how the good people around you react the same way as religious fanatics everywhere; automatically and aggressively defending their mental-emotional identity, and its reflection in the world.

This identity, the pseudo-reality of the cult personality, exists in a realm of binary categories, and so depends upon the existence of *enemies*. The goody can no more exist without a baddy, than left can without right, and so antagonists must be manufactured at the same rate as justifications. While the cult is excluded from power, those who have power or who support or aspire to it—the king, the government, the establishment—are obvious targets, but as soon as the cult gains power it must instead *generate* moral panics (these days; rape culture, white violence and hate crimes on the fanatical left, and communism, terrorism and extremism on the fanatical right*), witch-hunts and a series of denunciation campaigns.[†] Today this means anyone who questions the need to quarantine billions of healthy adults in order to save the lives of a few octogenarians. Tomorrow it will mean something else.

The supreme power is the distributed state-corporate nexus to which powerful cult-members tend to aspire. Fanatics are not interested in radically altering the hierarchical structure of the system, or of dropping out of it,[‡] rather they desire to play the dominant role or occupy the top spot within it, at which point

---

* Not, of course, that women aren't raped, racial minorities attacked, buildings bombed, or nutty ideas disseminated. 'Moral panic' means the creation of a denunciatory environment using real crimes as a pretext.

† Lupus Dragonowl, *Against Identity Politics*.

‡ Completely dropping out that is, not just dropping out to form a new mini-state.

the state becomes Marxist, Buddhist, feminist, black or Jedi, the commissars jump ship and join Oceania, and the oppression rolls along, as was, with different *labels*, but the categorical *structure* intact and all its contentions uninterrupted. The state of yesterday's Maoist, today's republican and tomorrow's leftist (see myth 30), are all ultimately the same, for ultimately there is no difference, psychologically, between religious extremists. They are all uptight, stiff with discontent, resentful, agitated, up and down like a roller coaster, yet defiantly self-assertive; all attributes of ego, upon which every cult on earth is and has been, built.

Ultimately, there is no difference, politically, between the states that religious extremists end up creating; because they are all religious states. There is no contradiction, whatsoever, in the concepts of 'gay state', 'feminist state', 'black state', 'atheist state', 'socialist state', 'Islamic state', 'democratic state', 'rajneesh state', 'scientific state', 'totalitarian bio-fascist state', 'Jewish state', 'capitalist state', 'professional state', or 'fully automated luxury communist state'. They are all composed of powerful people telling powerless people what to do, or in more advanced, distributed, states, tending a mechanism which completely dominates the lives of those who comprise it.

'Anarchist state' though—that doesn't make sense.

26

The Myth *of* Mental Illness

Mental illness does not exist. Selfishness exists, sadness exists, fear and violence and addiction all exist, but they are not *medical* problems · · · They are automatically seen as medical problems by the system, which cannot allow individuals and their societies to take responsibility for their lives · · · The reason that the system cannot accept the true cause of 'mental illness' is because *actually* 'curing' it entails the revolutionary act of *improving reality*.

I LLNESSES are objective, physical states: alterations of cells, organs and tissues which cause or manifest as symptoms that can be detected with tests on the body. Schizophrenia, 'high-functioning' autism, obsessive-compulsive disorder, post-traumatic stress syndrome, narcissism, depression, anxiety, borderline personality disorder and *all* addictions and phobias are not, *ultimately*, physical states; which is how they can be voted into existence by the psychiatric profession. Schizophrenia, for example, was *invented* by Eugen Blueler in 1907; based on the prior invention, in 1898, of dementia praecox by Emil Kraepelin. These men based their invention on behaviour, and on their beliefs about that behaviour, not on changes in tissue caused by disease or any other discernible material fact. This is how every 'mental illness' since has been invented ('discovered' is the official term)—from homosexuality to attention deficit hyperactivity disorder to the latest collection of eating, non-compliant language and 'oppositional defiant' disorders. Such problems—and they are problems—may *cause* a physical alteration to the mind or the body, as learning the piano does, or playing computer games all day, but no causal link has ever been discovered between genes, nerves, tissues and mental disorder and, in most cases, no literal, physical correlation has been found at all. If they were discovered the patient would be passed over neurology; which is to say they would cease to become *mental* illnesses.

Mental illnesses, as Tomas Szasz demonstrated from every conceivable angle, do not exist, any more than dream illnesses exist. Problems certainly exist; despair, alienation, fear and anxiety exist, selfishness and laziness exist; but they are not *illnesses*. They are *automatically* assumed to be *physical* illnesses by those who have a vested interest in ignoring the *social* and *personal* causes of psychological and behavioural problems. Such people fall into two broad groups. One group comprises those who are unwilling to live responsibly and meaningfully. These we call 'mentally ill' PATIENTS. The other group comprises those who have been granted immense power over patients; wealth, status, exclusive access to diagnostic machinery and treatments, the power to drug and imprison people against their will and even the power to determine what is real. We call these people 'mental health' DOCTORS.

Both groups instinctively reject any suggestion that personal and social problems might have personal and social causes. The possibility that traumatic childhood experiences lead to 'mental illness', or that 'trauma' doesn't really exist, or that verbal abuse during childhood leads to 'personality disorders', or that diet can adversely affect mental health, or that schizophrenia is more common in modern, urban settings, or that pre-civilised peoples do not suffer from our mental health 'illnesses', or that society drives us out of our wits, or that there *might* be a *teensy* bit of malingering dishonesty behind phobias, syndromes and other 'conditions' are, despite all being the truth,* instantly and reflexively dismissed or rationalised away by the medical profession and by their dependent clients, for the simple reason that if it were ever accepted that *we*, and not phantom illnesses, are responsible for our problems, doctors would be out of a nice job, patients out of a good excuse, drug companies would lose the billions they make from tranquillising us and the state would have no reason to coerce and confine problematic citizens.

It is true that all illnesses that are not properly understood are, to some extent metaphorical, but when the symptoms are mainly physical, it makes sense to go looking for a physical cause. It does not make sense to go looking for a physical (genetic, bacterial, viral, structural) cause for, say, Christianity, homosexuality, boredom, fear of birds, depression, psychosis,

---

* See, e.g. *Traumatic exposure and posttraumatic stress disorder in borderline, schizotypal, avoidant, and obsessive-compulsive personality disorders* by S Yen et al, *Childhood verbal abuse and risk for personality disorders during adolescence and early adulthood* by J. G. Johnson et al, *Household food insufficiency and mental health in South Africa* by K. Sorsdahl et al, *Does population density and neighborhood deprivation predict schizophrenia?* by A. Sariaslan et al, WHO *Report on Disability, Living in America will Drive you Insane—Literally* by B. Levine, *Depression as a disease of modernity: Explanations for increasing prevalence,* by B.H.Hidaka.

schizophrenia or laziness; unless you want to pass up your responsibility or imprison or anaesthetise people against their will, or unless you are a religious devotee of scientism (see myth 23).

When members of the medical establishment are confronted with a problem which is mainly mental or behavioural they go looking for a physical cause and they rule out personal and social solutions, preferring pharmaceutical interventions and ego-appeasing therapies. They never actually find a definite physical cause, despite their many mendacious claims, which is why they* have to vote 'diseases' into existence and why they diagnose on the base of behaviour; masturbation, anal sex, hallucinations, weird language, alcoholism, anarchism, unemployment, low grades, socialism... This leads to a series of preposterous fallacious contradictions whereby patients are said to have illness x because they display symptoms (i.e. behaviours) y and z; which are caused by x. John can't sit still, therefore he has ADHD. How do we know he has ADHD? Because he can't sit still! This doesn't faze psychocrats, or put them off their desperate search for literal and physical causes of psychological suffering, for the simple reason that *solving mental problems is not good for business*.

What *is* good for business, and for the authoritarian state, is to medicalise all psychological problems, all disabling fears and all psychotic desires in order to remove 'undesirables' from society, integrate discontents into the market, via monetised narcotics and therapies, and shunt from view the cause of misery— the system and the ego which feeds it. In the past, the medical myths used to subdue undesirables, have included drapetomania (the 'disease' of wanting to flee from slave owners), kleptomania and hysteria, now somewhat out of fashion. Today such baseless myths include, 'schizophrenia', (a hypothetical disorder which no test exists to detect and which many psychiatrists do not believe in), 'attention deficit hyperactivity disorder' (an inability or disinclination to be schooled), 'oppositional defiant disorder'

---

* Many authors of the DSM-IV for example, upon which psychocrats the world over base their diagnoses of what is and is not a disease, had links with the pharmaceutical industry (Cosgrove et al., 2006). Fewer authors of the DSM-V had demonstrable links, but the fundamental fraudulence—the medicalisation of social and individual problems in the service of the market system—remains.

(refusal to accept unjustified restraint or fraudulent authority), 'narcissistic personality disorder' (anyone we don't like), 'explosive disorder' (because it's useful to pathologise people who are angry with us), 'bipolar disorder' (extreme moodiness) and the smorgasbord of fetishised phobias available to justify not having to clean the bathroom or shit in the woods. Soon poverty, unemployment, offensive language, unprofessional behaviour, genuine character and presence will become disorders to be electronically detected and medically treated. For our own good.

The modern system is, essentially, a pharmacratic, or medicalising, system. Just as land and labour must be ripped from context in order to integrate them into the market, so the body must be rationalised and all its problems medicalised. In THEOLOGICAL SOCIETIES, *religious authority* claims control over the souls of men and women, and those who wish to assert non-religious autonomy are persecuted as heretics, in 'COMMUNIST' SOCIETIES *centralised authority* claims control over land, labour, surplus and so on, and those who wish to assert non-communist control over their own resources are persecuted as 'capitalists', and in 'CAPITALIST' SOCIETIES (the pharmacratic state) *professional authority* claims control over the drugs, medical care and 'rational attitude' of the citizen, and those who wish to assert non-capitalist control over their own bodies, minds, drug-use, medical care, communities or environments are persecuted as patients, or, if their assertions enter too forcefully into the objective realm, lawbreakers.

Ultimately, of course, it's all the same thing. The sickening system. It is impossible for professionals and their dependent punters to accept the role that the system has in the cause of unhappiness, or in the formation of their attitudes towards it. They *must* therefore produce a predictable litany of justifications for their coercive interventions; 'Depression must be an illness because drugs have an effect on it' (so slight sadness is a physical illness because ice cream cheers me up?), 'Denial of mental illness equals denial of people's problems', (automatic conflation of 'suffering', which clearly exists, with 'mental illness', which nobody has ever discovered), 'We know that schizophrenia has genetic causes' (we don't), 'The division between mental and physical is an illusion' (and so unicorns somehow exist?), 'I knew someone who was depressed and they discovered she had a brain tumour—therefore depression is a physical illness' (a logical fallacy; the discovery that some bachelors are secretly married does not make bachelorhood and marriage coterminous), 'Mental illness must exist because doctors can treat it' (and devils must exist because priests exorcise them?) and, finally, 'mental illness must exist because there is consensus on what it is' (just as there was once consensus on what witches are; verification is not validity). Such arguments are essentially religious in nature (see myth 25). That genes cause depression, that love is a chemical, that smoking is an illness rest on the same kind of 'evidence' as that the body of Christ is a wafer, that Joan of Arc is a witch or that Rasputin was possessed by the devil; which is to say, on absolutely no evidence at all. Pointing this out, if you are a patient, results in more 'treatment' (more drugs, more therapy and more incarceration*) and if you are a non-patient, in denial, ridicule and attack.

This taboo, that the authority of psychologists and the pseudo-science of psychology rest on religious illusions rests upon the wider taboo, of the entire medical-disciplinary wing of the capitalist system, that the best way to deal with so-called 'mental illness' is to *improve reality*. For the doctors, therapists, politicians, managers, academics and journalists of the capitalist market system, 'society' may be to blame, but serious attempts to deal with the stress, loneliness, confusion, boredom, fear and alienation of living separated from our communities, our nature and our own selves by allowing us to return to these domains, is out of the question. You are unhappy because of a fall in your serotonin levels, or because you don't have a sufficiently well-qualified therapist, or because you're not doing enough meditating. It can't be because you're forced to spend your life running on a hamster wheel with lead boots. What you need, sir, is cognitive behavioural therapy and a mantra! You'll stay on the wheel, and keep the boots, but feel less miserable about it. Getting off the wheel is as unthinkable, as unsayable, as the greatest taboo of all in psychology, the word guaranteed to strike fear into the heart of every mental-health professional; *sanity*.

---

* Which involves the classic catch-22 of incarceration; you can only get out once you have admitted that you should be locked up.

27

The Myth *of* Psychology

Psychology is a pseudo-science; it has more
in common with economics, statistics and
law than with biology · · · Psychology is
used to make money for large corporations
and to suppress dissent; but by far the most
important function for the late-capitalist
psychologist is to expose the human mind
to bureaucratic surveillance, measurement
and control · · · Exploring human nature,
investigating consciousness and recognising
sanity are taboo activities for psychologists;
and therefore *'insane'*.

T
HE STATE-CORPORATE RELIGION OF PSYCHOLOGY is, as Karl Popper pointed out, an activity which can never be falsified and, as both Emmanuel Kant and Ludwig Wittgenstein pointed out, can never be objective. It is, in other words, a pseudo-science, like economics (see myth 2). Its spurious validity rests largely on statistics ('the science of the state'*), with which it has been, since its inception, intimately connected. Unlike a true science, psychology lacks any firm theoretical basis, has no established body of facts to draw upon and cannot make reliable predictions about the real world. It cannot even define its own subject matter.

Psychologists refuse to draw evidence about the nature of psychological truth—consciousness—from the only direct source they can ever have of it; their own conscious awareness of their own lives, which is why they have nothing meaningful to say about sanity. The objectivity they rely on—which they *must* rely on in order to join the scientific fraternity they so ardently wish to claim legitimacy from—is a sham, a monumental fraud, based on the ceaseless diagnosing, classifying, naming, categorizing, quantifying and measuring of *behaviour*, upon which they invent the fictional medical categories they call mental 'illnesses' (see myth 26).

An enormous number of young people now study psychology. Are they taught about the nature of consciousness, or encouraged to consciously experience the world? Are they helped to understand the effect of coercive systems upon consciousness?

---

* 'The young science of the state initially concerned itself with collecting demographic and economic data. Accordingly, it became known as *Political Arithmetic* in English, and later took its name from the German *Statistik*. Here begins the numerical disciplining of people and the social spaces they inhabit into various boxes, categories and packages.' R. Roberts, *Psychology and Capitalism*.

Does self knowledge play any part in their courses, or true love, or genuine creativity, or nature, or techniques for enhancing spontaneity, or for divining conscience, or for critically responding to official narratives? Are they encouraged to take responsibility for their unhappiness or to help others to do so? Do those thinkers and writers who have worked in the field and said anything meaningful about such matters—Reich, Laing, Fromm, Szasz, Peele, etc.—make it onto the syllabus? No, no, no, no, no. Instead, students are taught to medicalise problems, to label strange behaviour, to fear their own thoughts, to detest alternative ways of living or perceiving, to psychologise away problems of an ethical, social or political nature, to ignore the evidence of their own conscious experience and to view the world through the insane prism of the mutilated, modern mind. Those students who graduate in psychology, get a PhD and rise up the psychocratic career ladder, are characterised, like all successful professionals, by extreme subservience, stultifying lack of culture, an inviolate sense of institutionalised superiority and intense mediocrity; evidenced, in the case of psychologists and psychiatrists, by an inability to make original utterances about the human condition.

Psychologists are not employed to investigate human nature, consciousness or the reality of human life on earth, all of which provoke annoyance, anxiety and dread in professionals. The priorities of their employers lie elsewhere. Firstly, psychologists are employed to expand the category of 'the mentally ill' in order to expand the market for therapies and drugs. Secondly, related to this, their job is to place all responsibility for the frustrations of living in a punishingly inhuman world upon measurable elements of the human body (brain, genes, chemicals, genitals and whatnot). The idea that individual consciousness, much less society, is responsible for human misery and rage must be annihilated.* Thirdly, psychologists are employed by large

---

* "'I see you don't like doctors," I said, noticing a peculiarly malevolent tone in his voice whenever he alluded to them. "It is not a case of liking or disliking," he said, "They have ruined my life as they have ruined and are ruining the lives of thousands and hundreds of thousands of human beings, and I cannot help connecting the effect with the cause... Today one can no longer say: 'You are not living rightly, live better.' One can't say that, either to oneself or to anyone else.

corporations to make us buy more, which amounts to inducing a constant state of desire and anxiety in consumers; particularly young users of modern tech. Fourthly, alongside perfecting technologies and strategies of consumption, psychologists are employed by corporations and other institutions to control and select compliant operatives ('gifted students', 'team players', 'boardroom material' and the like). Next, related to this, the state employs psychologists to refine methods of social control and to identify threats to the market system (facial recognition is one of the most heavily funded areas of psychological research). The sixth job of psyche-professionals is to support state-military operations by enhancing the power of professional murderers (official term: SOLDIERS) to kill and torture. The seventh unspoken bullet point on the job spec of psychologists is to construct official narratives that reconcile humans to living meaningless, hopeless, atomised lives, adrift in a hostile universe (see myth 32).

This mission, creating one of the deepest ideological foundations of the system, contains two superficially antagonistic goals. The first is to take responsibility for the destruction of reality from the state-corporate system and place it squarely onto the shoulders of ordinary people, who then are expected to bear the entire load of the world's problems. If, that is to say, your anxiety, depression and rage are anybody's fault; they are *yours*. We are all, as 'the father of psychology' Sigmund Freud taught us, inherently violent, neurotic and fearful addicts. We have always been so, and we always will be, and it's up to society to domesticate us into 'ordinary unhappiness'. Indeed. But when we look closer, we find, along with this thoroughly Hobbesian view of the universe (a torture chamber that strangers must battle with each other to survive in), a psychological 'reality' that also, in key respects, completely lets individuals off the hook; for it is either a few scapegoats who are to blame for our woes (rogues, narcissists, perverts, paedophiles* and foreigners), or it's the magic of 'mental illness'. Problems are not due to the

---

If you live a bad life, it is caused by the abnormal functioning of your nerves. So you must go to them, and they will prescribe eight penn'orth of medicine from a chemist, which you must take! You get still worse: then more medicine and the doctor again. An excellent trick!'" *The Kreutzer Sonata*, Leo Tolstoy.

* Who, incidentally, are regularly conflated with hebephiles and ephebophiles.

system, or to our own cowardice, stupidity and irresponsible selfishness. No, it's because of *baddies* and *demons*. The world tells you that it is your fault, but you are not responsible, when the truth, as always, is the precise opposite; it is not your fault, but you are responsible.

The image of human nature disseminated by psychocrats and infocrats—helpless babes who must be continually watched over, supervised and disciplined—is not considered to be an invention or a theory. It is a *fact*. Psychologists are just 'telling it like it is'. The 'is', however, that psychologists 'tell it like', upon closer investigation, turns out to be life in a repressive, unnatural, sickening and profoundly coercive system which cannot function without stunted, obedient, cowards. Psychology graduates have repeatedly 'discovered' that human beings are selfish, stupid, insensitive, easily led, crude, docile and lazy—in short *both domesticated and in need of domestication*—by studying people in Western, Educated, Industrialized, Rich, Democracies. Nowhere is it noted, in the literature of psychology, that such people are deeply and disturbingly W.E.I.R.D.*

Thus we are told that without the system there would be no work, no growth, no freedom. Why? Because people are inherently selfish, violent and lazy. And how do we know this? Look at how people behave. Where? In the system!

Thus we are told that humans are selfish, violent and stupid because we are animals, which are also selfish, violent and stupid. Which animals? Animals in zoos of course, and laboratories, and marginalised, degraded habitats. Or pets.

---

* D. Lancy explains; 'Joe Henrich and colleagues challenged the very foundations of the discipline (of psychology) in arguing that psychologists fail to account for the influence of culture or nurture on human behavior. From a large-scale survey they determined that the vast majority of research in psychology is carried out with citizens—especially college students—of Western, Educated, Industrialized, Rich, Democracies (WEIRD). They note that, where comparative data are available "people in [WEIRD] societies consistently occupy the extreme end of the... distribution [making them] one of the worst subpopulations one could study for generalizing about Homo sapiens" (Henrich et al. 2010)'. Fromm is more succinct: 'Modern academic and experimental psychology is to a large extent a science dealing with alienated man, studied by alienated investigators with alienated and alienating methods'.

Thus we are told that there is no escape, no alternative (see myth 33). The universe, the world, all life, consciousness and everything we experience are literal components in a literal mechanism, one that guarantees endless toil and suffering. And how do we know this? Actually, we don't know this, but we'd prefer *you* didn't know *that*. Better not to worry though. If you have problems and frustrations, just go and see a professional to discharge your pent-up anguish; someone who refuses to have any relations with you outside of a brief, market-transaction, who never divulges personal information about themselves, never criticises you and certainly doesn't love you, who charges you hundreds or even thousands of pounds an hour for their 'services', which amount to a brief and highly artificial system-sanctioned relationship in which, for a few moments, you can feel like a King or a Queen. We're talking about psycho-therapists, but the same can be said for prostitutes. Not really much difference.

If whoring isn't your thing, you can do three Hail Marys, or an hour of yoga, or some transcendental meditation, or get smashed, or attend a support group, or positive think your way to untold riches, or faff about in an alternative reality; all firm favourites of management. Perceiving the sickening system, perceiving the puppy that suckles from it, or actually being well? Okay, fine, but just as entertainment, if you don't mind, just for a lunch hour, just for a 'philosophical chat' or to offload your feelings of frustration and despair. Not for life; this we would prefer not to deal with.

This is not a new phenomenon. 'Therapy', in the sense of integrating the individual into society and of managing sane deviations from official definitions of reality,* is as old as civilisation. All civilised societies have a theory of 'sanity' and of 'madness' and a series of techniques for 'curing' the latter so that the challenge to the social order that she represents is mitigated and she gets her mind right. These techniques include arousing guilt by stimulating broken identity with 'normal' people ('think of your poor parents!'), overcoming resistance by offering a shoulder to cry on, teaching 'patients' the true nature of the objective world (the nature of the gods, the nature of the mind),

---

* P. Berger and T. Luckmann, *The Social Construction of Reality*.

stimulating subjective states which this world depends on (such as anxiety, craving, and moral responsibility), 'conceptually liquidating' everything that lies outside of the conceptual universe of *our* world (alternative world views which are, by their very nature, not to be taken seriously; the babblings of maniacs, sub-humans, barbarians, terrorists or whatever exclusionary label is flavour of the month*) and, finally, guiding the mind of the doubter towards the terrifying consequences of deficient socialisation; namely to highlight—and broadcast—the terrible fate of genuine dissidents and mystics.

What *is* new, is the move away from repressive techniques of conditioning to an entirely *permissive* approach.† This is the most insidious, and entirely unconscious, purpose of modern psychology and psychiatry—to make the implicit, mysterious, unspoken or unspeakable life of the psyche explicit, literal, legible and manageable. This is of the utmost importance to the system. Just as every crumb of land must be measured and mapped, and children must be inculcated into a life of self-conscious accountability, and women must be forced to conform to manifest, male styles of abstract engagement with sensuous experience, and everyone on earth must be named, numbered and fixed in definable place, so our innermost feelings, urges (particularly sexual urges), intuitions, intimations and inspirations must be brought into the light; confessed, declared, analysed, written about, researched, recorded and posted. This way the nightmare of life as it actually is, or you as you actually are is banished from the manager's mind, and the unruly outsider (the deviant, the child, the woman, the foreigner) can be brought under legal, academic and medical professional control, without any need for centralised state-corporate repression.‡ Modern therapy and the justifying architecture of modern psychology allows us to 'express ourselves', to 'reach our potential',

---

* The 'fundamental syllogism' works like this; A. The neighbours are fools, B. The neighbours are anarchists, therefore C. Anarchism is foolish, and therefore not even worth engaging with ('*I don't debate with fools…*' or homos, Jews, trans-phobics, genocide deniers, atheists, heteros, [add exclusionary tag here]) for it is, by its very nature, beyond sense and reason. Ibid.

† Critics like Szasz and Laing are mistaken here; Foucault is a surer guide.

‡ Michel Foucault, *The History of Sexuality*.

to achieve 'emotional freedom'. In so doing we do not escape from the system, but enter more fully into it.

28

The Myth *of* Professionalism

The prime directive of professionals is to deprive ordinary people of the means to feed, entertain, heal, educate, regulate and rule themselves. Everything else they do is secondary · · · Individually professionals may be *nice*, and, within the constraints of the system, they may even do good, but the ultimate consequence of their activities is disorder, sickness, stupefaction and boredom · · · The late-capitalist phase of the system sees subjugation to professional control internalised, and with it, a servitude that can hardly be imagined, let alone overcome.

P ROFESSIONAL DOCTORS MAKE US HEALTHIER; professional teachers make the world more intelligent; professional policemen, soldiers and lawyers make us safer; we need professional architects to build our towns; we need professional farmers to produce our food; we need professional artists to produce our culture; and we need professional psychologists and psychotherapists to determine the nature of sanity and even reality. Who tell us these things? Professionals, and their dependent clients.

Modern professionalism has its roots in the power of priestly elites who, for thousands of years, have placed themselves between the individual consciousness of ordinary men and women, and the mystery, generosity, intelligence, and, ultimately, the conscious reality of the context or situation they live in. It has always been intolerable to priests, and to the elites they serve, that ordinary people have direct access to reality—the reality of death, for example, or the reality of sexual love, or the reality of nature—which is why they have always sought to *intercede*, in the name of divine authority, and to *dress up*; to dress up themselves in important-looking robes and important-sounding titles, and to dress up the truth in a religious dialect remote from ordinary speech. When, at the end of the medieval period, divine authority started to lose its power, the modern, secular, professional was born; identical in nature and function to the priest, but instead of appealing to *divine* authority, or using a *religious* dialect, or dressing up in *priestly* robes, appealing to *scientific* authority, speaking and writing in a *technical* dialect and dressing up in *professional* gowns.

The modern professional—the modern doctor, lawyer, teacher, policeman and technocratic manager—was born with the scientific-management revolution of the late nineteenth century which saw capitalist enterprises conglomerate into immense super-corporations overseen by an army of professional 'knowledge workers', and vast areas of human activity handed over to their ministrations. The skilled craft of the ordinary worker was broken up and its direction given to rational planners employed to manage production lines for the body of the now decapitated labourer so that they could carry out intensely specialised micro-activities with nothing but the thinnest dribble of conscious input, if any.

Likewise, the long project of the system to 'free' local communities of their power to feed, educate, care for, entertain and protect their members, reached its 'natural' conclusion as armies of scientifically 'educated' professionals took over the business of communal administration and with it the silly belief that ordinary people can take care of themselves. 'Education' came to mean compulsory attendance in a small (then virtual) room where children are inflicted with a centrally administered syllabus for ten to twenty years, 'health' came to mean access to jealously guarded diagnostic equipment, vaccines and narcotics, 'locomotion' began to be understood as the need to own a car, and 'development' was simply unthinkable without systematic dependence on massive, *massive* quanta of energy. That stupidity might result from being forced to 'learn' in an unreal, unpleasant environment divorced from ordinary society, and consume therein intensely abstracted market-friendly techniques; that ill health arises from an unhealthy environment*; that it is changes to the environment that improve health—which the medical profession has resisted since its inception†; that

---

* Cancer, heart disease and diabetes hardly existed two hundred years ago. Those diseases that did exist (TB, smallpox, etc.) were not just reduced but totally [albeit temporarily] eradicated and not by professional technique or specialised understanding of aetiology but by *environmental improvements*. The environment also causes cancer, heart disease, diabetes and all other modern illnesses. Improve the world and they will vanish. Until then doctors can tinker and 'improve' all they like, but nothing, essentially, will change.

† Smallpox vaccination became effective when it became part of wider culture and was applied independently of professional delivery. The doctors involved in developing and promoting these vaccines were considered quacks by the established professional hegemony of the time. TB was already on the decline when the vaccine was developed and had almost vanished by the time the first sanatorium

crime, suicide and madness are all consequences of systemic alienation, atomisation and inequality; that it might be possible to live within reach of our needs, to use tools that we can fix ourselves, to power our lives with the sun or wind; all such ideas are unacceptable to the capitalist professional class, for whom professionalism is synonymous with existence.

In the real world: *Hospitals make us sicker.* They deprive ordinary people of the means of diagnosing and treating themselves (even denying them, in many cases, the freedom to give birth or to die) and their privileged employees systematically ignore the cause of sickness, which is the very system that grants them power. The medical system pushes narcotic fixes in lieu of cure, eliminates or denigrates meaningful responses to pain, medicalises personal and social problems and proliferates oppressive lock-ups (official terms: CARE-HOMES and MENTAL-HEALTH CLINICS) in order to deal with the social jetsam that nobody has time to care for—all at massive profit to their providers. The idea that sickness comes from the unconscious, monocultural system, and health from independence from it, forms no part of medical training, nor can it. Individual, unique human beings, embedded in their environments, do not exist for the health profession—only cases, or instances of categories —nor does the mysterious totality of life into and from which such individuals pass. 'Life', for the medical profession, is an aggregate of probabilities which must be managed to lessen statistical risk, or flatten curves, in order to improve functional— essentially mechanistic—'health'. Such a nightmarish picture of humanity has been taken up and internalised by the consumers of this horrifying 'health', walking-talking bundles of symptoms who will stop at *nothing* to ensure that risk is minimised.

---

opened. Cholera, dysentery and others also peaked and declined independently of clinician's control. In addition, improvements in antiseptic hygiene which helped eradicate the ailments of industrial modernity were actively resisted by the medical profession of the time. The two men behind it, Joseph Lister and Ignaz Semmelweis were actively persecuted; the latter giving his name to the widespread tendency of medical institutions to reject new paradigms in health. History has demonstrated, time and time again, that the medical profession is resistant to meaningful changes to society if those changes threaten that profession. Doctors, pathetically clinging to their jobs, are all too happy to acquiesce.

Roads slow people down. High speed transport, under the pressures of capitalist expansion, inevitably places the necessities of life unnecessarily further and further away. Feet become a burden or, at best, a means by which to reach a car which, aside from its fetishistic powers of consumer enticement, becomes a necessity for every form of material transaction (at least until the internet, and automated production and delivery systems, become sophisticated enough to take over). With more and more people being forced to travel further and further away journey times inevitably increase until the productive population are spending two or three hours a day crawling along at half the speed of a bicycle.

Power stations exhaust us. The system's appetite for energy is insatiable. It uses everything available and then demands more. Social relations in a society which is completely dependent on energy-hungry machines, are inevitably dictated by the technocratic stress of fuelling and maintaining them, along with the unimaginable power of those who control (and will do everything in their power to control) energy sources. When well-being is yoked to the capacity to consume oceans of energy, those who have access to the central management such a system demands increase their power, speed and comfort at the expense of society as a whole, which is forced to subsume human needs to the demands of technocratic education, the consumption of mechanical slaves, constant warfare over energy supplies and the hyper-growth of kafkaesque bureaucracy.*

Security make us insecure. A society that must rely on professional law enforcers external to the community is one that is unable to deal with its own problems. When these law enforcers are in the pay of the state-corporate system, justice must take second place to defending the needs of the system. Individual policemen and army personnel, like any other professional, may well be decent folk (see myth 15), but they are employed by the system, *to protect the system.* There are two inevitable consequences of this. Firstly, the process of realising justice becomes slow,

---

* See the mighty Ivan Illich; *Medical Nemesis, Energy and Equity, Celebration of Awareness,* from which many of the points in this chapter have been taken. Familiarity with Illich's arguments is a prerequisite for understanding the modern world. See also David Cayley's work on Illich's life and thought.

expensive, burdened with middle-men and, ultimately, unjust (see myth 14), and, secondly, human beings become completely incapable of dealing with disagreements and differences; infants, effectively, who are forced to go crying to mummy and daddy when problems occur. The fear of 'disorder' and alternations between violence and apathy produced by 'law and order', are also inevitably fomented by other professional activities which subordinate human beings to entirely passive—and highly ordered—roles, such as providing municipal housing to poor people rather than giving away land and building materials, or allowing the homeless to occupy unused buildings; unthinkable to both capitalists and socialists.*

Management annihilates meaning. Management serves itself. Many people claim to understand this yet, at work, or in dealings with the state, ask themselves over and over again why 'they' have made such and such a preposterous decision. *'Why have they…? Why don't they just…? I don't get why they would…? But why can't they…?'* Stop right there! Large hierarchical organisations whose prime directive is to grow more and more powerful by controlling more and more life, necessarily proliferate bureaucratic functions and functionaries which exist solely to convert life into data.† Only by naming (and fixing names), measuring (and standardising measurements) and recording (everything that happens, forever) can nature and people be completely controlled; the objective of the perfect management system. If the data do not exist, or there is not enough of it, no matter; the manager either creates tests, laws, benchmarks, targets, indices, reviews, meetings, presentations, surveys and portfolios to produce more or, very often, she simply does next to nothing but cling to a privileged but wholly pointless administrative position.‡ That such 'practices' greatly impede the activity of the managed—and create even more frustration, violence, alienation, apathy, anxiety and anomie—is not just irrelevant; *it is the entire point.*

---

* Colin Ward, *Cotters and Squatters, the Hidden History of Housing*.

† James C. Scott, *Seeing like a State*.

‡ David Graeber calls this MANAGERIAL FEUDALISM; the multiplication of what are essentially idle royalty within the corporate court. The huge influx of these useless, but incredibly well-paid administrators was due largely to the colossal influx of empty cash-power that financialisation injected into capitalist institutions.

Naturally, in an intensely managed world—in which everything, including language, which is to say, *thought*, is under specialised control—none of the realities of professional life can be seriously considered, or even mentioned. They appear astonishing, ludicrous, 'utopian', or, if it looks like enough people are taking them seriously, a grave threat which must be brutally extinguished by the international professional priesthood, which will stop at nothing to protect its vast power over human life.

Professionals, it can be easy to forget, wield extraordinary control over ordinary people, who can do almost nothing of social value without professional validation, and who find that everywhere they turn to grasp reality—in art, in justice, in consciously inhabiting the body, in love-making, in spontaneous innocence, in self-knowledge and even in death—the self-serving authority of the expert stands before them. The reason it is easy to forget the immense and pervasive power of the educated middle-man, is because professionals, who dominate education and media, *never mention it*. They know that their authority rests on illusory credibility, on quasi-addictive dependency and on inculturated irresponsibility (the belief that nothing can be done without professional intercession; that it is *teachers* who educate us, *doctors* who dispense health, *lawyers* who solve problems, *politicians* who run the country—not us), and they know that the beliefs they indoctrinate us with,* despite being drummed into children from moment one of their 'socialisation', and despite being more widely accepted than any religious belief in history, are actually more fragile than snowflakes. And so even the suggestion that people are not born to be passive consumers of professional services, that they do not need successively more complex tools by which to live or a cadre of intensely institutionalised monomaniacs to determine their needs, must be treated as outrageous heresy.†

As we enter the final stages of the system the ancient professionalism of the priest, the classic professionalism of the

---

* Unconsciously of course. Professionals, like all coercive parents, just think they are generously 'doing the right thing' for the benefit of their clients. They care; which is why they are so surprised and baffled by the 'ingratitude' of those who refuse their altruistic ministrations.

† Ivan Illich, *Disabling Professions*.

enlightenment, and the modern professionalism of industrialisation, give way to an even more pervasive and oppressive form of management; the postmodern professionalism of post-industrial society. Institutions—closed, bordered, slow, rigid—are not well suited to immaterial, networked forms of production, surveillance and control,* and so many tasks previously managed by institutionalised professionals become automated and 'distributed'. This automation process combines the artificial intelligence of powerful computers with the artificial stupidity of powerless people, forced to watch, teach and discipline themselves in order to engage with online work (including 'job seeking') and 'society' (talk to friends, pay bills, consume culture, etc.). Automated and semi-automated surveillance, data gathering, classification, rating and performance management systems demand constant *self*-management (and self-censorship) to successfully engage with. Productive units in modern economies must now master techniques of time-management, anger-management, self-branding, self-control and emotional labour which formerly a professional expert imposed. Modern people, motivated by anxiety, precarity and rootless momentum, must construct the corporation of the self and launch it alone upon the high seas of the late capitalist market. They must be their own workers, supervisors, CEOs and shareholders, which allows actual elites and upper management to fade into the background while the tasks of lesser professionals (teachers, journalists, designers, pilots etc.) get absorbed by AI, dumping their bewildered practitioners into the mass of precarity.

The ongoing death of the middle class is much bewailed—by the middle class. It would be funny, were it not that the halfmen once employed to oversee the school, the barracks, the church, the office and the asylum are to be vaporised, diffused through the worldbrain and then installed in your mind.

---

* Byung-Chul Han, quoting Gilles Deleuze, *Postscript on the Societies of Control*.

29

The Myths *of* Pseudogender *and* Monogender

The self-mastery of masculinity and the
mystery of femininity are both existential
threats to the system, which cannot allow
men to be men or women to be women
$\cdots$ The first consequence of living in the
system is *pseudogender*; gender as a sexist
fact, which leads, in turn, to *violence*, as the
sexes *no longer* understand each other $\cdots$
The second consequence of living in the
system is *monogender*; gender as a feminist
spectrum. This leads to *boredom*, as the sexes
can *only* understand each other.

MAN IS BORN SPLIT from a conscious, contextual presence which woman never really leaves. This split— the division of an *absolute* embodied experience of reality into a *relative* emotional-conceptual lattice of this and that, here and there, me and you—is what we mistakenly call 'intelligence'. Woman is also capable of cutting herself off of course, and susceptible to being split too, but her intelligence is ultimately more immediate, spontaneous, apt, selfless, creative and absolute; all qualities which the system denigrates or actively punishes. The world refuses to recognise female-type intelligence, in women or in men, *as* intelligence for the simple reason that the world was made by insane men.

In a sane world, man strives to reintegrate his cut-offness into an embodied reality that most women never entirely abandon. This mission, which takes man about forty years to realise, is what we understand as 'becoming a man'. Women do not *become* women in the same way.* She embodies a primary *intelligence* which he, merely *clever*, strives, for much of his life, to realise. When he ceases to strive in this way, she loses her respect for him and eventually, as his attention becomes corrupted by its rootless, relentless self-referentiality, she begins instinctively— often unconsciously—to hate him for his inveterate selfishness; a hatred, or distrust, that lodges deep within her psyche; reappearing once a month. All this wounds man, and, if he has any integrity—if he is what we might call 'a real man'—inspires him to raise his game, the two of them working together towards a mutual state of embodied dignity and psychological freedom manifesting as gendered sanity, togetherness or that rare state of unity in difference, COMPLEMENTARITY.

---

* Unless society 'pre-splits' them. Then we find socialised women on much the same dreary mission as men. See *Self and Unself* for further discussion.

In an insane world such reintegration is denied man. His self, and its cleverness, are the be-all and end-all. He still strives, but not now to consciously master his self and integrate it into the context, but to *control* his self and, through this control, subordinate the context *to* his will, his fucking will that is; to impregnate every woman on earth. To achieve, in other words, extrinsic, worldly, COCK-POWER.

A widespread premium on extrinsic male power leads to a society formed of male hierarchies, which is to say, warfare for top positions in a pyramid of sexual selection filtered by the approval of women who desire extrinsically powerful men and who use their *own* extrinsic CUNT-POWER (using youth, beauty, fertility and the vague promise of sex) to acquire top cock. Men and women in such a society come to resemble self-informed *caricatures* of maleness and femaleness; the men being openly aggressive, hyper-rational, sexist, filthy and obsessed with domination and the women being vain, bitchy, utterly unreasonable, masochistic, physically feeble and obsessed with manipulation. These identities, sometimes known as 'traditional gender roles' are not gender. They are PSEUDO-GENDER; clichés built on a *pre-modern* civilised system that rewarded such exaggerations.

As the system progresses, those within it become more and more cut off from their innate, natural, conscious and gendered connection to the natural or social context. All that is innate, natural, conscious and gendered is then completely ignored or actively (albeit unconsciously) perceived as a threat, and exterminated. Man is denied all opportunities to engage in his odyssey and woman is denied the capacity to embody, or to recognise, her inborn intelligence, let alone express it. A new form of madness begins to develop in which the entirely unnatural, or disembodied, thrives; the MONOGENDER.

Initially, as only a small group of elites can cut themselves off from contextual reality, gender begins to dissipate in only the highest classes of society. As power spreads, and more and more people can *afford* to live an entirely egoic life, so monogendered characteristics and priorities begin to spread down to the middle classes; the middle men who organise the expanding system. In the most decadent phases of societies such as Greece and Rome such middle-men were still very few. In the *modern* world, they represent an enormous number of people. Most people in the

West have almost nothing to do with nature, with society, or with their own bodies. Everything they experience comes through the mediated market, which is incapable of recognising, valuing or promoting any kind of *genuine* difference, complementarity, self-mastery or mystery.

What the advanced market recognises is an insane form of maleness—hyper-abstraction, intense egoism and explicit violence—blended with certain market-friendly attributes of depraved femaleness—subservience, emotional volatility, passivity and implicit aggression. These attributes are, ideally, to be found in every genderless 'body' on earth. This it calls 'DIVERSITY'.

Note that the term monogender does *not* refer to a breakdown of 'traditional gender-roles'. Such sexist, pseudo-gendered, pairings *do* get roundly—and correctly—rejected by the professional class, but along with these our *innate* gendered dispositions and sensitivities are also effaced. Natural, innate gender and unnatural system-friendly pseudogender are then indistinguishable. Gender, complementarity, and all forms of innate maleness and femaleness appear, under such conditions, 'sexist'. The monogendered woman begins to ambitiously fight her way up through male hierarchies to 'battle sexism', while her ally, the monogendered man, denigrates all hierarchies as sexist (an integral part of postmodernism: see myth 24) while, allied to increasingly powerful pseudo-male women, creating independent hierarchies of his own.

Two apparently opposing cultural forces turn out once again to be essentially the [oppo]same. The pseudogendered are motivated by a desire to scramble up established rankings in order to gain access to a maximum number of female automatons addicted to men who possess power over the flesh pyramid; while the monogendered are motivated by a desire to create their own hierarchies predicated on the fantastic idea that gender does not really exist. The rejection of 'sexism' by monogendered feminists is made to appear revolutionary and progressive, but turns out to be the same sad fear of fundamental difference and shoddy lust for extrinsic power; the only kind that pseudogendered sexists *and* monogendered feminists understand. The innate need for men to master themselves, to achieve or be worthy of a state which women—sane women—never leave, the miraculous complementarity of gendered domain (his extrinsic genius and her intrinsic genius) which has united lovers for millennia* and LOVE, a state which, for obvious reasons, is never intelligently addressed or expressed by either monogendroids or their sexist counterparts; all this is invisible or reduced to cliché and sentiment.

I mentioned 'monogendered feminists'. Note that we are *not* talking here about women who help out other women, or who value femininity, or who are repulsed by the insensitive, self-loving, power-hungry, half-blind, hyper-abstract children who call themselves 'men'. Nor are we talking about so-called 'first-wave' feminists, who fought for the vote. Despite being misguided (as democracy is misguided) this clearly made *some* kind of sense (as, indeed, voting occasionally does). There are all sorts of feminism, just as there are all sorts of democracy. When I say 'monogendered feminists' I am referring to women who are estranged from nature, from society, from their own bodies and, most tragically of all, from their own mysterious, innate, terrifying and loving femininity. I am referring to women, and men, who belong to a club which is founded on gaining power within the civilised system and on justifying the appalling gender-deformities that the modern system creates. This is pretty much mainstream, or 'third-wave' feminism, the kind you read about in the Guardian or the New Statesman; although many of the views of second-wave feminists, such as Germaine Greer, radical ('fourth-wave'?) transgender activists and many other unhappy folk also fall under the term as I use it here.

Returning to pseudo-gender. Sexists deform gender by caricaturing it, by focusing only on those qualities, feelings and ideas which reinforce extrinsic power. Man is a man, says the sexist, and woman is a woman, and we all know what that means; he protects his gal, pays her rent, hurtles round the world on magic carpets fucking other women and never cries; while she gabbles on, takes care of the kids, gets emotional and frets about her shoes. He cannot perceive her competence, her intelligence

---

* See e.g. *Sex equality can explain the social structure of hunter-gatherer bands* by M. Dyble et al, and *The Cambridge Encyclopedia of Hunters and Gatherers*. As I mention in the Introduction, we can never know for sure how people lived tens of thousands of years ago. *Ultimately* our only guide is self-knowledge, tempered by what facts there are; facts which indicate that domained sexual equality was the norm.

or, most terrifying of all, her depth without turning his entire world on its head, and so he keeps her in what he deceitfully thinks of as 'her' place while immersing himself entirely in his own cut-off play-palace.

The masochist ally of the sexist, sadist man, the doormat woman, is terrified of standing on her own two feet. She is dependent on his power and his attention—what dwindling morsels he offers after the honeymoon—and she is hypnotised by the fantastic belief that one day her love will change him,* that he will love her again like he used to. Meanwhile, she contents herself with artfully directing his priorities, buying shit she doesn't need, overeating, daydreaming her life away, fussing over her instagram account or taking what love she can get from children and animals (her substitutes for true love; just as business and sport are his).

The sexist world-view is consecrated in all 'fallen' ideologies, which are founded on the assumption that women are, with the notable exception of mummy, whores; interested in nothing nobler than protection for their unweaned child and ever-ready to deceive men to slope off with a more powerful penis. No sooner had man formed his first civilisations than myths damning diabolical woman appeared to justify his fear and consequent subjugation of the strange, wild intelligence she embodies. Over the course of ten millennia superstitions evolved into religions which then evolved into science (specifically evolutionary psychology), but the sexist attitude to women remained essentially the same; men are superior to women or, in the case of modern, monogendered feminism, the male mind is superior.

Yes, you read that correctly. Modern feminists *exalt the male mind*. Conditioned by male styles of awareness, or wishing to succeed in the male world, they exalt man's cut-off hyper-abstract egoism—insane hyper-focused, hyper-rational, scientific 'intelligence' or 'realism'. Compelled to substitute her embodied presence with intellect, anxiety and ambition, she becomes estranged from her own feminine nature which she perceives as a threat; or, at best, childish, naivety. She may wear lipstick, watch weepies, have children or even be attracted to domineering apemen, but her strange and awful intuition, her radical

---

* It might, but I wouldn't count on it.

generosity, her miraculous presence, sensitivity and love are as alien to her as nature is. A genuinely intelligent monogendered feminist is a contradiction in terms—they have no idea what feminine intelligence is and they never express or support it.

In order to be able to think and act as men do, such feminists uncritically accept fundamentally male styles of experience and perception, and then, to justify their profitable self-alienation, seek to efface gender completely. There is, they assert, no such thing as masculine and feminine. Innate sex differences, which have been discovered 'at every level of analysis',* are a patriarchal conspiracy, and all the classics of art and culture which express innate gendered differences and the mystery of their complementarity, along with all the evidence we have that men and women lived in egalitarian *gendered* societies for 99% of human history; are all lies. The 'truth' is that 'gender is a spectrum', that society determines gender and we are all free to choose our own gender identity (or fuck whoever we want†), held back only by the existence of nefarious 'gender stereotypes', which (despite being mostly accurate) limit our 'freedom'.

---

* Sex differences between men and women have been discovered at every level of analysis. There are sex-differences in how our brains work—in the amygdala, hypothalamus, and hippocampus—and in basic neurochemistry. Our cells are different, the chemicals in our bodies are different, our bones and muscles are different. See, amongst many others, Saraswat et. al., *Evidence supporting the biologic nature of gender identity*, Amber Ruigrok et al., *A meta-analysis of sex differences in human brain structure*, Simon Baron-Cohen, *The Essential Difference* Melissa Hines, *Brain Gender* and Ivan Illich, *Gender*.

† This is the thesis of the popular *Sex at Dawn*, by Christopher Ryan and Cacilda Jethá; that gender is a modern, social invention and that our 'natural' state is therefore one in which men and women think and behave like men, having sex with whoever they please. The outrageous bias and sheer incompetence of their argument (notwithstanding a few decent central chapters) is exhaustively detailed in *Sex at Dusk*, by Lynn Saxon, which despite itself being a biased (and BIASTIFIED; see Introduction) account of human psychology, resting entirely on the insane hyper-objective scientism of Neo-Darwinism and its inflated assumptions about the role of genes in evolution, is a far more measured, complete and fair account than Ryan and Jethá's which, as Saxon correctly points out, 'reveals itself as a contemporary middle-class, child-free, sex-obsessed, male fantasy projected back onto prehistory'.

These 'truths', alas, aside from being incompatible with science, art,* all of human [pre] history and the sane gendered experience of loving couples, also contain a couple of nasty contradictions which feminists would prefer not to explore. The first is that women seeking access to the male world, to 'traditionally male' top jobs, are forced to claim that gender is the result not of nature, but of nurture, in order to justify a position in the system gained through the exercise of their will. Yet, oddly, they are unwilling to entertain the possibility that a world created by men, which forces everyone within it to act and think like men—insane men at that—masculinises women and estranges them from their embodied femininity.

Another contradiction inherent in the ideology of feminist monogender revolves around the totemistic notion of 'diversity'. The Monogender Myth has it that we are all the same, that differences between men and women (and between black and white, straight and gay) are *really* illusions. Unfortunately, because those who promote such ideas are all very keen on getting good jobs, they also have to promote the idea that institutions must accept women, black people and homosexuals in equal number. Why? Because we need diversity. And what does diversity mean? It means we are all different!

Feminists and their allies are unwilling to explore these contradictions, to accept that men and women are different and therefore possess different sensitivities and skills, to explore the real reasons why men are more violent and more easily (and catastrophically) addicted to porn and VR, to accept that sex differences tend to be greater in individualistic, gender-egalitarian societies,† to address the parlous state of young men in today's world, or to admit that they are attracted to men who behave like men; who are courageous, who can perceive when no *does* mean no, and when it *actually* means, 'try in a better way', who can master themselves and the skills that males excel at, such

---

* Women have had the chance to be queens, prime ministers, presidents, CEOs, consultants, judges and army generals, but sitting alone in a room with a guitar and writing a song equal to 'Pennies from Heaven', 'Sunday Morning' or 'I Want you Back' has somehow been denied them.

† See *Taking Sex Differences in Personality Seriously* by Scott Barry Kaufman, which provides a good, measured, general overview of the science of sex difference.

as making maps, building houses, writing symphonies, hauling slag and taking super-sensitive *manifest* charge.

This intellectual dishonesty, along with the strident emotionality and loveless unconsciousness of feminism, is based on a masculine experience of power within the capitalist system, the entire locus and point of prominent feminist discourse. Not a day goes by without an opinion piece published in the corporate press lamenting that women do not have access to positions of capitalist power, or exalting notable capitalist fiendesses (such as Hilary Clinton, Margaret Thatcher or Julia Gillard), or demanding that all references to gender be expunged from our culture; yet, oddly, not *quite* so much attention is given to raising up the powerless classes (see myth 4) composed of several *billion* miserable women, to levelling structural hierarchies, or to meaningfully addressing the problems that men and women have living with or loving each other within the confines of capitalist 'civilisation'. Love is completely ignored by monogendered feminists. They never use the word, or, if they do, reduce it to the usual red herrings of compromise, companionship and sexual desire.

Woman has had the vote for over a century, she has participated in the male economy for half a century, she has had access to top jobs for a quarter of a century, and soon she may well achieve complete equality within, or even dominance over, the system. And yet the system remains unaffected. Prominent modern systemacrats are falling over themselves to promote equality, monogender-rights and 'gender-intelligence'. And yet the system remains unaffected. The mythos of the world—its movies, novels, newspapers and adverts—are full of powerful, fuck-hungry women dominating contrite, emasculated men. And yet the system remains unaffected. Funny that.

Remove the distorting influence of the system, its insane hyper-egotism, its [consequent] separation from nature, its hostility to embodied awareness, its destruction of culture, its fundamental sexism, its gender-effacing priorities and characteristics (domestication, human and animal, is well known to reduce sexual dimorphism), its limited selection of remunerative tasks and its total ignorance of love and you remove everything that creates the warped sexual psychology it rewards; which is why prominent defenders of monogenderism have no interest, whatsoever, in meaningfully criticising the system, or its roots, any more than their pseudo-gendered sexist counterparts do. If they did, if gender-rights crusaders made any *real* effort to deracinate the world-brain, they would uproot the cancerous tree they wish to climb.

A note on Criticising the Left

M ANY PEOPLE ON THE LEFT who have read up to this chapter will have been nodding and sighing with appreciation only to discover *what!? He's against us!* The fact that I have spent the majority of the book criticising the racist, sexist, disabling, elitist, unnatural system will go out the window when they read that I am *also* criticising the so-called 'radical' left. How can it be? We're the good guys! *We* would never construct an identity out of our beliefs, huddle in identity-reinforcing groups and violently suppress outsiders. Look, we're the *victims* here. We're innocent.

Victims you may be (or may not—a lot of radical agitation is made by extremely comfortable folk), but innocent? I think not. Innocence comes from independence from the system and from its egoic roots; something which large numbers of socialists, feminists, leftists and radicals have no interest in. They are trying to change the system so that it gives *them* power, prestige and comfort, and thus leave its foundations unaffected, even unexamined.

It goes without saying that I believe the sexism of the system, the kind outlined in this chapter, along with its racism, its hatred of any kind of difference (such as men who have sex with other men), its suppression of true creativity (genius and scenius), its obliteration of nature, its violence towards children, its unending brutality towards the poor and the psychological abominations that the system allows to own and run the world are all worse than a few entitled nobs noisily declaiming in the paps on the subject of gender-neutral toilets and the 'right' biological men have to give birth, or a few menopausal hags squashing dissent under the banner of 'feminism' (or taking revenge on a male world that no longer pays her court), or a few [white or Uncle Tom*] university students demanding 'safe spaces' or publicly swooning at the 'n-word'.

My point, in this chapter and the next two, is not that leftism (feminism, socialism, anti-racism, etc, etc.) is worse that rightism (sexism, capitalism, racism, etc, etc.), but that it is *misguided*. It is, for the most part, aiming at the wrong target, for the wrong reasons, and in the wrong way. Of course it is right to stand up against violent racists, dogmatic priests, corrupt bosses and so on, but the target, as this entire book is attempting to show, is not *them*. It's not 'the right' or 'men' or 'sexists', or 'racists'. It's not even the hyper-wealthy, the professional class or capitalists. Even if rich, right-wing, sexist, racist, professional men are currently in capitalist power, the problem, and the target is not old, fat, white, heterosexual men in suits. It the system; and *the system* doesn't *care* what colour, sex or shape you are, or what ideology you follow. Many of the cruel, cynical, mentally and spiritually-deficient moral vacuums in charge, they care—but the system doesn't.† If *you* care, then you are barking up the wrong tree. In fact it's not a tree, it's a lamppost, and by the time you get to the top, the lights will be out.

---

* I am referring here to black people who are given access to the media platforms of the system and then use that access to explicitly criticise racism (or the 'racist system') while implicitly sucking up to the civilised system which makes slaves of us all.

† The people in charge of the system might lock up socialists or persecute environ-mentalists, but, as we have seen in the *Myth of Truth* and as we shall see in the next three sections, the system *encourages* you to fight them, to rebel, to be a 'radical'.

30

The Myth *of* Catastrophic Offence

The religious instinct to treat both words
and ideas as real leads to the creation of
powerful and power-serving religious *taboos*
· · · These taboos actually *serve* the system;
by ignoring power, which is the source of
violence, and by raising the wall between
what can and cannot be officially said. This
permits the violence of power-relations to
be concealed by gentility, politically correct
language, advertising campaigns and other
totemistic presentations · · · Questioning
totems is intolerable to groups which are
jockeying for first-position within the system,
whether they are on the left or the right.

WHEN SOCIETY IS RUN BY PRIESTS, any idea which criticises their God, or their right to rule in His name, is deemed 'heresy'. When society is run by uptight, nationalist capitalists, any idea which throws their sadistic power into question is judged to be improper, unpatriotic or hysterical. When monogendered feminists, homosexuals and metrosexuals gain or are granted power, any idea which questions their foundational ideology, that gender does not exist, becomes unsayable. When drug pushers and mind police are granted the power to determine reality, invent phantom illnesses and implicitly conspire with malingerers, so-called 'ableist slurs' enter the lexicon of the damned. And when a few members of hitherto excluded racial minorities are granted their own big desk, then 'racist language' is given the power to instantly render all within earshot subdued and tyrannized.

As soon as women, homosexuals and racial minorities were fully admitted into the workplace, so feminism, LGBT, anti-racism and disability rights campaigns became integral elements of [late] capitalist ideology. But it is not simply as a capitalist advertising campaign, or in straightforward defence of group-power that criticism of any woman must now be rendered 'sexist', or criticism of any black man 'racist', or criticism of any politician 'abusive', or criticism of the conceited, the selfish, the lazy or the stupid 'ableist'. There is another reason why modern states and corporations—the most dishonest, repressive and destructive organisations ever to have existed in human history—are scrupulously fair, respectful and tolerant in their use of language and publish guidelines on the correct language to use when referring to disabled people, women, 'people of colour' and members of the LGBT 'community;' another reason why, although the global south is poorer than it has ever been, black people are more marginalised than they have ever been, ordinary people are more disabled than they have ever been (less able to use their legs to move, or use their mouths to speak and be heard, or use their hands to do things), and femininity is more rigidly suppressed than ever before; another reason why we are less able to use words that might offend women, the poor, black people or the disabled. Corporate power is hyper-vigilant about offensive language because, in order to conceal its inherent, *implicit* racism, sexism and classism, it *must* be scrupulously just in its formal, *explicit* speech and behaviour.

There are two reasons for this; for taboos on 'offensive language' (on insulting prophets, calling girls 'chicks', rape jokes and so on) and for continually decamping from one word to another 'safer' one (e.g. from 'the n-word', to 'black', to 'person of colour'). Firstly, the sanctity of taboos upholds the religious belief upon which the system is founded; that words, ideas and emotions are as real as things and that a bad word can smite those who hear it senseless (particularly women for some reason) as if from a percussive blast. In this way can all the lies of the system, conjured from thin air, be given the material ground that credibility demands, while all intellectual criticism and verbal mockery be banished *as acts of violence*.

Secondly, taboos don't just ignore the source of racism, sexism, etc, but, ultimately, they raise the wall between formality and informality higher. Children, friends and a few banished comedians will continue to use non-standard words, but we must now use the *correct* word in public. This actually *serves power*. Without the formal smokescreen of inoffensive language, the actual repression and bigotry of criminal state-corporate activity would be visible. Thus a standard matrix of prohibitions is employed to conceal capitalist power-relations and personal egoic insanity behind gentility. Only a stupid or angry slave owner uses racist language, only a drunk upper-manager calls his wage slaves 'plebs' and only an ageing comedian calls women 'birds'. An elite, racist, sexist system is far better served by limitations on such language, for the same reason that the most abusive parents never explicitly suppress, belittle or even criticise their children.*

* R.D. Laing put it this way: 'Rule A: Don't. Rule A.1: Rule A does not exist. Rule A.2: Do not discuss the existence or nonexistence of Rules A, A.1, or A.2'.

This is how 'racism', which actually means indiscriminate, prejudiced hatred of or violence towards *an entire race* ('I can't stand black / white people') has come to mean bias, criticism or antipathy towards *a group of people* who are of the same race ('I can't stand *those* black / white people'). Wealthy and powerful people, and their occasionally well-meaning professional servants, seek to conflate the two in order to redefine popular resentment of their privilege into forms of racism. Thus criticism of Israel, or animosity towards isolationist groups of *wealthy* Saudis (Jews, Russians, whoever) or revolutionary ire directed at the dominance of institutions by certain races (old, white, Anglo-Saxon CEOs for example) must all be understood as 'racist'. Such misdirection is not difficult, as those who express their frustrations at privileged groups, or at immigrants shipped in *by* privileged groups to destabilise local workers, frequently make the same error; assuming that, for example, *rich* Brit is synonymous with *Brit* (or *White Author* is synonymous with *White Man*, or *Bogan* is synonymous with *Australian*).

Concealing *actual* prejudice and ensuring that just criticism or even doubt be conflated *with* prejudice or violence (disagreement with a zealot is taken as proof of guilt) is why Western governments and public figures bend over backwards to accede to demands for correct usage and to express contrition for semantic transgression. Modern power is quite happy for language to be policed, books banned, free speech curtailed, criticism criminalised, 'racists' sacked, 'sexists' reprimanded, a rigidly policed taxonomy of spectres take the place of reality and words conflated for the things they represent. The system is also quite comfortable with a 'radical' movement which requires a massive and powerful pyschocratic-punitive legal apparatus to make them 'safe' from 'abuse', from 'hate speech', from various forms of 'phobia' and from catastrophic thought crimes which stand in for 'all the things I don't like'. The system, in other words, welcomes the modern LEFTIST.

The modern leftist (extreme versions of which are called 'SJWS' and 'INTERSECTIONALISTS'), usually some kind of [political] feminist, gay rights activist, anti-racism campaigner or member of a racial minority, complains about privilege, yet is typically a member of the privileged classes (ideally with a working-class accent). The modern leftist complains about 'victim-blaming' yet never criticises the system which relentlessly suppresses the idea that the environment causes conflict, crime, physical ill health or outright madness. The modern leftist complains about 'objectification' yet sees the entire world and everyone in it as a collection of categories; you are not an individual, you are 'white' or 'a man'. The well-to-do leftist regularly expresses 'solidarity' [i.e. intense identification] with those most affected by the system (the global poor and excluded) while making demeaning professional interventions in their lives and patronising pronouncements about how they should resist the system. The modern leftist complains about 'fragile egos', yet demonstrably possesses a self so extraordinarily delicate and brittle, it can shatter at (be traumatised, triggered, even infected by) a word. The modern leftist complains about 'being silenced', yet shuts down all criticism immediately and ferociously with arguments largely based on belittling interlocutors, or ruling out their entire view based on a single piece of information, rather than on making a persuasive case. The reactive leftist regularly meets fact, knowledge and truth* with feeling†—'what you are saying is irrelevant, because it makes me feel threatened, offended and angry; and because you do not belong to my category, you can *never* understand this feeling'—a minority version of the standard mainstream position; reality is what we say it is. The modern leftist has a great deal of difficulty speaking for himself; opinions are prefaced with *'as a'* [homosexual, white man, writer, mammal]. The modern leftist believes himself to be cruelly abused, not just constantly harping on the actual insults he receives ('see how awful they all are! look what names they call me!') but constantly interpreting as derogatory pretty much anything that is said about him (or about groups with whom he identified). The institutional leftist believes herself to be a crusading radical while aspiring to state control or professional advancement, regularly supporting centralised, hierarchical or artificially distributed power, happily working for a large corporation, or implicitly supporting apparently opposed ideologies (e.g. the absurd collusion between feminism and Islam). The postmodern leftist often claims that knowledge is a product of

---

* Which are not the same thing.

† Actually, *emotion*. See *The Apocalypedia* and in *Self and Unself*.

one's race, privilege, gender and so on, yet demands that her *intensely* relative philosophy* take first place on the institutional syllabus. The modern leftist—black and white, male, female and transgender, able-bodied and disabled, socialist and capitalist— is *terrified* of the total abolition of the system.

These characteristics, along with their herdlike self-reinforcing groupthink, their uniformity of opinion on matters of importance and the astonishing mediocrity of their intellectual output, would suggest that the modern leftist is, in a general sense, a morbid, masochistic infant with no self-confidence, beset by a chronic sense of inferiority, bitter, reactive, essentially uncreative and without a sense of humour. Individuals vary, one to the other, and, tragically, a massive number of decent, intelligent, easy-going, gentle and genuinely creative people are attracted to leftism, as it seems to offer fairness, freedom, kindness and so on, without too many inconvenient sacrifices. Unfortunately, this is an illusion. Reform is impossible.

The mirror image of the left-wing identity politician, fundamentally identical but for superficial details reversed, is the *right-wing* identitarian. There is no *fundamental* difference, for example, between white supremacists and modern third-wave feminists. The identity is different, as is their proximity to state power, as is their general intelligence and behaviour (*obviously* the knuckle-dragging goon is a different beast to the effete identitarian) but the character is the same; absent, which is why the identity is clung to so desperately. Both modern leftists and rightists see the world as a collection of categories, both rely completely on the system and refuse to critically examine its foundations, both believe, despite ten millennia of evidence to the contrary, that world-society can be controlled (through autocratic rightist edicts or rational leftist plans), both yearn for power or the security that power-relations offer, both are, in lieu of anything deeper than identity, extremely up-tight and, consequently, both fly off the handle when their identity, or the religious ideology that is based upon it, is intelligently criticised. Truly, they deserve each other, which is handy because while one exists, so will the other.

---

* The philosophy of the modern left is an extreme form of 'nominalism', the magical idea that if you change what something is called, you change the thing itself'.

31

The Myth *of* Reform

Reform is the lightning rod and relief valve
of the world system. It deflects desire for the
overthrow of the system into negotiations
for re-arranging its constitutive elements
· · · The principle actor in reformist projects
is the ambitious, professional *stagversive*
· · · Stagversives may be good people, and
their work may lead to more people living
in more comfortable cells, but they have
no interest, whatsoever, in freeing men and
women from the prison.

O CCASIONALLY WORKERS GET CHEESED OFF with carrying out meaningless tasks for a meaningless system, with being systematically exploited and robbed of the power to determine how they work, with dragging themselves back to the storage units they call 'home' in order to dream of more classrooms and corridors, and they begin to express their frustration and anger in indifference, resistance to scheduling, sabotage, high turnover, neglect, abseenteeism, presenteeism (WORKING TO RULE; doing no more than is contractually necessary and precisely following all regulations), hostility, rage or madness. The entire purpose and meaning of management is to devise ways to counter such rebellion, to replace the people the system uses with machines, to make men and women satisfied with their alienated confinement, or, at the very least, unable to effectively resist it, and to paralyse them with fear of official enemies (or official viruses). And yet, still, periodically, even the most 'efficient' management system falters and the slaves threaten their masters—then it is time for REFORM.

Reform is the emergency mode of the capitalist system when faced with widespread radical opposition; a means of releasing the steam of revolutionary pressure without changing the mechanism which produces it. It comprises three stages, each of which is carried out with great fanfare; 1. *Wave money.* The simplest and, in the long run cheapest solution to discontent is to chuck a few more bananas at the monkeys. Most men and women will swallow their principles for a pay rise, furlough cash or a tax cut. 2. *Grant limited or superficial reforms.* The second stage is to make a few limited concessions, pass a few laws that ease the burden, allow clients to fill out complaint forms, put a comments section on the website and hand out a few upbeat stickers. 3. *Grant temporary reforms.* Finally, if nothing else works, give in and wait. As long as the system itself is unaffected, it remains in charge and can bide its time until a more opportune moment comes to 'roll back' vernacular freedoms and traditional, contextual rights.

The key actor in the process of reform is, naturally, the reformist (a.k.a. STAGVERSIVE or professional activist / leftist). This is an institutional employee, usually a journalist or elite academic, who makes a wage or diffuses her frustrations by pushing for change without criticising the host organisation (the company or government he or she works for), without seeking to remove the state and, critically (and this applies to unofficial leftists) without attacking the root of the system. This she does by focusing on secondary solutions to secondary problems. Intolerance, the glass ceiling, violence towards women, the erosion of civil liberties, digital addiction, bad science, corruption, financial speculation, paedophilia, unpleasant working conditions, the decline of the honey bee, unjust politics, anti-Semitism, lack of diversity and the rise of fascism are all fair game for, generally, the system opposes these things too.* Redistribution of wealth, systemic exploitation of land and labour, thought control in a democratic society, radical self-knowledge, truthful utopia, genuine revolution, profound insurrection, unconditional love, the reality of death, consciousness and other terrifying 'subjectivities' are well off the menu for the 'radical' *and* her system.

Likewise, giving workers the power to vote for employee of the month, beer in the office, wacky Zoom avatars, gay bosses, community spirit, bean bags in the coffee room, amusing posters, sexual innuendo in the coffee room, family days, staff discounts, limited control over production, anarchist-trousers and, for the miserable millions building the profits of Amazon, Apple, Walmart, Primark, Cargill, Bechtel, Aramco, Ikea and Tesco, a *slightly* higher wage than they could find elsewhere— yep! Allowing workers the chance to control the entire production process, as men and women once did, by mastering craft, allowing them control over surplus, allowing them power over management, allowing them to take back control of their fates from professionalism, meaningfully integrating the company with the environment, and genuine, human spontaneity and generosity—*no, no, no, no, no.*

---

* See T. Kaczynski, *The System's Neatest Trick.*

Although those in power make an immense fuss about the slightest stagversive activity, the system actually requires reformists in order to effectively function. It needs, above all, obedience (which it calls non-violence, community spirit, etc.) from everyone, whatever their colour, gender or sexual preference, and privileged 'radicals' are happy to serve by campaigning for tolerance, inclusion, trans-rights, equal pay and whatnot. Left-wing journos, market-friendly radicals and career leftists provide and even police the limits to acceptable discussion; any idea left of the liberal press is, *ipso facto*, insane. They are a lightning rod for genuinely revolutionary unease, channelling demands for a different system into inconvenient but, ultimately, harmless, amendments to the current one, such as endless bickering about the number of crumbs the poor should be served on the welfare table; a 'debate' which keeps left-wing politicians, trade unionists and liberal journalists nice and busy while society slowly, but safely, rots.

A similar function, on a smaller scale, is played by everyday cynicism, fantasy and even comedy. Ordinary men and women, living entirely conventional and brutally predictable lives of domesticated subservience frequently deal with their inhuman routines and herdlike consumption of spectacular drugs by mocking *them*—the stiffs, the weirdos, the others or those fools out there. 'We're different', say the suburban couple, 'we can laugh at the world'. 'I'm different', says the bank clerk, 'I'm *really* an artist, a dreamer, a revolutionary, mad!' Such attitudes strengthen the power of the system, which panders to a sense of specialness and actively encourages the irresponsible, ironic or marketable distance from the world that daydreaming,* escapism, cynicism and irony open up.

Without the eco, female, 'radical', artistic, comic, cynical and philanthropic veneer of free speech created by stagversive *care* for minority rights, the environment, working conditions, corrupt politicians, fat cats and so on, the fundamentally repressive and

---

* 'We may be startled to find that the person in the office next door, whom we had always pitied as a pathetic 'unreflective accomodator to routine', is not only busy distancing himself madly from all around him, but is doing so in exactly the same way as we are... We are [all] trapped again in routine, the routine of distancing'. S. Cohen and L. Taylor, *Escape Attempts*.

iniquitous nature of the system would be easier to perceive. As it is, elites can point to their pinko chums in the newspapers and movie studios and say, 'look how free our society is!' That stagversive columnists also help pull potential radicals into the advert saturated pages of The Guardian and the New York Times just happens to be by-the-by.

If reformists ever do reach positions of power they find themselves forced, by the structure of society, to subdue and oppress those they dominate and to serve the needs of the system. As Michael Bakunin noted, this partly explains how 'the most raging rebels become the most cautious of conservatives as soon as they attain to power'. It matters little whether the power is in a capitalist corporation, a professional hierarchy, a democratic parliament or a socialist trade union. Authority (the authority of power, that is, not the authority of presence, character, intelligence or experience) corrupts. A little work is required to deal with the bad dreams and guilt that authority entails—crusading convictions must be reshaped, whispers of conscience suppressed—but no biggie. A marvellous sense of mission, a swollen pay cheque, and the arousing energies of mass attention all carry the newly promoted effortlessly through their midnight doubts. For a while.

Some stagversives gain their power by being granted it from the ruling elites they oppose. One of the most terrifying sights for authority has long been a large, violent crowd, or the prospect of one. Rioting mobs intent on upturning the system can be suppressed, but a far more effective technique is to appoint powerful leaders and spokesmen, which automatically funnels attention towards tractable, manageable interactions. There is always the danger of the wrong kind of leadership arising though—one that refuses power, inspires the people to listen to the voice of their own conscience and freely act on it for themselves. That won't do! What authority wants is the *right* kind of revolutionary; someone who will negotiate; or, failing that, someone who, if they gain power, will keep the basic structure of the system intact.

The archetypical reformist, who gave his name to the quintessential reformist movement, was Karl Marx. Marx was a brutal authoritarian, famously manipulative and an enthusiastic proponent of war, work and progress, all governed by classically Graeco-Judaic deterministic laws, filtered through the totalitarian scholastic jugglery* of Georg Hegel. His attitude towards nature was domination, his attitude towards the peasantry and the urban poor was contempt[†] and, crucially, his attitude towards an organised, central state was... that *he was in favour of it*. He simply added, to his contradictory declarations about the state, the proviso that it should eventually be run by workers and should vaguely aim to 'wither away'. Meanwhile; 'there can be no talk at present of achieving communism; the bourgeoisie must first come to the helm'. Marx detested those who *actively* opposed the principle of statism (that is to say, anarchists) and who sought revolution beyond the authoritarian bounds[‡] of his vanguard; upon one of whom, Pierre-Joseph Proudhon, Marx performed one of the most disgraceful hatchet jobs in intellectual history, and then stole his ideas (notably the surplus theory of value[§]). Finally, Marx had absolutely *nothing* meaningful to say about any matter of real importance to men and women outside of economics and the effects of capitalism.

Marx would not be revered as he is if what he had said had not contributed so much to the human library. Marx's

---

* Schopenhauer's words.

† The *lumpenproletariat* was his dismissive term for the latter; although he believed that all men were, faced with the 'forces of history', dispensable.

‡ Bakunin put it this way; 'Marx is an authoritarian and centralising communist. He wants what we want, the complete triumph of economic and social equality, but he wants it... through State power, through the dictatorship of a very strong and, so to say, despotic provisional government, that is by the negation of liberty. His economic ideal is the State as sole owner of the land and of all kinds of capital, cultivating the land under the management of State engineers, and controlling all industrial and commercial associations with State capital. We want the same triumph of economic and social equality through the abolition of the State and of all that passes by the name of law... We want the reconstruction of society and the unification of mankind to be achieved, not from above downwards by any sort of authority, nor by socialist officials, engineers, and either accredited men of learning—but from *below upwards*, by the free federation of all kinds of workers' associations liberated from the yoke of the State'. [my italics]

§ Marx, of course, like all writers, great and small, took an enormous amount from all kinds of people (Blanqui, Fourier, Saint-Simone, etc.). The point here is that he took key ideas from the very man he was pillorying and *misrepresenting*.

critique of capitalism contains many peerless observations, and the Marxist tradition contains some veritable masterpieces,* but Marx's plan for revolution (communism that is; hatched with his capitalist friend, Friedrich Engels), was the very model of self-seeking reformism, which explains all of its salient features; its record of catastrophic failure, megalomaniacal corruption, enervating compromise, state-capitalist exploitation of the working classes, obliteration of nature, cockeyed priorities,† conspicuous disinclination to make the slightest change to the basic structure of the bureaucratic / technocratic system and rampant, unconscious, egoic groupthink.

All forms of Marxism, communism, trade unionism, authoritarian, democratic, Fabian, parliamentary and 'eco' socialism, along with syndicalist forms of anarchism, are, in these respects, identical to capitalism, feudalism and fascism. If one evolves into another, *nothing changes.* That socialist movements often comprise decent folk; that socialist states, trade unions and syndicates *do* occasionally offer vital protection against extreme forms of [private] capitalism‡; that communist critiques of capitalism are often superb; all this is, ultimately, irrelevant. None of the political systems of the so-called left have, despite lip service, any interest in doing away with the entire system, nor are their ideological priorities fundamentally in any kind of conflict with it. The left wishes to preserve property rights, professionalism, money, progress, work, iniquity (either centralised state power or artificially distributed corporate-technocratic power) and all the other foundational components of the anti-world. This is why kindly, fair, compassionate socialism so frequently ends up looking like a classic totalitarian nightmare. You would have to be raving mad to oppose the NHS, or higher pay for teachers, or more welfare for the poor, or unconditional UBI, or higher

---

* The works of Mumford, Ellul, Braverman, Illich and Chomsky for example may or may not be 'Marxist', but they certainly draw from Marx's well, as do I.

† Such as seizing the means of production, for example, in a late-capitalist world in which *everything* is a means of production, or placing revolutionary action almost entirely into the hands of *workers*, with everyone else relegated to a support role; an approach also favoured by anarcho-syndicalists.

‡ I myself have, out of sheer desperation, voted for socialist leaders and mooted unionising at work.

corporation tax, or more council homes, or more jobs for the working classes—indeed it usually is nutters who do oppose them—but all of these initiatives strengthen the second most totalitarian institution in world history; the state. That the *most* totalitarian institution in world history—the capitalist corporation—makes much the same criticisms, and rushes into the breach when socialist states are dismantled, does not make them any less true, or any more right wing. The fact is that, despite their protestations to the contrary, their individual good nature and sympathy for the poor, the good they do fixing people's teeth* and providing bike-lanes, and, in many cases, their enthusiastic flashing of radical credentials, socialists are engaged, usually from positions of extraordinary privilege, in the task of organising, from the top down, *a bearable system*. They are thus bound, forever, to futility, contention, repression, exploitation, ruinous technical progress and stultifying compromise with technocratic power, constant interference in people's lives and proliferating bureaucracy; in short to totalitarian FASCISM.

A fact of history which socialists are keen to forget, or to excuse, is that fascism originated, at least to some extent, in Italian socialism. It was first branded 'right wing' by the Soviets in Russia in order to distance the 'right' kind of socialism (their own; Lenin's, Stalin's, Mao's) from the 'wrong' kind (Hitler's and Mussolini's), a definition taken up, with added emphasis on hyper-nationalism and morbid romanticism, by Roosevelt (a fascist) and Truman; but, despite their foundational capitalist elements and their reliance on the support of capitalist landowners, all these polities were based on powerful, 'classless' states (Mussolini and Hitler both had massive support from workers, managers and owners; if anything it was the capitalist class, unhappy about rising wages, who were least enthusiastic), generous nationalised welfare (health insurance, public housing, etc.) unionised workplaces† (Mussolini's unions were called

---

* Including mine, by the way. I use the NHS, have benefited from state hand-outs and had *lovely* teachers. I'm not an unlovely teacher myself, although I have noted, time and time and time again, that the only people who can be taught anything are those in no need of teaching.

† Hitler's semi-socialist unions, the German Labour Front, replaced independent trade unions.

fascio, hence *fascism*), 'social justice', democracy,* technocratic progress and other such left-wing-friendly initiatives.†

'Oh, but that's the *wrong* kind of socialism!' cries the reformer, who wants a national health service, heavily unionised workplaces, a powerful professional-class, mass democracy, money markets, [green] industrial technology and a profligate welfare state, but also, magically, a reality in which these unnatural, anti-human techniques and institutions somehow give power to nature and to human nature. It doesn't matter what reformists say, or how nice they are, when their actions inevitably strengthen authoritarian, hierarchical systems, radical monopolies and dehumanising tools which create forms of control that, functionally—*actually*—are no different to those which private capitalists, centrists, [neo] liberals and company stooges brazenly extol. Leftoids either do this unwittingly, or, with varying degrees of shiftiness, they suppress their awareness of the disastrous consequences of what their instincts to do good end up producing when channelled through the state, or through technocratic institutions. Castro's Cuba is, quite obviously, nothing like Mussolini's Italy, and clearly Podemos is not headed towards National Socialism, and, while we're at it, obviously Corbyn is not Lenin. The point is, their systems ruin man and nature for the same reasons that capitalist, feudal and totalitarian systems do.

When the socialist state, academy or guild has completed its work, it is, firstly, entirely run by the kind of people able to force their way up the immense authoritarian hierarchies that states entail, and eliminate opposition (Stalin, Kissinger, Blair, etc.) and, secondly, and more importantly, *it is still an institution*; which is to say, *a system-integrated conglomeration of enforced habits.* Institutions control by creating and compelling people into pre-defined patterns of conduct; system-friendly cliches. The specific laws, processes and players are irrelevant. The institution,

---

* Hitler and Mussolini were both democratically elected (and had the overwhelming support of ordinary people, who rarely felt any sense of 'oppression') although both immediately took steps to dismantle the possibility that they could be democratically ousted (common behaviour for democracy-enthusiasts), or that their plans could be significantly interrupted.

† Nazi animal welfare policy, for example, was the best in the modern world.

by forcing people into institutional habits, *automatically* destroys spontaneity—which is to say conscious response to the context, which is to say *humanity*—through existing in and as the system, making any kind of structural reform completely futile. Add to this the overwhelming dominance of the modern technocratic market system, upon which all institutions (and therefore all habits within them) are *completely* dependent, and the ridiculous futility of socialist reform, of changing this or that law, of voting for this or that nice guy, of protest and petition, becomes clear.

Think of it this way. You can have a socialist in charge of an oil tanker, the kindliest old captain imaginable; but to what end? Oil tankers are vast machines, which can only run on and transport equally vast quantities of poisonous crude oil. While we are forced to work on oil tankers, only a fool would vote for a capitalist captain; but what good can a socialist captain actually do with this ship? Can he use it to transport people? Fish for crabs? Can it be 'scaled back'? Can he use it for *anything* on a human scale? He cannot. No matter how fair and friendly the captain is, the time comes when we need to stop listening to what the company tells us to do, take our tanker to a country where people know what to do with scrap metal, and then smash the damn thing up.

In opposition, reformists, who are either keen to essentially preserve the system or are simply too cowardly to radically oppose it, tend to extol entertaining, celebratory, largely passive forms of protest ('*Great day out at the march! Twitter storm tomorrow guys!*') along with quietest philosophies of complete pacifistic acceptance; an approach which has always been tremendously popular with power. Quiet reflection, meditation, godliness, good-hearted simplicity, peacefully loving the police and the like have been praised by princes and kings—and, obviously, by their professional, priestly, employees—since the dawn of history. Pacifism and 'being nice' are, in their place, terribly good for business,* although nowadays mindfulness is the thing; using ancient (and potent) techniques of self-mastery and acceptance to suppress the conscience, rage, fear, despair—and,

---

* Pacifism at home that is; all that loveliness is rapidly defenestrated when it's time to butcher baddies abroad who, coincidentally, are sitting on an underground ocean of oil.

most horrifying of all, the urge to dispel them with *action*—which prostituting oneself to a dystopian cyborg evokes. Much better to do a bit of yoga or mass-meditate with breast-feeding mums than blow up a dam or take down a power station. Co-opting such techniques, and the perennial philosophy they are built upon, also persuades would-be dissidents of their 'self-indulgent', 'introspective' uselessness, and deprives potential miracle workers of the incandescent essence of revolution; their own conscious—and utterly subversive—experience.

Such experience, despite being the wellspring of actually effective revolution, plays at best a secondary role in reform. For reformists it is, first of all, *society* which must change—through the actions and plans of states and professionals. Those with a yen to change society through law, policy and command like to believe that society is relatively simple thing, that the effects of tinkering with it can be predicted, that there will be no unforeseen side effects of their actions, that it is possible to gain actual, meaningful power over large numbers of people and that entrenched self-interest and the power conferred by money, property and institutional status can be overcome—that all we need to do is to replace the baddies in charge with goodies—while ego, money, property and professional institutions continue to exist. Most absurdly, they believe, or act as if they believe, that the dominance of the technocratic system is a secondary concern, and need not be considered when campaigning for political change. History, science, the wisdom of people who understand how the world works, all available evidence and common sense say otherwise, but nevermind all that. Reformists aren't interested in seriously considering reality, or civilisation, or the ultimate point of their activity, any more than doctors are, or teachers, or politicians, or academics, or journalists. The lovely sense of purpose they get from their work, the day to day hustle and bustle, the *nice* system-friendly ideology they base their articles and even their personalities on; all of this would crumble if they turned their minds to 'paradigm disputes'. That it is *the system* which is in charge of society, that society can *never* be rationally controlled, shaped, planned or designed without unforeseen catastrophe, that the most powerful autocrats, the fastest computers and the most benevolent and moral crusaders are completely impotent before the forces of society, nature and the global system in which they are constrained, that it is rank futility to appeal to kings, governments, CEOs, bureaucrats and other leaders to solve the problems of the system they depend on for their power; all this is heresy of the first order for the reformist, and to even suggest such a thing in her presences makes her quake with anxiety.

Reformists and leftists have no interest *whatsoever* in discovering what the system really is or how to actually overcome it. It doesn't matter that the ideology of professional minds is heading towards some kind of marvellous multicultural paradise and that of thick-skulled nationalists is heading nowhere; because ideology is irrelevant to what actually happens in the world, just as what a man says about himself is irrelevant to who he actually is. Leftists *say* they want love, peace and harmony, they *say* they want the same thing as genuine anarchists—a stateless, classless (and possibly even low-tech) world—but who they are, how they think and what they do, *serves the system*. They are every bit as pathetically servile before its needs as capitalists and rightists are, every bit as uptight and mediocre, every bit as violent; just clever about it, and clean. Neither group has the slightest real awareness of their own conscious self, nor do they have any interest in allowing humanity to create, from the bottom up, a world formed by its own hands. The prospect of allowing the intelligence of nature to intelligently guide ordinary people terrifies them; and it will continue to terrify them until *they* are on the bottom, and forced to use *their* own conscious self to build something meaningful with *their* own hands.

32

The Myth *of* Meaning

There is no meaning in the system, nor can there be. The system only understands, and only *can* understand, expansion · · · Meaning is the result of *conscious being* and of *purposeful doing*, both of which are impossible within the system and violently suppressed when they appear · · · The perfect system is therefore comprised entirely of unconscious people performing meaningless tasks.

W ITH EVERY PASSING YEAR fewer and fewer people need to be persuaded that life in the system is mean- ingless, although many are still convinced that the consolations, addictions and surrogates they use to fill the void that system-life creates, are overflowing with purpose.

Meaning, or reality,* comes from two places,† CONSCIOUS BEING and PURPOSEFUL DOING. Conscious being refers to the experience of consciousness that precedes, or is aware of, thoughts, emotions and separate sensations. This pristine sense of 'I' is occasionally sensed, or felt, after a long refreshing sleep, before all 'my' ideas slot into place, or in moments of stillness, when I am stunned by beauty or when, perhaps for no other reason than a walk in the park, I feel, all over my body, a profound *rightness* with life. Recognition, or *knowing* what is happening, takes me out of this experience into ideas, names, words and objects, which are all *relative* experiences; which is to say, known through relation and comparison. I know what the idea 'The big cloud above me' means by references to various relative scales, such as big-small, white-dark, fluffy-hard, above-below, here-there, and so on, but no such *abstract* knowledge is involved when the big cloud above is *actually* raining on me, or when I hug someone I am completely in love with, or in moments of sporting brilliance, when I am one with the ball, or after a hard day's work when I step into the shower. Neither do I make relative assessments in moments of great shock, when I am stunned, by pain or loss or even embarrassment, into a full experience of what is. In such

---

* We are not, therefore, talking here of rational, intellectual meaning. There's certainly little of that in life. Tolstoy said, 'the only absolute knowledge obtainable by man is that life is meaningless', but he was conscious there is an ineffable, intimate *truth* to life, and that is what I mean here by 'meaning'.

† Or, rather, one place seen from two different perspectives.

moments time seems to slow down and sensations become more vivid. This is because conscious being is not a partial, mental event, located in the head, but a complete physical one. The entire body is conscious—an experience which we register as vivid, bright, intense, actual and full of meaning; while mind-made time, as we normally experience it, is a relative mode of experience which takes our attention away from the conscious body and into *ideas* of the past and the future.

Naturally there is no problem with time, with thinking and feeling, or with picking separate objects out of the blended present. They are all useful tools; indeed the first tools that humanity ever used. The problem appears, as with all tools, when they take control of the user. When woman can no longer experience her body directly without thinking, without feeling time press upon her, without a restless need to do or to buy something; when man cannot experience the present moment directly, when all experience comes via the thinking mind, when the strange, elusive intensity of life is instantly translated into comprehensible ideas, plans, desires and theories; then confusion and unhappiness become constant companions, the planning and recollection of time-awareness become endless anxiety and worry, and all talk of the radical awareness of conscious being sounds silly, self-indulgent and, in a complete reversal of the fully sensate truth, abstract. It also feels, to the relative self, uncomfortable, weird, worrying.

For ten millennia or more, the tool of the self has been in charge of human affairs,* working to eradicate the threat of selfless consciousness, and the threat of the selfless CONTEXT with which it is indissolubly blended. Selfless† states of conscious being, such as empathy, spontaneity, creativity, presence, or any other uncensored response to the context, have been unconsciously perceived as existential dangers of the first order by every monarch, state, party, priesthood, profession, government, board of directors and irresponsible parent‡ that has ever existed.

---

* I call this 'self-in-charge' EGO, by which I do *not* mean the Freudian 'ego'. For Freud the 'ego' was different to the instinctual 'id' and the hyper-rational social 'superego'. In truth there is no real difference between these divisions; they're all ego.

† Or 'self-soft', what we might call 'tool-less', states of being.

‡ See *How to Brainwash Your Children* in *The Apocalypedia*.

This threat becomes greater with each successive generation. When the organs of the system—INSTITUTIONS—are still young and 'within reach' of those who created them, laws, habits and customs are still, at least partly, informed by the context; they are still relevant to society as it is, and those who created them still have some kind of power over them. But when a new generation appears, for whom institutional processes have become divorced from their original context, the 'way it's always been done round here' on the one hand doesn't seem to make so much sense, while, at the same time, through expansion and reinforcement, seems more real than it ever has. Key texts—once questionable and mutable—become fixed and sacred; pioneers—once human and responsive—become deified and beyond reproach; and, most insidiously, unspoken norms become *reality itself*, breach of which is perceived, by specialised elites now in charge of this objectified reality, as, at best, impudence, and in more serious cases, as sacrilege, madness.*

Because the original meaning of the institution cannot be so readily accessed by new generations, a great and ever greater effort has to go in to interpreting, explaining and teaching 'the way it's always been done' to them, and coercing or punishing deviance, which, notwithstanding the monolithic mind-shaping organs of the system, is surprisingly straightforward. It is easy to instil compliance because, as the system evolves, the matrix of institutions† which comprise it covers more and more aspects of life. The language, the science, the 'facts', the recipes, the laws, the habitual actions, the justifying myths and the pre-defined roles that form the warp and weft of institutional life increasingly define, construct, control and predict everything the individual does; and, consequently, everything he can *think* about what he does. This is how the handed-down reality of the institution becomes reality itself. The mind can find no escape, and all attempts at escape feel like depravity, insanity or just plain silliness (although this does not mean that silly, insane and depraved acts are effective escapes). In other words, because you

---

* P. Berger and T. Luckmann, *The Social Construction of Reality*.

† These institutions, the 'sub-institutions' (departments, classes, and so on) within them, and their 'sub-universes' of meaning, are frequently at odds with each other and jockeying for power; which gives a false impression of 'diversity'. Ibid.

can think about the human world you are fooled into believing it is somehow sensible or right. Knowledge about the world *is* the world. You can, and probably do, criticise the constituent elements of the system—the government is bad, our institutions are failing us, civilisation is falling apart—while, *through* the criticism, remaining an integral part *of* that 'world', which, therefore, still somehow makes sense, feels 'right', maybe even is 'worth fighting for'.

This is how all attempts at rebellion get effortlessly subsumed into the mythos of the system. The original thought, the inspiring slogan, the radical art, the rebellious speech are all manifestations of conscious revolt; and as manifestations—definable, storable, saleable, controllable intellectual objects—they are *automatically* co-opted.

Likewise, everything we feel and do is absorbed by the system; once it has been made explicit, measurable, literal; graspable by the mind. Ambiguity, intimacy, vagueness, paradox (not to mention the great ungraspables, love and death) cannot be allowed into the advanced institution. They must be interpreted, confessed, recorded, posted, *available*. The biological model of mental illness, the mapping of all life, the systemic suppression of artistic truth (and the exaltation of entertainments in which the ineffable plays a subservient role, such as sport, cooking, travel, and all kinds of mediocre music and drama), the bureaucratic profiling of every person, action and emotion on earth (abetted by therapy, education, confession and digital communication), and the absorption of the incomprehensible, the elusive and the unpredictable into the crude literalism of science, indeed all literalism (postmodernism, feminism, blokeish common sense, etc, etc.), are all unconscious moves, fuelled by unconscious threat of the abyss, in this totalising, totalitarian, direction.*

---

* Craft too, sane specialisation, must eventually go out of the totalitarian window, along with local and even national difference. Genuine individuality is automatically 'hollowed out' by the monolithic pressures of institutional modernity. The certificates of professional expertise remain, the flags and football teams of national 'identity', the symbols of local pride (animals, plants, craft processes) but the private and particular reality that these things refer to is long dead, merged with the systemic mass.

Perception of this threat has to be unconscious, for consciousness is the threat. Consciousness, and [active experience of] the context it illumines, is the *only* escape from the pseudo-reality of the system. This is why the system ceaselessly works to suppress consciousness, along with all its qualitative manifestations, while never recognising that this is what is happening. Dissidents are silenced for security, systems men are promoted for their talents, background music is played for entertainment, motorways are built for transport, cellular networks are made more powerful for 'communication', refrigerators are manufactured for convenience, forests are felled for profit, society is uploaded for efficiency, unruly folk are tranquillised for their own good, spontaneity is banished for propriety, children are locked up for their safety, everyone is under constant surveillance for their own protection, laws which curtail psychedelic drug use, handling of dead bodies, free sexuality and self-sufficiency are passed for dignity or decency or some such other thing and technologies (or rationally-organised activities) proliferate which demand standard responses and suppress, ignore or punish impulse, individuality, reverie or fully sensate awareness (such as driving a car or using a phone or playing a video game) so that we can all live 'normal' 'happy' 'lives'. All these reasonable, fair, fun, beneficial and logical activities end up suppressing consciousness, dulling the senses, separating men and women from their own nature and from each other, and sucking the incarnate joy from life; but that's neither here nor there for the system, or for those who serve or willingly submit to it, none of whom are capable of directly recognising what they have lost.

The second (and secondary) source of meaning, after conscious being, is purposeful doing. This means exerting oneself to achieve a meaningful goal. For the history of mankind—*millions* of years—this has entailed feeding, clothing, heating and housing oneself, forming close bonds with the members of one's society, finding a mate and raising children, truthfully expressing experience and playing; and all autonomously, consciously and with an immense amount of skill naturally acquired from nature and culture* without compulsion, or even instruction.

---

* The distinction between the two, like that between work and play, being a modern, and artificial one. See P. Descola, *Beyond Nature and Culture*.

Needless to say, none of this is acceptable to the system, which must force humans into entirely subservient roles, and, in order to do so, must remove their capacity to provision, care for or express themselves. In a highly developed system, people find that no skill, whatsoever, is required to keep themselves alive.* Only obedience. They find that they are unable to have direct relations with their fellows, which makes them feel lonely; they find that, in matters of cultural achievement, skill is a positive handicap, which makes them feel inadequate; and they find that they are prevented from directing their own activities in any meaningful sense, which makes them feel frustrated.†

To counteract the prodigious loneliness, inadequacy and frustration that the system causes—and, handily, to generate further realms of market expansion—the system must provide people the opportunity to engage in *meaningless* activities; that provide nothing but solipsistic stimulation (porn, teevee, VR, drugs), that require minimal skill (modern art, modern university courses, collecting stickers, journalism), or minimal autonomy (schooled education, waged work, Disneyland), or, if they satisfy man's‡ need for independence, that have no bearing on the overall functioning of the system (cycling around the world, mastering yoga poses, getting in the Guinness Book of Records) or, if they satisfy man's need for a challenge, that actively support the system (winning the world cup, becoming CEO of Snapchat, wealth gathering). Humans must be encouraged to believe that all of these activities are just as 'meaningful' as genuinely purposeful doing.§ They must be persuaded to pour

---

* With the partial exception of professionals, who must be skilled in a fantastically limited—which is to say pathologically specialised and market directed—sense. See Jeff Schmidt, *Disciplined Minds*.

† T. Kaczynski, *Industrial Society and Its Future*. Kaczynski's analysis of the consequences of being deprived of purposeful doing is peerless. The role of conscious being does not, however, figure in his work; which explains the fact that he felt killing university professors was a good idea.

‡ And it does tend to be *man's* (see myth 29).

§ Not that these activities *are* totally meaningless. Rather they are not as meaningful as (indeed on a completely different level of meaning to) purposeful doing. If they were genuinely purposeful, they would not be allowed. As Kaczynski says, '*we can do anything we like as long as it's* UNIMPORTANT'. There's a parallel here with

their personalities into such hobbies and ambitions (which, again, in a totalising environment is easy) and, consequently, to violently reject criticism of them as personal attacks, thereby divorcing the cloud of oppressive futility and boredom that hangs over the planet from the surrogates and stand-ins for an authentic life which cause it.

The ideal, for a perfect system, is a world in which everyone is completely unconscious—unable to feel love, empathise, act spontaneously or honestly experience the present moment as it is, in all its mysterious intensity and strange intelligence; and in which everyone is totally dependent on the system—physically, emotionally and psychologically domesticated, deformed to fit its requirements and, ideally, not just unable to see their deformity, but actively celebrating it.

---

reform. Writing petitions, protesting in the street, voting, fretting over poor black people and girl's STEM grades and so on are not always completely meaningless either—but they are not in any sense revolutionary and, again, if they were, they would not be permitted (see myth 31).

33

The Myth *of* Eternal Necessity

The system presents itself as the only way humans can possibly live · · · Nothing else can ever be seriously attempted, or seriously suggested; because the system is *reality itself* · · · Anyone who does seriously attempt or suggest an alternative to the system is ignored, laughed at, disposed with labels, such as 'utopian', 'extremist', 'narcissistic', or destroyed.

THERE IS, AS MARGARET THATCHER famously told us, *no alternative*. The market system is the only system that works, or can work. Revolution will get you nowhere. Do you really want to live like a medieval peasant or a communist drone or a miserable dropout? The message is: You cannot win. The world cannot change. This is how it has always been, and how it always will be. This ultimate truth is common to all dominating systems. What is real is what is both necessary and inevitable. Nothing else has worked, because, look, here we are in the only reality which *is* working. See?

That there is a different way of organising society, one that takes the best aspects of pre-civilised egalitarianism, feudal conviviality and even, yes, perhaps even a little modern technology; that there have been glimpses of free and fair societies even in recent times; that the reason there haven't been more is that the system has crushed every one of them; that networks of mutual aid, based on our innate intelligence and generosity, have threaded through history; that humans are innately intelligent and generous—not to mention peaceful and just—as amply evidenced in the anthropological record of pre-agrarian societies; once again none of this can be seriously considered or acted upon.

Likewise, utopian thought must be limited to superficially tinkering with capitalism. A radical alternative to the system, which naturally, effortlessly and completely returns power, freedom, conviviality, complementarity, responsibility, autonomy and the natural world to ordinary men and women; which seeks to revolutionise consciousness from the dominating ideologies of the system and the dominating influence of the so-called civilised world; which allows labour and land to form themselves into the miraculous playground they could easily be; which sources its inspiration from the scenius and genius of utopias and utopians past and present; all of this must be confined to the vaguely amusing fantasies of unrealistic dreamers.

The standard means of disposing of such dreams is, firstly, to brush them off instantly, without reflection ('*I threw the book across the room!*'); secondly, to laugh at them ('*hahaha, no cars! no laws! no money!*') or at the person who expresses them ('*hahaha, ridiculous shoes!*' or '*hahaha, he's criticising society and here he is participating in society!*') or at the first nutcase that can be found who agrees with them ('*hahaha, one of his followers is a fruitarian!*') or at the style in which the ideas are presented ('*unfocused word salad!*'); thirdly, to pay hasty, unreflecting, but highly reactive attention to them (freaking out at trigger words); fourthly, related to this, to focus laser-like on isolated utterances divorced from their context (the entire point), basing fantastic misrepresentations upon them ('*you're criticising the left, therefore you are an ally of the right*') or highlighting irrelevant errors ('*he understands nothing; look, he got a number wrong*'); and finally to continually demand rational details. To ask, for example, how a functioning Utopian system would handle selfishness, the distribution of surplus and nuclear weapons.

Most rational questions like this can, as we shall see, be answered (*people*, as opposed to systems and institutions, would handle them), but the point is that a move from qualitative critique to quantitative detailing, *removes the quality*—the point, the context and the ring of truth. Imagine talking to a learned seventeenth century English farmer about his unhappiness with feudalism, or this 'capitalism' thing he was suggesting, and then asking him how an international high-tech debt economy which depends on infinite 'growth' is supposed to function. Imagine presenting to him the image of a modern computer processor factory plonked in the middle of Stuart Hampshire and asking him what he would do with it, how he would propose to run it, how would it integrate with the economy. Imagine protesting that 'people would never understand' or that 'the gentry aren't going to like it'.

All ridiculous; and capitalism is something which is, in essence, based on fact (it is describable, quantitative) and egoic emotion (it demands anxiety, craving and violence to function). How much more ridiculous to ask such questions of a critique which comes from a source which is prior to, or greater than, such facts and fears: an ultimately *unmanageable* reality; the quality of life and our innate sense of it.

But of course quality—the intelligence that precedes ego—is what the system was built to annihilate and supplant. This is why we have the nightmarish sense that love is going out of the world. We do not have direct relations with our fellows, or with our environment—everything goes via the system—which provides a constant watertight excuse for treating everyone in the world *as* an object, as entries on the books; as clients, staff, patients, punters, the population and the people. And as the totalising system replaces all direct relations, so it takes on the status of reality itself, a.k.a. 'the real world', a 'realistic' realm of practicality, necessity and normality, where 'tough decisions' have to be made, to be sure, where impressive share dividends necessitate scorching the planet bare, sadly, tragically. But that's just how it is. Get real!

It is, says the system, 'unrealistic' to feed the poor, to redistribute wealth, to let the wild flourish or to dramatically reduce energy consumption. It is unrealistic, in other words, to improve reality. This is like saying it is unclean to clean a dirty floor, because by cleaning it you are removing its current level of cleanliness. The current level of reality in the system is no reality at all, but *that* is 'the real world'. Do you see? It doesn't matter if you do or if you don't, because, as we have seen, the alternatives to unreality cannot even be perceived, let alone imagined. You may *believe* that there is something wrong with 'capitalism' and we need this thing called 'socialism', you might protest, you might hate all the *really* bad baddies, you might even riot; but Thatcher spoke true, unwittingly of course; no alternative can be imagined. Imagination within the system *is* the system. It has always been so, since ego took control of consciousness, but now the system has colonised every last corner of experience. Precarity, technophilic addiction, a constant diet of drugs, unnatural diet (of food and information), lack of meaningful activity, loneliness, total estrangement from the wild, being forced to consume a dead culture, relentless monitoring, assessing, training and testing, and the diffuse background anxiety of living in a portacabin which is hanging over the edge of a cliff combine to block out the light completely. The system now *constantly* reproduces itself, in the mind of system man and system woman, *as* the system. Any genuinely revolutionary movement, any great art, any natural expression of humanity which comes from outside of this waking nightmare, even an accidental moment of honesty, strikes the system mind as nonsense, non-truth, non-reality; unrealistic.

'Oh yes, money is evil, but we all need money don't you know—without it we'd starve!' 'Oh yes, the law is an ass, but without law there would be anarchy!' 'Oh yes, capitalism, awful isn't it? but look at Stalin. Socialism doesn't work, does it?' 'Oh yes, sounds lovely your Utopia, but who's going to organise it? How can we vote for them? What exactly is your plan for bringing it about' 'Oh yes, I know, there is absolutely no hope that politics can make the slightest difference to your life, but what else are you going to do?' 'Oh yes, overcoming my self, I did that once. Did nothing for me'. Such objections appeal to objective facts, objective realism,* the illusion of reality produced by the system mind and, over ten millennia of history, projected *into* reality as the world. And how can you oppose the world? You'd have to be off your rocker! Can't you see that it is *unrealistic* to put inspired teachers in schools and great artists on television and let them say what they want? Isn't it *obvious* that nobody is interested in genuinely radical alternatives to institutional dominance of the commons, that they aren't vote winners? Don't you realise that without the system—the state, capitalism, socialism, whatever—we would all be murdering, raping and exploiting each other? There would be anarchy!

This word, 'anarchy' can only indicate the nightmares of hell for those who rule. Nevermind that enormous, well organised societies have existed without states or central control,† nevermind that we have been murdering, raping and exploiting each other only since the beginning of the system and the invention of states and that the perfected corporate-state is the most exploitative there has ever been, nevermind that we know in our hearts we do not need the system and its laws to rule over us and, finally, nevermind that cooperation, not competition,

---

* Mark Fisher called this *Capitalist Realism*, although Fisher, a statist, technocratic, democratic, professional socialist, had zero interest in critiquing the all-embracing nature of the entire civilised system claiming that an effective revolution was impossible without a 'party structure'.

† James C. Scott, *Against the Grain.*

predominates in free nature—that only a madman, or a scientist, could find nature fundamentally, or even mostly, violent.*
Nevermind all that. 'We need the system' say those who know full well that this is the precise opposite of the truth. The system needs us, and it always has.

---

* A madman or someone who has never really spent time in the wild; in the ocean, in the woods, on the mountainside, where stillness reigns, just as it does in free men's hearts. Storms of violence—even, yes, of selfishness—these there certainly are—and pain; but only in the system do they *rule*. In the early system that is— the system of gangs and lords. After that, all is suppressed, the peaceful and the violent, under a desert of civility and wealth. For a while.

a

A Brief Account *of the* Future

'The illusion of freedom will continue as long as it's profitable to continue the illusion. At the point where the illusion becomes too expensive to maintain, they will just take down the scenery, they will pull back the curtains, they will move the tables and chairs out of the way and you will see the brick wall at the back of the theater.'

Frank Zappa

An account, not a prediction. Nobody knows what will happen and nobody has ever known, but it is possible to describe where this civilisation is leading; the same place as every other before it.

THE SYSTEM IS AN ENORMOUS MACHINE, built from humans,* for the dual purpose of excluding reality from conscious experience and pumping power into the hands of a few rulers, owners and managers. The civilisations which comprise the system all originate in the unnatural† insanity of the ego, from which they grow, with unnatural insensitivity, violence and speed, ignoring all natural limits, becoming larger and larger, and more and more complex,‡ until they take on a frightening, momentum of their own which cannot be comprehended, much less controlled. In the beginning, when the civilisation is young and manageable, all is restraint, foresight and heroic energy. As the power and extent of the civilisation is consolidated, this energy is redirected to management, commerce and intellectual and artistic pursuits. Complexity grows, and bureaucracy (and more management) grows to deal with it. More and more people and things are subjugated to the needs of the system, and techniques of coercion and discipline (including

---

* And, of course, from the nature that humans are part of.

† The system would have it that there is and can be no such thing as 'unnatural' (or any of its synonyms; see myth 24), as all created things exist in a natural universe or are arbitrary inventions of individual minds. The unnatural systems-man cannot perceive the *principle* of nature because he has no access to it, and so can only recognise appropriations, imitations or impersonations of natural quality, which is why utility, beauty, intelligence and honesty always strike him—instantly, viscerally—as useless, ugly, stupid and dishonest, and why he can only perceive the value of greatness once it has died.

‡ More institutionalisation, specialisation, stratification and at greater scale.

reform, welfare and so on), grow to deal with rapidly expanding inequality and revolutionary ire. Eventually the civilisation (or the AGE or ERA; for civilisations comprise self-similar epochs which also rise and fall, or surge and slump) enters a period of terminal decline and inevitable fall.

The fall of every civilisation is greeted with epidemics of suicide and murder, every imaginable form of perversion and misery, riots, civil unrest, warfare, addiction, gambling, weird religions, preposterous superstitions, widespread insanity, ecological exhaustion, withering of structure, disease, contention, intense materialism, groupthink, and the production of pus: these aren't 'bad luck', any more than liver failure, bone disease, degenerating physical power and whatnot are 'bad luck' when a diseased individual body reaches the end of its life. Not that there is anything natural about the body of the world, any more than there is about the cells which comprise it, all of which are inherently unstable, wasteful and ruinously destructive of the natural ground they depend upon.

As the end draws near, the usurping head employs a series of predictable and increasingly desperate measures to keep the disintegrating body together. These include extreme violence and brutally punitive legal practices (including outrageous rents and taxes), escalating super-production of bureaucracy, monitoring and systems of surveillance and control, frantic technical development (to manage out-of-control complexity), intense hostility towards genuine culture, serious reflection and honesty (which are correctly perceived to be more threatening than any terrorist or barbarian group), hyper-stimulating displays of distraction (to keep revolutionary frustration pacified), frantic monument building, financial bubbles and insane speculation, total insensitivity to what is actually happening in the world and an ever more desperate and pathetic reliance on imported labour and faraway supplies, which gradually dwindle to naught. Such painful symptoms and deleterious solutions—along with all the misery, fear, violence, confusion, boredom, discomfort, illness, craving and lack of vitality that they create*—were present, in

---

* Note that 'awareness of what is happening' is not on this list. When people begin to be aware that the show's over the exponentially replicating horror of utter ruin is one minute away.

varying degrees, at the decline and fall of every civilisation (and eras) before ours,* but this being the first total and totalising world civilisation, we find ourselves faced with the epitome and pinnacle of sick—and exponential—decay.

*

A T THE END OF THE FINAL WORLD CIVILISATION, humanity reached a point where it was surplus to requirements. The system had never wanted it and, with the advent of artificial 'intelligence', robotics, cybernetics and so on, it no longer needed it. Human beings could only be conceived by the system as consumers and producers, which, ultimately, meant completely depriving them of nature and society. This was done through forcing *all* natural processes through the machine world (making love, giving birth, eating, dying) and all social interactions through the automated-digital WORLD BRAIN (education, health, benefits, tax registration, shopping, entertainment and all other market transactions). A perfect Phildickian nightmare.

The gap between intelligence and artificial intelligence narrowed and closed. Not because computers became more intelligent (they merely became smarter) but because humans became less conscious. This AI was used to process the oceans of information gathered by the mandatory hardware of the system—personal computers, smartphones, scanning cameras, nanotech, advanced microphones, body-sensors and VR headsets. This somatic data combined with various other institutional records to provide the artificially-intelligent Kafkaesque corporate-state with a complete, automatically managed, database of every manifest aspect of every citizen (not to mention every particle) on the planet. At the same time, the hospital, the prison, the asylum, the corporate-state, the bank and the school blended into one artificially 'intelligent' mono-institution that was indistinguishable from virtual society. This ensured permanent and continual medical, 'mental health' and 'social care' interventions;

---

* See, for example, J. Tainter, *The Collapse of Complex Societies*, A. Durant, *The Lessons of History*, J. Glubb, *The Fate of Empires and Search for Survival*, O. Spengler, *The Decline of the West*, C. Ponting, *A New Green History of the World*, E. Cline, *1177 BC: The Year Civilization Collapsed*, W. Orphuls, *Immoderate Greatness: Why Civilizations Fail*, Jared Diamond, *Collapse*, and W. Kötke, *The Final Empire*.

permanent and continual 'education', training, assessment and advancement through the ranks of credentialisation; permanent and continual surveillance, tracking, recording, monitoring and measurement.

The autonomous virtual system, or electronic worldbrain, thus domesticated, disciplined, coerced and punished everyone in the system, instantly. There was four stages of this Orwellian intervention. Firstly, the anxiety and obsessive perfectionism engendered by existing in a constantly surveilled, nuance-free, hyper-literal, electronic super-spectacle massively intensified, subduing the population further; stimulated, as ever, by a range of consciousness-pacifying medical, moral and environmental INVISIBLE ENEMIES (terrorists, demons, diseases, mental illnesses, evil ideologies and moral scourges). Secondly, non-standard thoughts, beliefs, acts, facial expressions and emotions, along with a decline in work enthusiasm, were instantly recorded and punished—first there were upbeat messages on the phone to cheer up, then access to resources and opportunities for advancement magically dried up (doors, both literal and figurative, would not open), then the individual magically dried up too. Thirdly, overt rejection of the system was instantly diagnosed as a life- or society-threatening illness, physical or mental, and neutralised by automated algorithms programmed to identify, target and neutralise 'dissent', which could be suppressed by locking out radicals from education, travel, banking and so forth, and 'sickness', which could be dealt with in the maximum-security hospital system. Finally, severe revolutionary threat was wiped out by bio-medical authorities, private security forces and military drones programmed to swiftly track down and eliminate 'security threats'. All of this happened automatically, which is to say, quickly, completely, coldly and with continual, innumerable, horrendous and freakishly weird errors.

With every subversive word, deed, gesture and emotion—every rejection of systemic literalism, relativism, conformity and upbeat obedience—monitored and punished, and with society, nature, *reality itself* obliterated, what damp sparks of life left in the inner world were extinguished. Model citizens were then indistinguishable from androids; courteous, flexible, plausible, hard-working team players with no recognisable conscience or consciousness. Perfectly unempathic madmen who applauded the destruction of mankind in the name of security, safety and health. Model, masked, citizens were also necessarily hyper-anxious, prone to catastrophic overreaction, tense, needy and dependent on consumption, narco-stimulation, spectacle, attention and constant institutional intervention; but these were all supplied, for a price. Smart drugs, epic virtual porn, fantastic immersive video games, daily hits of micro-fame, titillating tech-updates, horrifying news and shopping were provided to fill the hole where 'I' used to be. Eventually, these coalesced into a totalising pan-pornographic narco-spectacle, a ceaseless horror show of apocalyptic news, live-cams, sex, violence, lurid fantasy and hideous weirdness, beamed 24-7, into everyone, everywhere, all the time. It was effectively impossible—and illegal—to ignore this spectacle. Ever faster, and ever madder it became. REALITY APATHY set in—people longer cared about what was real or not—accompanied by a massive intensification of the dreadful symptoms of living in an intensely surveilled solipsistic pseudo-reality. No past, no future, no present; an unnatural hypervivid, hyperawake sense of cultureless untime, crippling, insane self-consciousness, paranoia, extreme emotional agitation, ultra-violence unmediated by the slightest sense of empathy, frightening strangeness, catatonic living death and complete psychological breakdown. Humanity went out of its mind. The young were most severely afflicted, terrorising and dismaying their elders, who, as ever, blamed everything but the system, and everyone but themselves.

For nearly a century the world system had been in a state of terminal decline; the parlous, macabre and mind-numbingly boring state of affairs we knew as 'late capitalism'. As energy ran out, and debt bubbles could no longer be paid off with their own interest, the system started to crash, openly consuming itself as it fell, cannibalising government, public services, nature and even the misery and madness of collapse. Desperate attempts to dam the river of consumption, by locking down the world into an horrendous digital supermax, dragged out the misery for a few more years until, as the body of the world entered its death throes, systemic power, now perfectly uniting the most inhuman aspects of capitalism with the most brutally authoritarian state-systematisation of socialism, began to consume the root of human existence — the body itself — while automatically crushing all dissent, all consciousness, all humour, all 'offence', all character and all forms of vernacular freedom (using ecological collapse and the usual range of health and security panics as a pretext). Humanity was uploaded, exterminated, sold into new forms of slavery, or just left to rot, as infrastructures broke down and everything ceased to work.

As the oceans were dredged dry of life, as they were filled up with poisons and plastics, as water sources were degraded, as topsoil was stripped away, as old-growth forests were cleared, as energy sources were exhausted and the earth stripped of 'resources', as oceans heated up and permafrost melted, as land was cleared and covered with chemicals, as a colossal, almost unbelievable number of species went extinct, as the world covered the earth completely, so a series of devastating 'natural' disasters struck. Floods, famines, droughts, wars, pestilences, financial crashes, on an unimaginable scale, struck. Elites attempted to deal with this by locking the planet down, but they could only contain the people for so long. As the cage cracked up, the repressed terror and madness of humanity broke free and the horror, the horror, was everywhere.

Why!? We had created a global civilisation, and for what? So the whole thing could come crashing down into the ocean, bringing unimaginable misery upon the earth? What purpose could such suffering possibly serve? The answer—in truth, the *solution*—was and is simple. *Only suffering changes man.* Only loss, death, despair, desolation, sickness, ill-treatment, indignity and, as Nietzsche wrote, 'profound self-contempt, the torture of self-mistrust and the wretchedness of the vanquished' really change ordinary men and women. *Extra*ordinary people change through the good thing, and through the self-mastery that yokes them to it; the joyous source of the world. But such types are few and far between. For the *masses*, there is no hope; because all they have is hope, and habit, and expectation, and desire, and possession, and progress, and business, and money, and all the other illusions of the egoic system.

That man had to be *dis*illusioned was not, quite obviously, a message which could find very much popular support in a world of illusions, but then no message worth hearing ever does. The *individual* knows that the evil and pain and suffering she has gone through has not been for naught. Being sensitive and kind—those rarest of qualities in the civilised system—the individual finds no pleasure in the idea that everyone has to go through hell to reach heaven.* But pleasure is besides the point. Indeed '*why* must suffering occur?' is besides the point. The point, the eternal point, is only ever and always, after hope has been taken away; *what*.

As civilisation fell, more and more people could see *what* was in front of their eyes. This seeing, they were astonished to discover, is why it had to happen at all.

---

* Or earth, which is the same thing.

b

Anarchism *at the* End *of the* World
An Introduction to the Instinct that Won't Go Away

'And now we'll pull down every single notice, and every
single leaf of grass shall be allowed to grow as it likes to.'

Snufkin

Primal anarchism is the only way of life that has ever worked or ever can. It is the only actual alternative to the pseudo-alternatives of the left and right, of optimism and pessimism, and even of theism and atheism. That being so you would expect it to be widely ignored, ridiculed and misunderstood, even, perhaps especially, by nominal anarchists.

What is Anarchism?

Anarchism is the rejection of *domination*. In a primal anarchist society—which means of course in the anarchist herself—nobody is dominated by anyone or anything else. This does not mean, as we shall see, that there is no *authority*.* What anarchism rejects is authority with the power to control or coerce the individual against her will.

There are two crucial exceptions. The first is that, in refusing domination, the anarchist necessarily has to restrain those who dominate—force and control—other people. Rapists, murderers, bullies and, less directly, thieves seek to dominate others, and so they must be prevented from doing so.

The second exception is that the anarchist is justified in restraining those who do not have control over themselves. There is no coercion in preventing young children, sleepwalkers and drunkards, for example, from walking over a cliff. If someone has control over themselves and insists on throwing themselves from a cliff, then an anarchist would let them do it.

These two exceptions partially answer two of the most common objections to anarchism. The first is, who or what, exactly, is going to stop thieves, rapists and murderers from harming me? and the second is, who or what is going to stop

---

* Which makes the literal meaning of anarchism—absence of a chief—misleading.

the mad, the sad and the stupid from harming themselves? To which the anarchist ordinarily replies 'people'. Not the state, not professional experts; *us*. This answer, of course, is incomplete and leads to further objections. To respond to these we need to recognise those elements of the world which control individuals against their will, elements which would need to be removed to create a *fully* anarchist society, one that is *primally* free. I call these the SEVEN DOMINANTS. They are, in roughly ascending order of subtlety and pervasiveness:

1. The [autocratic] monarchy.
2. The [capitalist-socialist] state (which includes its money, law, property, police, etc.).
3. The [totalitarian] corporation.
4. The [democratic] majority.
5. The [professional-religious] institution.
6. The [technocratic] system.
7. The [mental-emotional] ego.

It is difficult even for anarchists to recognise that these are all *inherently* coercive forces. There are no anarchists who support the monarchy of course, and very few who support corporate control, but anarchist support for the state and its various techniques and institutions is surprisingly widespread (voting, campaigning, supporting its wars*), as is anarchist support for democracy (trade unionism, anarcho-syndicalism and other forms of 'direct democracy') and for professionalism (professors Chomsky, Graeber, Bookchin, et al.[†]). The system and the ego are so subtle and pervasive they often do not figure in anarchist literature at all (with the honourable exceptions of Lao Tzu, Chuang Tzu,[‡] Leo Tolstoy, William Blake, Henry Miller and Ivan Illich[§]). That anarchists ignore or support the coercive power of

---

* Usually on so-called 'pragmatic' grounds. This is why Kropotkin supported and Chomsky supports (indeed, worked for) the state.

† Graeber and Chomsky are social democrats, essentially; workist technocrats.

‡ And, arguably, of Jesus of Nazareth; provided that you discount his rather dubious Church-friendly pronouncements (dubious in the sense that they are unlikely to be his) and those of the mystifying authoritarian propagandiser, [St.] Paul of Tarsus.

§ And the less honourable exception of Max Stirner, who was, insanely, *for* the ego.

dominants, or that they—we—are often forced to compromise, does not make such support an anarchist position any more than some vegetarians having a crafty bacon sandwich makes eating pork a vegetarian position.

Despite what anarchists may or may not think, it is indisputable that the seven dominants are coercive; that they control individuals, and nature, against their will. It is indisputable that kings coerce their subjects, that states do the same, and that possession of property, financial wealth, the ability to write or manipulate laws, the strength of the majority, specialised, technical expertise, professional authority and systemic conformity all confer power to dominate—sometimes even *domesticate*—people. It is also indisputable that tools beyond a certain size and complexity enslave men and women and compel them to think, act and even feel in ways alien to their better nature; for them to serve the car, for example, or transport system, or the farm, or the school, rather than their own, or nature's, instincts. Finally, it is indisputable that the restless mind and emotions take control of conscious experience and cause men and women to do, say, think and feel things they don't really want to; cause them to hate, for example, get angry and depressed, or worry. 'I' may want to stop wanting and worrying, but, if I am honest, I can see that 'I' am not in charge here. My stupid self is.

It follows that a philosophy, *the central tenet of which* is that all forms of coercive domination are wrong must—despite inevitable lapses and compromises—set itself against the autonomous power of states, corporations, property, professionalism, money, law, democracy, monarchism, tools and the inherently needy and violent, obsessively wanting, worrying and planning, mental-emotional false self.

This attitude, to people who have lived in dominating systems, seems strange to say the least. The kind of hyper-radical independence that anarchism describes seems so far from the experience of ordinary people that those proposing it might as well be describing the best way to live on Jupiter; and yet, in fact, anarchism is not just the original state of human society, it is also the way that most of us live already, at least during those times when we are happiest. We are anarchists in our love affairs, in our friendships, and even occasionally in the very teeth of the system, at work. When the boss is absent and everyone gets together to work out how on earth to sort out the mess he's created, occasionally, for a fleeting moment, we glimpse a collective so simple and effective it slides under our attention. But then the boss returns, and the ordinary world of work returns, or of politics or police or teachers or money, and someone tells us they are an anarchist and we find the idea, if not ludicrous, at best confusing. Surely...

Objection 1. Anarchism is inhuman.

What is the *primal* core of human nature, underneath all the systems of domination that compel us? If nobody and nothing is controlling us—including our own emotions and thoughts—what's left? How will we act? Will we tear each other limb from limb? Steal, fight and fuck our way to the top of the pile? Will we go insane?

Authoritarians—*genuine* authoritarians that is, those who support the seven dominants—answer 'yes'. Human nature is *ultimately* violent, selfish and stupid, they say, and so we need kings, states, corporations, democracies, laws, experts and the control of the dominating mind or emotions to prevent 'anarchy'—a word they interpret as something close to late medieval hell, in which human-shaped monsters run around eating each other. Libertarians—and again I am talking about *actual* libertarians, those who refuse to be coerced by anything—answer 'no'. Humans certainly *can* be violent, selfish and stupid, but *ultimately* we are peaceful, generous and intelligent creatures.

Ordinary authoritarian people respond to such an idea by telling us to 'look around—look at people, look at the news—we are *obviously* violent, selfish and stupid'. Authoritarian psychologists agree; they point to the many, many experiments which have shown that people are violent, selfish and stupid. Authoritarian philosophers also agree; they say that there is no order, or meaning, or intelligence outside of the seven dominants. They have very complicated theories to hide their basic distrust of nature and human nature but that is what the authoritarian attitude is based on.

The libertarian might then point out that the 'people' who surround us, those whom authoritarian people complain about and authoritarian psychologists study, have been raised in a world dominated by force. To say that we need authoritarian forces because people who are dominated by authoritarian forces are violent, selfish and stupid is a tautology. It's not unlike saying we need to put birds in cages because birds in cages are dangerous.

The primal anarchist does not base her view of humanity on how the people around her think and act, but on her *own* nature. In this she is no different from the authoritarian; the difference being that when she looks within herself she finds that although she certainly can be a liar, a coward, a fool and a sadist, that *ultimately* she trusts her instincts, that *ultimately* she is peaceful, generous and has good sense. She goes on to reason that others must be the same; a conclusion borne out by her most intimate relations, which demonstrate to her that absence of control and force *is not disorder*.

Objection 2: Anarchism is chaos

One of the most common authoritarian objections to the lifting of all constraint that anarchists seeks, is not just the *fear* that anarchism is synonymous with chaos but, as those who control culture inevitably shape the definition of words, *the written fact*. The word 'anarchy' means, in the dictionaries of the system, disorder; despite the fact that actual anarchists, with a few insane exceptions, have never been opposed to order. The question which anarchists seek to ask is what order, or whose. Anarchists believe that the only society worth living in is based on some kind of *natural order*, that which naturally or intuitively regulates individual and collective life. For authoritarians this does not exist. They see no evidence of it. What they see in 'intuition' is erratic emotionality. What they see in nature is, principally at least, warfare, fear, pain, hierarchical struggle, pecking orders, alpha males and so on. For such people nature, and human nature, may contain organised elements, but the natural world is essentially a neverending, chaotic battle of all against all. Nature might be finely ordered, formally beautiful and good eating; but it cannot be trusted. To organise a society therefore must entail suppression and control of our natural instincts. Result; people become resentful, bored, stupid and violent… which is to say *disordered*.

'But look how neat everything is! Look how well your phone works! Look at how nicely tarmacked the M25 is'. One of the reasons it is hard to perceive the chaos of the system is that it is *formally* ordered. It all looks good—provided you look in the right place. Everything, for example, looks good on paper, because it is has been priority one for the system, since the invention of writing, to ensure that everything in heaven and earth is *legible*—capable of being named, measured, standardised and controlled. Everything also looks good when it is dead. A modern farm is the epitome of order because nothing lives on it but one, hyper-ordered crop bred to depend completely upon equally ordered synthetic inputs (the same applies to the modern city and the modern computer). Finally, everything looks good when you don't have to pay attention to what isn't so good. We do not have a direct relationship with our fellow humans, or fellow creatures, and so we are spared from perceiving the bedlam that reigns beyond the office (flat, farm, factory or shop). All important interactions go via the system, and so we do not have to deal with, or even perceive, the *cause* of our formal order (the actual lives of people who build our computers, for example, or the animals which fill our burgerbuns) or its *effects* (where our rubbish and shit actually go when we're done with them). The people of the affluent West live in an antiseptic sphere of mini coopers, Dyson vacuums and self-service checkouts. Everything seems to us, just as it did to the ancient Greeks and Romans, just as it did to the comfortable, happy, little men of 1930s Nazi Germany, who had no idea of the horror their comfortable lives were based on, so very nicely arranged. We are confident in ourselves because we are confident in the safety and order of our surroundings; what lies outside the gates is not really worth paying serious attention to. We know that *something* is wrong out there, or we intuitively feel it, a distant rumble of thunder during the picnic, but it terrifies us, and so we turn to the consumption of reassuring neatness to push the anxiety away. Not that there is anything wrong with organising your record collection or cleaning your kitchen or collecting stamps or poring over maps; but that the system must manufacture toys which soothe the anxieties produced by the chaos which is the by-product of toys which soothe the anxieties produced by the chaos... of domination.

Dominate the land with industrial technology, dominate the people with repressive laws, dominate your children with rigid 'discipline', dominate women with physical power or intellectual scheming, dominate your life with strict plans, goals and systems, dominate the darkness with 24/7 light; and what happens? On paper it all works out fine. In the real world domination produces chaos.

Domination, however, is not the same thing as *power* or even *authority*. The ocean is powerful, but anarchists do not protest the tides. Likewise old people sometimes have, by virtue of their experience, immense authority; but only a fruitcake would oppose age on principle, or refuse to listen to its wisdom. There is a crucial difference—reflected in our language—between being *in* authority and being *an* authority. In the first place your power comes from *holding* a position, which is, by definition, an inflexible role or rank, and in the second your power comes from *being in* a position to use your knowledge, experience or sensitivity; then, when the circumstance changes, the power evaporates, as of course it should.

Fixing power into roles and ranks has the same effect as fixing names into titles, meanings into definitions and guidelines into laws; they become unable to respond to what is actually happening. Result: fabulous inefficiency and, once again, unmanageable chaos, as everyone knows who has worked in an organisation bound by titles, definitions, laws and fixed power. Those at the bottom, actually facing the actual situation, find they are unable to deal with it, while those at the top not only have no idea what the situation is, they are terrified by the power of those who can see what needs to be done, and fanatically suppress any attempts to use it.

In an anarchist group whoever has more ability or sensitivity than the others naturally 'takes the lead'. Nobody with any intelligence, anarchist or otherwise, would refuse to *unthinkingly obey* an experienced sailor in a storm.* Indeed, the hallmark of ability and sensitivity is that neither compel. One word from a

---

* Although there are few people capable of discerning real authority in a system which brutalises sensitivity. That we all drown at the behest of the cretins who are popularly exalted as philosophical, artistic, or moral authorities is less of a worry to systemacrats than that someone who knows what they are doing finds the helm.

true leader and everyone does as they please. Once we remove compulsion, then ability and sensitivity naturally take over as sources of honoured and respected authority. Thus a primal anarchist society is, actually, *full* of leaders.*

Just as anarchism is not antithetical to authority, power and order, so it is not incompatible with what *appear* to be laws. A common complaint on anarchist discussion boards is *'this isn't really an anarchist forum! look, you've got rules!'* The question is not the existence of rules, but their *fluidity* (how much they allow for contextual exceptions), their *boundary* (the freedom one has if one disregards them) and their *purpose* (to what end this or that regulation). Anarchist 'laws', unlike those of the system, adapt to the intelligence of the individual, and the multitude of exceptional situations she finds herself in, allow dissenters to do what they like beyond their boundaries of application and, crucially, serve the non-egoic truth.

That's all well and good, you might be thinking, but what will we do about the lazy people, those who will not work, the thieves and the criminals, those who steal what others have or produce? The anarchist answer is that we've been supporting such people for millennia. We call them the elites. When people work for themselves and with their fellows, without coercion or control and under reasonably promising circumstances, they do not tend to leech and steal from each other. Of course there will always be some who do, but when they are not in power they can be easily dealt with.

The fear that we cannot take care of ourselves without the police† or that we cannot heal ourselves without doctors is

---

* 'In any one tribe there may be a hunting chief, work chief, dance chief, women's chief, age grade chief, and fishing chief. These leaders function only in specific contexts and for limited periods of time; usually, their primacy is based on capacity in the particular activity. It does not carry over into the round of daily life; and, almost everyone in the society is, at one time or another, in a "chiefly" position'. *In Search of the Primitive*: S. Diamond.

† The police were invented to track down slaves, control large, defiant, crowds and protect shops; which, combined with more modern functions of surveillance, intimidation, making life unpleasant for unemployed people on the street and filling in forms, remain the principle tasks of the police. Coming round to your house after it has been burgled and being nice is really just a PR exercise.

identical to the fear that we cannot feed ourselves without the supermarket. Take schools.* How, the authoritarian asks, will we educate our children without them? The objection, like all objections to anarchism, isolates the institution in question from context and consciousness. It says; given that reality is as it is (a collection of scarce things), that society is as it is (enemy territory) and that people are as they are (selfish apes or sinful gods), if we remove institutions which protect us from reality, which organise society and which regulate people, then everything will go to the dogs. And, given *those* assumptions, everything would.†

A world without schools demands an educational society; in which nature, and the activities of adults within it, are freely available to children. Opportunities to learn—meaning opportunities to work and to play—are, like everything else in nature, *abundant*. When children can join adults in their orchestras, workshops, libraries, laboratories, kitchens, teams, theatres, farms and football pitches; they learn. The reason that children are not allowed to learn their culture in this way, through direct contact with reality, without the ministrations of a credentialised middle-man, is because that reality is wild.‡ It can be influenced, understood and used—not to mention adored—but it cannot be dominated. It is this—and not the prospect of millions of children vegetating in front of their playstations—that horrifies those who are addicted to institutional control.

Likewise, when work is pleasurable (or at the very least meaningful), when rest is available, when the wilderness is close at hand, when ordinary people have access to the tools and techniques of health, when they can self-diagnose and self-medicate, when they can learn to deal with pain on their own, when they

---

* Meaning without syllabuses, state-compulsion, credentialism and so on. No need to get rid of the buildings, some of them are rather nice. They could even be used, of all things, for instruction and study.

† At least initially. Weeds ravage fields from which artificial controls are lifted

‡ Or chaotic—although I prefer not to use this word as the chaos of nature is more like the 'chaos' of chaos theory, a paradoxical state between unpredictable chaos and intuitively appreciated and generated (rather than merely mind-made) order. For the educational and organisational power of wild chaos see R. Sennett, *The Uses of Disorder*. See also I Pearse and L. Crocker *The Peckham Experiement*.

can die on their own; when, in short, society is healthy, there is no need for professional doctors. There is a need for people who naturally specialise in complex procedures and risky techniques, just as there is a need for people who naturally specialise in intensely funky drumming, but in an anarchic society everyone has rhythm.

Objection 3. Anarchism is Violent.

If the first thought, on hearing the word 'anarchism' is 'chaos', the second is likely to be 'violence'. Both associations have been relentlessly promoted since anarchism became a force to be reckoned with—as it was for large parts of the nineteenth century—but the idea of the moustachioed fiend creeping through the shadows was first disseminated and sensationalised after several heads of state were assassinated by anarchists at the end of the nineteenth century. The trope has evolved over the years—today the cartoon bomb is usually carried by some dude wearing a *V for Vendetta* mask—but it continues to be defined by indiscriminate, juvenile violence.

The essence of the problem was first identified by [the famously socialist] George Orwell, who complained to his anarchist friend, George Woodcock, that there is nothing to stop groupthink from dominating anarchist societies with the same coercive force as the state does; and indeed this is just what tends to happen. A certain kind of idiot is drawn to anarchism, just as a certain kind of idiot is drawn to classical music, team sports or Hello Kitty. Their idiocy simultaneously reinforces itself (through stigmatising outsiders and glorifying insiders) and degrades itself (through stereotyping and stereotypical behaviour) leading to the ready-made cliché easily sensationalised and spurned by opponents. Violent young atheists wearing anarcho-acceptable [ideological] attire, reading Palahniuk, playing hardcore music in violent demos, living in filthy squats* and sharing dank memes fantasising about exterminating pigs, are not hard to come by, but they no more represent anarchism than Cliff Richards represents Christianity or Margaret Thatcher represents women. In fact, a large proportion of great anarchists were pacifists, some of them

---

* Not that there is anything wrong with squats.

rather extreme (Ghandi, for example, was an anarchist*). Not that pacifism is necessarily anarchistic either, or that violence[†] is not sometimes necessary (it certainly is—particularly against property). Total and complete pacifism is, actually, an impotent, immoral and very often racist absurdity (even Ghandi, like Martin Luther King, wasn't against armed insurrection when pacifism could not work[‡]). Even those who suggest Native Americans, Jews and Laotians should have sat around holding candles, 'bearing witness' and positively thinking their way out of genocide would violently defend a four-year-old daughter from attack.

Blanket characterisation of anarchism as 'violent' (or 'childish', another common put-down) on the basis of the restless, cliquey child-minds it attracts, or on the occasional use or recommendation of violence (justified or otherwise), is not just a caricature, it is also a *tad* hypocritical coming from a king, a capitalist, a socialist, a mandarin, a commissar or any other representative of the system. A more violent way of life than we have now, or have ever had within the system, is nearly impossible to imagine (see myth 13).

Objection 4: Anarchism is parochial.

Another doubt which people commonly have about anarchism is its capacity to work beyond small groups of a few hundred. Critics point out that, okay, tiny groups of pre-agricultural folk and minute radical outfits on the fringe might be able to handle life without coercive laws and the like, but how on earth are we to organise a global post-industrial society informally?

We aren't. It is impossible. A world *such as we have* cannot, of course, be run from the bottom up. What kind of world *can* emerge from anarchist principles is, however, an open question. Large-scale anarchist co-operation and free international exchange are perfectly feasible and would lead to an extraordinarily complex world; just not one overruled by czars, commissars, rigid

---

* According to Woodcock in *Anarchism: A History of Libertarian Ideas and Movements*.

† A word, incidentally, which is notoriously difficult to define.

‡ See Peter Gelderloos, *How Non-violence Protects the State*, for a flawed but thorough and convincing critique of *totalising* pacifism, and argument for the use of violence *in certain situations*.

plans and fixed laws. Anarchism, in fact, is no more antithetical to complex federations, than it is to leadership, authority and law. What it opposes, once again, is hierarchical *control*. Anarchist federations are, in fact, hierarchical;* just extremely flat ones in which the power of the level above is zero; with those at the peak able to do little more than recommend and relay. This doesn't mean they are ineffective (as advisory bodies are in the system) any more than your grandmother is. As the influential anarchist Colin Ward has pointed out, the international postal service and railways are both massive anarchist structures, with no central control whatsoever, as were a great number of pre-civilised societies, some of which were enormous. And we have even glimpsed—alas only for a few moments—a scaled-up anarchist society in modern times, in revolutionary Spain. This lasted a short time, was riddled with compromise, violent opposition from the fascist right *and* the communist left, and all the chicanery and confusion one might expect from such a radically permissive experiment; but there were many astonishing examples of spontaneous, peaceful, organisation and generosity—again, on an extraordinary scale—in anarchist Spain.†

You might be asking yourself what's to stop a powerful state overwhelming a weak informal anarchist federation? Almost nothing. Does it mean that our immune system is wrong or faulty because a bullet can kill us? Genuine anarchism prevents authoritarian hierarchies from forming; it can no more protect us against the vast militaristic states that have spent millennia organising themselves than an ant's nest can defend itself against a nuke. That doesn't make anarchism ineffective or powerless though, as we shall see; in fact quite the contrary.

A related objection is 'if domination arose from anarchic societies, what's to stop it from arising again?' Putting aside the

---

* Some hunter-gatherer cultures are also hierarchical. The word 'hierarchy' is normally used in an entirely negative sense; hierarchical processes are always said to be predicated on *force*. For this reason the word is probably best not applied to anarchist federations.

† You wouldn't call the slums of India, Brazil or Pakistan 'successful' in the sense of allowing people to live well, but in that they have allowed them to live at all, under horrific circumstances, has not been down to any kind of central planning. They often exhibit some of the finest examples of anarchy in action.

contradiction that 'we need domination to prevent domination', putting aside the fact that actually it is incredibly difficult to dominate people—the system took over forty thousand years to establish a foothold that required, and still requires, enormous effort to maintain, and putting aside the possibility that humanity can learn as individuals can—can have ignorance blasted from its broken heart, and grow up—there *does* remain the possibility that the system could grow again, that the cycle could begin again. But so what? Is that going to stop you? Are you going to stop eating because you'll only get hungry again, or stop exercising because you'll only get fat again, or stop loving because you'll only be betrayed again?

Objection 5: Anarchism is uncivilised

This one is correct. Anarchism, insofar as it is effective and consistent, rejects the entire dominating machinery of what we normally call 'civilisation'. For most of human history such societies were the norm and, until recently, there were innumerable remnants from that time which displayed, in varying degrees, the consequences of living in a genuinely anarchistic manner; societies in which egalitarian social and sexual relations were the norm, as was enjoyable work, absence of scarcity, no money, no warfare and very little suffering, at least as we experience it today. Certainly nothing like clinical depression, schizophrenia, psychopathy and so on. That humans were long-lived, healthy and happy *is the consensus position* amongst those who study ancient or primal people. There were problems of course, tensions, disagreements, even murders—and of course the wild is a brutally unsentimental companion—but in the absence of property, specialised power and whatnot, interpersonal problems could be dealt with. Likewise there were disagreements and doubts about what should be done, but these were not resolved by means of a vote which a minority was compelled to submit to; indeed very often they were not resolved *explicitly* at all.*

---

* 'Those who have lived among savage or barbarous peoples... have related how they have attended native councils, where matters in which they were interested were being discussed. When, after a time, the English observer found that the people were discussing some wholly different topic, and inquired when they were

Problems were resolved in a way which is almost unimaginable today; by looking, together, for the *right* thing to do.

The idea that the most successful social organisations in history should serve as some kind of model for what we should collectively aspire to, goes by the much-maligned name of ANAR-CHO-PRIMITIVISM (or PRIMALISM); the *general* rejection of civilised forms of organisation such as industrial technology, centrally controlled cereal cultivation, institutional hegemony along with the psychological priorities which underpin them. Despite the caricatures which critics invent (*'using a phone! what a hypocrite!'*), primalism does not entail the ludicrous refusal of *all* technology (such as fire, pottery or even agriculture, which predates the horrors of state-run farms*) or demand anarcho-primitivists take off all their clothes and go and live in a tree; and it certainly doesn't entail, as some critics like to believe, a recommendation for the extermination of mankind. It simply recognises that coercion and control run deeper than kings, parliaments and corporations pushing people around; that we are domesticated as much, if not more, by our tools,† as we are by those who have power over them, and that a functioning society *must* be based on the non-democratic egalitarianism, sensitivity and wildness of our ancestors. As such, anarcho-primitivism *is* anarchism.

Quibbles over terminology aside, primal societies are not the only ones which demonstrate that we do not need money, usurious systems of debt peonage, hyper-specialisation, entrenched networks of professional power, bureaucracy, law and similar civilised techniques to live well together. People around the world, from the middle-ages up to the present day, have functioned on informal, decentralised, systems of decision-making, taking care of their lives, working, playing, educating themselves and dealing with conflict without the

---

going to decide the question in which he was interested, he was told that it had already been decided and they had passed on to other business...The members of the council had become aware, at a certain point, that they were in agreement, and it was not necessary to bring the agreement explicitly to notice'. W.H.Rivers

* J.Scott, *Against the Grain*.There have been, in Peter Gelderloo's words, 'resolutely anti-authoritarian and ecocentric agricultural societies'.

† Particularly our high tech tools but also the hyper-complex 'tools' of social organisation that build pyramids and feed Pharaohs.

interference of dominants. Money supplies have dried up, police have vanished, governments have broken down and people have found that life has not just gone on as before, but has been far easier and more pleasant. Ordinarily, this happens during a crisis, such as when the banks shut down in Ireland in 1970, or in the early days of the British, French, Russian, Chinese and Hungarian revolutions, in the spring days in Prague in 1968 and in the breakdown of communism in the former USSR, not to mention in the middle of natural catastrophes, when people have often found, in spite of all the horrors that attended these events, collective intelligence, resourcefulness and conviviality. This has surprised them, just as it does us, who are used to seeing the breakdown of 'society' portrayed as brutal chaos. Such chaos does exist of course, but usually *only when dominants still exist*. It is not the absence of civilisation that causes riots and violence during times of social crisis, but its presence.

Peasant societies the world over, some of which are extremely complex and widespread, also demonstrate that the various machines of civilised coercion are not necessary to organise life. Groups living on the periphery of civilised states—the barbarians and the 'backward' folk—have successfully conducted their lives along broadly anarchist lines, while resisting centralised control, for millennia.* Again, they haven't been without their decidedly non-anarchistic internal problems, but to those who wish to look, they are also evidence of the genius and harmony that is possible among people working together outside systems of control.

Anarchism works, and there is important evidence to demonstrate that it works. Ultimately, however, evidence is secondary, even tertiary. You don't need evidence to reason that theft is impossible in a society in which nobody owns anything, police are unnecessary when there are no laws to uphold or borders to defend, a teaching establishment is redundant when

---

* J. Scott, *Weapons of the Weak*. Some large-scale radical movements of the middle ages were also broadly anarchist. Indeed the so-called 'dark ages'—the period *before* the stereotyped late medieval period of starvation, servitude, intolerance, poverty and plagues—were only dark to *states*, who were unable to control them. Many medieval towns were not exactly anarchist, but, after having thrown off their lords, were independent and egalitarian to a level unimaginable today.

society itself (not to mention nature) is educational, and medical professionals have nothing to do when the causes of sickness and madness are removed. More than that, and most important of all, you don't need evidence to know that *you* do not need governments and institutions to tell you what to do and that, ultimately, *you* are no different from *them*.

Objection 6: Anarchism is unrealistic.

If we accept that anarchism is a viable approach to our lives, and that it is not best represented by the Sex Pistols, or by the many middle-class voices who have co-opted anarchism for their own middle-class ends, there is another—and for many decisive—objection to realising a genuinely anarchist way of life; that it is utopian pie in the sky. Given that we are about as far away from an anarchist world as it is possible to be, how on Earth are we to get there? Given that the whole world would have to be anarchist, or concentrated technological power would soon overcome everywhere else; how are we to create an international anarchist paradise?

Once again, we aren't. In the first place, on the foundational recognition that nature, including conscious human nature, is inherently intelligent—a *living* intelligence moreover, that is responsive to a phenomenally complex and ever-changing context—anarchist strategies for organising society are *necessarily* extremely weak. People will, when unconstrained, create their own unique federations, associations, cultures, traditions, fluid guidelines for living, styles of working and so on. To be sure we can speak of certain attributes a free, functioning anarchist town or farm or theatre is almost sure to have; ego-dissolving rituals, small groups federated into weaker large ones, tools that ordinary people can fix and use, presence of the wild, love of craft, freedom of women and children, leaders taking the hindmost, etc. Finally though, we don't know how innumerable people in innumerable situations are going to set about organising their lives. And thank God we don't.

On top of this, we face the titanic world-system as it is. Bringing that down and allowing anarchism to grow is impossible for us. As it stands it would take centuries to change our institutions (by some estimates around 400 years to change our energy systems*). Add to this the power, the extent and the invasiveness of the state-corporate technological system and its professional, political and military organs of control, then perhaps multiply by the domesticated passivity, sickness and fear of the masses and lay that against how polluted the planet is, how little tree cover is left, how much CO_2 is in the atmosphere, how rapidly the ice caps and permafrost are melting and the oceans heating up, how much time we have left before we run out of oil, rare-earth metals, fresh water, fish and top-soil... then heap on top of all that, if you are capable of perceiving it—and few are—the basic abomination of the world, the depths of dissolution and darkness we now live in, so far from collective intelligence or joy that they appear as dreams within dreams within dreams; if they appear at all. And then, finally, consider what it means to situate all this as a *process*, consider the phenomenal relentlessness of the system; how it grows continually, picking up the pieces of failed civilisations and institutions, improving on previous techniques, pushing inexorably onwards, spreading indefatigably outwards, colonising, rationalising, fixing, defining and controlling more and more, and more and more. We are on the edge of doom and the system is not merely growing, it is, like the compound interest that drives it, growing *exponentially*. It never stops, never sleeps and never, ever, gives up—it is the evil, inhuman supermind *par excellence*. It is so complete that just as it makes the most radical of us guilty hypocrites (*'hohoho, look at this radical wearing shoes made in a sweatshop!'*), so, as it disintegrates, it suffocates and scatters not just its supporters, but its opponents. The radical, forced like everyone else to suckle from the satanic tit, is not strengthened by the weakness of the system, but weakens with it.

Now, after all this, consider what readjustment can achieve, what reform and change and marches and articles can do to stop this Leviathan for good, so that it *never* picks up its tools again. *Nothing*. Consider how absurd, how blind, it is to suppose that we can legislate our way out of this, or, even more ridiculously, technologically steer growth down 'eco-friendly' channels; indeed that anyone can ever rationally control society. Consider what

---

* Changing from non-renewable energy to renewable would require an obscene amount of energy, not to mention far more resources than we have.

actually needs to be done to prevent the short-term annihilation of the natural world and, with it, our so-called civilisation; immediate and massive negative growth, redistribution of wealth and power, colossal scaling back on energy usage and a radical dismantling of the state-corporate system (both capitalist and socialist)—and all of this everywhere, pretty much *immediately*. What needs to be done? The system needs to end. For good. And who is going to do it? We, those of us who even want to understand the problem, are stupendously weak. A few scattered oddbods set against a mechanism, ten-thousand years in the making, which has invaded every last recess of the natural world and the human mind. It is everywhere at all times, in all people. It is the polluted body, the restless emotion and all thought based thereon. We don't stand a chance.

We don't—but I know someone who does!

We have an ally in our long struggle against the Zone of Evil, an ally which is to the system, as the system is to us; unimaginably more powerful. Powerful on an epic, universal scale. This ally goes by a few names, but we'll use here the one closest to common understanding; NATURE. Nature is a more effective activist than man; and she, unlike us, is not one for discussion. Nature does not vote, or protest, or write petitions, or form unions, or write stern letters, or launch social media campaigns. She prefers to effortlessly sweep the world away.

The system thinks it understands nature because it can measure and describe every measurable and describable aspect of her; the so-called 'objective' world of things and events (external form) and the so-called 'subjective' world of thoughts and emotions (internal form). Because it appears, to the system, that everything is form, philosophers of the system regularly claim that everything is natural. The word 'unnatural' has no meaning for them because they are incapable of experiencing the *principle* of nature, which precedes and comprises form. 'Natural'— the natural order that primal anarchists strive to base society upon—describes the consciousness which *precedes* internal form, and the context which *comprises* external form. It is this natural principle which produces the natural blackbird and guides it to naturally respond to the worm. Lack of consciousness, and separation from the context, produces the unnatural crop duster and guides it to respond unnaturally to the worm.

Natural organisation is impossible for the egoic self-informed mind to grasp. The mind is an *either-or* mechanism. It perceives *either* wave *or* particle, *either* here *or* there, *either* order *or* chaos. Nature, like consciousness, is *both-and*. It is *both* wave *and* particle, *both* here *and* there, *both* ordered *and* chaotic. When the anarchist asserts (without, or ultimately without either-or evidence*) that nature should reign over scientific method, transport, education, farming, city planning or anything else in life, mind—to the extent it is informed by mind (or by the mind-made system)—*objects*. It creates an object of nature; a *thing* over there, dis-ordered, out of control, wild, *chaotic*, which must be isolated, dominated, *ordered* before we bring it over here. The idea that nature can organise society with the same intelligence and beauty as it organises tree crowns and mycelium networks is *unthinkable*.

The nature that is coming to blow the world away is not, then, merely the formal hurricanes, floods, draught, diseases and freezes that, even as you read, are waiting in the wings, not merely the waves upon waves of displaced people sweeping across the earth or the unimaginable civil warfare soon to come, it is also, and ultimately, the super-intimate natural principle behind this cataclysm. Just bringing down the power lines and blowing away the government is not enough to free the mind. The system penetrates the deepest recesses of the psyche. From the moment it is born, the self is gradually moulded into a system-compliant form; through the corrupting (if well-meaning) influence of family—the erratic, emotional pain, and continual (if unconscious) repression of one's finer, subtler instincts— through the continual pressures of socialisation to accept, conform and submit to the requirements of the school, the office, the court, the parliament and the artificial hyperworld they are slowly being absorbed into; through habituation to the totalising simulacrum of the spectacle, continual exposure to its relentless propagandising and surrender to its addictive enticements, all tailored (again, unconsciously) to the particular anxieties and manias of the individual; through a life lived continually in mediated environments, in which no wild nature, no direct truth, no

---

* The anarchist honours the facts of evidence, but they are subordinate to the conscious context which is, ultimately, non-factual.

aesthetic profundity and, increasingly, no reality at all is allowed to penetrate; through total dependency on the system for all its needs, the self slowly turns into an emotionally over-involved, highly abstracted, highly distracted ghost creature, a bland, half-dead, entirely predictable, desensitized, appendage to the system with no way, whatsoever, of discerning that which is not self. Self, in other words, becomes ego, a self-informed mental-emotional mechanism which accepts completely the system's determinants of reality. It may rebel against narrow conceptions of 'the system', it may fantasize about all kinds of artistic and creative freedom, it may invent all manner of fantastic conspiracies to account for its misery and confinement, it may—indeed must—break down or drop out completely, but while the system-ego reigns over conscious experience, the ordinary world forever appears to *be* the ordinary world and not, as it is, every second, a standing invitation to gut-ruptured astonishment and self-shattering psychological liberation.

This profound conditioning is not, it is vital to grasp, just an intellectual belief, a question of 'accepting official narratives', (although it is that). Nor are we just talking of the anxiety and craving associated with emotionally-potent sociological conditioning and groupthink (although it is that too). The system-conditioned ego does not just reflexively spout the absurd scientific or religious nonsense of whatever cult, profession or state it belongs to, does not just think, feel or even act as the system does, but *sees and feels* systematically. The *entire self* is colonised. This is how the system—the discrete world of institutions and the diffuse hyperworld of the world brain—appears to merge with nature, with the passing of time. 'It becomes necessity and fate, and is lived through as such*'; an oppressive, all-consuming, normality. Unlike the normality of nature though, it is alien to us, beyond our capacity to meaningfully experience, influence or understand. In dreams it appears as a monstrous, intangible, dread and yet, upon waking, we defend it with our lives. This is why genuine moments of liberation feel like a kind of dying; because we are not merely overcoming the world out there, but the entire self that creates and sustains it, in here. It is also why, paradoxically, genuinely liberating experiences do not merely

---

*   Peter L. Berger and Thomas Luckmann, *The Social Construction of Reality*.

amaze the mind and excite the heart, but baffle, delight and stun the natural *body*. Genuinely revolutionary realisations reveal the heartbreaking, radical truth of forms, sensations, colours, flavours; of the pressure of the ground under the feet, the taste of sugar on the tongue, the phenomenal, incarnate fact that there is anything at all.

Your sanity certainly depends on your capacity to live, as far as possible, independently from the world-machine, and every step we can take to disrupt its operation or spread understanding of what it is and how it works represents genuine progress, the return of the good thing. Debilitating strikes (without reformist demands—simply refusing to clean, for example, wealthy houses, or take their rubbish away), 'white' (work-to-rule) strikes and presenteeism (doing nothing at work), wiping out records (the first and most important act of peasant revolts throughout history), collective refusal to pay rents or loans, disruption of the mechanisms of definition and control, establishing communes (and avoiding activist groups and especially 'democratic general assemblies'), disseminating the sweet truth and, most effective of all, finding and snapping, or jamming, the weak points that every overextended system creates (while avoiding direct confrontation); these are all meaningful and effective acts, as is planting parsnips, making charcoal, cleaning up the beaches, building a bomb-shelter, learning the bassoon and running naked through the supermarket singing 'Dancing Queen'. A committed and intelligent group might even, eventually, at the right moment, be able to deliver a disabling blow to the system.* Engaging in

---

* Kaczynski's, *Anti-Tech Revolution: Why and How* provides a readable overview of how such a group would need to be constituted and what it would have to do. His criticisms of half-arsed reformism are, as elsewhere, particularly useful. And funny. *But*, as discussed in the notes to myth 32, Kaczynski has close to zero understanding or appreciation of conscious being, or of the role that ego played in forming the system, or plays in maintaining it, or *would* play in screwing up the potency of a genuinely revolutionary group. Such a group, along the lines that Kaczynski outlines, may be able provide a service to the earth. Who knows? But I wouldn't endorse it. The kind of group that could really do what needs to be done, and with style, would be far gentler and more playful than Kaczynski seems to think. This doesn't mean they would be opposed to violence, or be wishy-washy. It means they would be human.

such genuinely subversive, non-reformist system-destructive acts is not an option for the kind and the conscious, merely living in the unworld compels them; but the most widespread revolt and the most meticulous preparation don't currently stand a chance of completely overthrowing the system. Only nature can do that; the spontaneous, unplanned and unplannable nature of human beings (the source of all really effective revolts) and, above all, the self-shattering principle of your *own* nature.

Although we might be able to deliver crippling injury to the system, and although, eventually, the pressure of suppressed nature and human nature will soon blow the lid off this dismal box, ultimately this is the only way to overthrow the self-informed system; to overthrow the self-informed self, or ego, which created and sustains it. As more people realise, learn to experience and express their own nature—an event inevitably interpreted as 'narcissistic' by the egoids plugged into the monolith—so the unimaginable power of natural people working freely together—a chaotic, informal, undemocratic, non-centralised, collection of radically natural folk who understand that only *an end* to the whole thing can work—will inevitably pull the system apart, as it has so many times in the past.

What this radical internal revolution actually means however—while being, in the end, astonishingly simple—is, to the ordinary, systemic mind, an extraordinary odyssey.

Objection 7: Anarchism is insane.

Many people refuse entirely to engage with politics, never read the news, and believe that, on every subject that comes under the rubric of 'politics'—such as immigration, social class, health, education or work—there is very little to say, as it is *all* complete and utter bullshit. This is pretty much an anarchist position.

There have also been many people in history, indeed for most of history if we look back to the beginning of human experience, who have not had to deal with anything like what we would call politics; with a state, for example, or with professional authority, or with war and taxation and news and technology and whatnot. Among such people are primal hunter-and-gathers, children, animals, plants and every other non-human thing in the universe. They are also anarchists.

Finally, there have been people, numerically few, but influential far, far beyond the ambit of their immediate reach, who have refused the moral, intellectual or social authority of their peers and have freely fathomed the depths of their own conscious experience. Such people we call GENIUSES. These might not be politically anarchist, and their work might be extremely sober and *ordered*, but in their approach to what they do, they were, as Paul Feyerabend has demonstrated, radically libertarian. We sometimes call their work anarchic too; the comedies of Monty Python, for example, the sketches of Reeves and Mortimer, the films of Emir Kusturica or Alejandro Jodorowsky, the thought of Jiddu Krishnamurti or Barry Long, the Moomin stories, the music of Can or The Residents, the drawings of Tomi Ungerer; any radical refusal of authority which excites our original, natural instincts greets us as form of anarchism. This is why so many great people are attracted to it. Georges Brassens, Percy Bysshe Shelley, William Blake, William Morris, Oscar Wilde, Mark Rothko, J.R.R. Tolkien, Lao Tzu, Jesus of Nazareth, Ludwig Wittgenstein, Leo Tolstoy, Albert Einstein, Charlie Chaplin, Ghandi all realised, in their own lives, that refusal of all constraint is the only way to further knowledge, experience harmony, live with any integrity, create something actually new or have fun.

This refusal is usually understood as a kind of negativity or as a kind of madness and, *strictly* speaking, that is the case. Anarchism is largely *defined* by what it is not, because life, the life that great anarchists revere, is not a definition. Reality, as everyone realises from time to time, is far stranger, subtler and more flexible than what can be said of it.

Anarchism, in the finest primal sense of the word,* resists definition because it claims that the only intelligence, like the only wealth, is life itself; the conscious life of each of us. The reason men and women do not need kings, princes, states, professionals, institutions and systems to rule over them is because the life within them is more intelligent, more apt, more sensitive, more forgiving and more creative than anything else — certainly any human authority. But this life cannot be rationally fixed. It

---

* 'Purist! Sectarian! Gatekeeper! Who are *you* to say what anarchism really is? To exclude those who don't fit your narrow definition?' My answer to *that* question is this entire book.

can be expressed, artistically, indirectly, poetically, musically, or with tone and glance and such ordinary, metaphorical arts of human interaction; but it cannot be literally stated. This is why the 'beliefs' of anarchism, as far as direct statements go, are so often negative, why anarchism is so often dismissed as 'just being against everything'. As nihilist.

Another reason that people accuse anarchism of nihilism is that anarchism is not a socialist or a capitalist approach to collective problems. The idea is this: 'You are criticising *our team* (communism, socialism, feminism, the nation, the market, whatever)—therefore you believe in *nothing!*' The system-state (like the system-institution or the system-corp), and socialist-re-formist plans for organising it, is all there is, or can possibly be, forever and ever. Anything else is 'nihilistic' (because the system is the universe) or, alternatively, 'insane' (because the system is sanity) or, perhaps, 'unrealistic' (because 'reality' is the Way Things Are and The Way People Are). Domesticated automatons unconsciously serving a technocratic state (or corporate, or feudal) system forever; *that* is reality. Oppose that, and you are by definition an unrealistic, insane, extremist, nihilist.

The egoic mind made the world that dominates us and so to say that we do not really need it quite naturally seems, to the mind, nuts. When pressed on what we *do* need, the answers that anarchists give seem equally absurd; because the egoic mind cannot quite grasp them. This 'ideological elusiveness' is, finally, why many people who are anarchists in so much of their lives, refuse to define themselves as such. When they start to *think* about their politics or their culture they find the think-able; capitalism, socialism, Christianity, humanism, feminism or some other ideology of the system. And when they *think* about anarchism, in its mightiest form, they find the thoughts that the system has placed there; it seems inhuman, or chaotic, or violent, or parochial, or unrealistic, or uncivilised, or mad.

And yet, life is anarchic, and all good things within it; including you. Take a look at your friendships, at your love life, at your attitude to nature, at your creative life (if you have one), at your play. How do you behave, in other words, independently from coercive systems of centralised power and control? Do you base your closest relationships on authoritarian rule? Do you vote when you are out with your friends? Do you write and rigidly enforce laws with your family? Do you refrain from engaging in loving activities until you are properly accredited? Is there *anything* socialist about your natural life? Do you create and jam and play and collaborate together democratically? I don't think so. There might be the odd 'show of hands', but by far the most generous, the most intelligent and the most enjoyable reality of collective and personal life is without any kind of domination; it lives mysteriously, naturally and spontaneously. Free.

This is why anarchism, in its profound and primal essence, is the instinct that *won't go away*. Nature is anarchic, children are anarchic, the free, creative mind is anarchic, the body is anarchic, all of humanity's beloved ancestors were somehow anarchic and all of human society, beyond the microscopic bubble of the [corp]state, is and has always been anarchic; hunter-gatherers, friends, lovers and most effective working groups. We are anarchists.

*

W HAT MIGHT A FREE anarchist society look like today? Imagine if we removed the state and all its laws, dismantled our institutions and corporations, made attendance at school voluntary, opened the prisons, abolished educational qualifications and all professional accreditation, allowed everyone access to all professionally-guarded resources, cancelled all debts, completely abolished the police, the army, modern industrial technology, money, banks and private property.* Imagine, in short, that we lived, now, 'as if the day had come'. It seems to us, considering such a prospect, that the result would be unbelievable chaos and suffering. But, even putting aside the fact that, outside a few comfortable bubbles, the world is *already* unbelievable chaos and suffering, it is still an irrelevant objection; because very soon there will be a crash that will do all this anyway. We have the choice between that kind of crash and one we organise ourselves. In either case it will be grim; but I know which one I prefer.

---

* All together of course. As discussed in myth 8, you can't rescue one element of life from the system, without destroying yourself.

by Darren Allen

Non-Fiction: Natureculturenothing Trilogy

THE APOCALYPEDIA

33 MYTHS OF THE SYSTEM

Fiction: Things Unsaid Trilogy

DROWNING IS FINE

PERPETUAL DAWN

Television Scripts

FIRED

BELLY UP!

Website & Blog

WWW.EXPRESSIVEEGG.ORG